P9-DEE-883

Living

In

Panama

Sandra T. Snyder

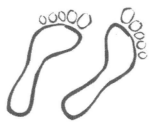

LIVING IN PANAMA
SANDRA T. SNYDER

PUBLISHED 2007
TANTOES, S.A.
PANAMA, REPUBLIC OF PANAMA

306
  S96   SNYDER, SANDRA T.
              LIVING IN PANAMA / SANDRA T. SNYDER. – PANAMÁ : IMPRESORA
        PACÍFICO, 2007.
              341P. ; 24 CM.

              ISBN 978-9962-00-156-0

        1. CULTURA POPULAR   2. PANAMÁ   I. TÍTULO.

PRINTED IN PANAMA BY IMPRESORA PACIFICO, S.A.

PHOTOS BY SANDRA T. SNYDER
COVER DESIGN: DAVID W. WILSON
COVER POLLERA: MARJORIE HERRERA

EDITORIAL BOARD:
DAVID FISHLOW
DONNA SANCHIZ
WILLIE K. FRIAR
IRIELA DOSSENBACH

COPYRIGHT © SANDRA T. SNYDER, 2006.
UNITED STATES AND PANAMA
ALL RIGHTS RESERVED

NO PART OF THIS BOOK MAY BE TRANSLATED OR REPRODUCED IN ANY FORM, EXCEPT BRIEF EXTRACTS BY A
REVIEWER FOR THE PURPOSE OF REVIEW WITHOUT WRITTEN PERMISSION OF THE COPYRIGHT OWNER.

CONTACT THE AUTHOR. COMMENTS ARE WELCOME
TANTOES@POBOX.COM
HTTP://WWW.LIVINGINPANAMA.NET

Dedicated to:

Ing. Dominador Kaiser Bazán

By the Same Author

Living in Panama
Spies, Crooks and Others Along the Way
Christmas at My House

Short stories:
The Disposal
Rainbow Dragon
The Peacock Feather

Little Cornflower

World War I Diary
of
Alfred Bruce Trickett

Editor:
The Jenkins Family History
In Jenkins Hollow in the Blue Ridge Mountains of Virginia

Business Office Orientation Handbook
For MediShare

Living In Panama

Sandra T. Snyder

Tantoes, S.A.
Panama, Republic of Panama

Table of Contents

Appendices

Living in Panama

Foreword

This little book is meant to serve as a guide to anyone coming to Panama to live. While the primary focus has traditionally been aimed at international executives relocating for business related to finance, the Canal, corporate assignments, import or export business, or diplomats, the same advice is relevant to the new influx of snowbirds and retirees.

The allure of Panama is allusive. To some it is the illusion of freedom and simplicity. Where it may seem that the laws of your home country are oppressive, the rules in Panama are flexible. They are a suggestion at best and a mild inconvenience in some cases rather than absolute. There is the perceived benefit of a better life for less money and in most cases this is true, but not all.

Panama has a very sophisticated, self-important image of itself. On many levels it appears to be modern and functional; but like everything else in Panama, appearance is what is important and sometimes there is not much depth. Up front, I offer you this advice and guidance: Panama is a small town trying to be a country and as a result it is possible to be a big fish in a small pond. For executives and diplomats cycling in and out of here and other places every few years, this can be an exciting opportunity. It can also be overwhelming.

Relocating to a foreign country is one of the most stressful experiences a family will encounter as they find themselves not only in a new country but using a new language, experiencing a new culture, as well as a new home, school and perhaps work. *Living in Panama* is aimed at helping these newcomers to Panama, whether they are here for business, as a student, a retiree, or snowbird coming to Panama for an extended time each year, as well as returning native Panamanians, who will also find the contents within these pages of great assistance.

ACKNOWLEDGMENTS

I wish to acknowledge the assistance of many members of the community who have helped make this publication possible:

David Wilson, Gale Cellucci, Rodrigo Marciacq, Dr. Charlie Garcia, Yvonne Lohrer, Dr. Wallace and Vilma Snyder, Daniella Stransky, Marsha Kat, Maria and Robert Boyd, Craig Owings, Craig J. Morrissey, Nixia J. Guerra, Jim Sayers, Aristides Hieldjo, Helene Breebaart, Terry McCoy, Edith Lohrer, Linda and Dave Cerrutti, Tom Ford, May Psychoyos, Floyd Skoubo, Clea Efthiamedies, Paul Smith, Carlos Barnes, Cedric Gittens, Ingrid Mayne, Marcela Porras, Caridad Charette, Alex Psychoyos, Julie Ford, Donna Sanchiz, Canadian Ambassador Jose Herran Lima, Mireya Edith Ouiros, Andrea McCarley, Pricilla Maloney, Rosalind McCoy, Sheila Teran, Melissa Bishop, Marinela Bouche, Marly Rios, Richard Vizor, Carlos Weil, Diego Madronero, Pablo Prieto, Marisa DeArco, Gerry Dowden, John Carlson, Margaret Mues, Lic. Kathia Mendez Barcia, Angel Bakx, Dale Jackson, Loretta Miller, Carol Steen, and Nana Horton.

Technical Resources:
Banking—Lic. Ricardo Cazorla
FOTW Flags of the World
Insurance - Lic. Howard Wenzel
Legal - Lic. Berta Thayer, Lic. Linette Landau,
   Lic. Alvaro Aguilar
Real Estate - *Espacios*, PKM Latin America S.A.
La Prensa
Weil Art Gallery, Carlos Weil

Introduction

Whatever brings you to Panama, a corporate move, retirement, returning to family, investment opportunities or as a tourist; you are in for a delightful surprise. I first arrived in Panama on a sailboat as my husband and I traveled from California to the East Coast of the U.S. via the Panama Canal. Arriving by sea allowed us to visit the numerous bays and small villages along the Pacific coast and to experience the flora and fauna and people of the more remote areas. You know you are entering Panama waters along the Pacific coast when you start to smell the flowers. If there is one image I always have of Panama, it is the fragrance of flowers that fills the air, not only in those remote anchorages but even here in Panama City in La Cresta.

Living in Panama is like stepping back a few years to a time when there was more emphasis on family and friends and more time to enjoy life. It is also a third-world country with a first-world façade. It is a large, modern city with all the conveniences but straining its limited infrastructure. In general, while the traffic may seem maddening at times, Panama is a relatively safe and sane place to live. This is the answer I give almost daily to those newcomers that ask me why I have chosen to live here.

Since I first started writing about life in Panama, the country has grown in many areas. The real estate boom is most noticeable followed by the influx of tourists and potential retirees from around the world.

Consequently, areas previously only thought of as weekend get-a-ways, farming areas or just plain rural are now becoming potential home sites to these newcomers. As a result of this change, this new edition of *Living in Panama* has been expanded to incorporate information about these newly discovered areas and the changes countrywide.

Within these pages are the answers to many of the questions you, as a newcomer or long-time resident, have asked at one time or another. It is meant to be a general reference for managing day-to-day life, as well as providing suggestions for researching further those subjects of particular interest to you. I have also included some helpful words you will hear in day-to-day use in Spanish, as well as reading recommendations.

Take time to smell the flowers and get to know the people. Relax and enjoy the life style.

And, remember, if you drink the water of the Chagres River, you will always return to Panama.

Sandra T. Snyder

Panama
2007

Living in Panama

In the 1920's before the introduction of inexpensive plastic buttons, about 20% of buttons manufactured in the United States were made from tagua nuts.

The Tagua Nut, commonly known as *vegetable ivory*, earned its name from its ivory-like color and texture. With the implementation of laws protecting the elephants from poachers for their ivory, tagua nuts have become a highly valued commodity by artisans and consumers alike. In Panama, tagua is skillfully carved by artisans into figurines, key chain tags, Christmas ornaments, jewelry, vases and buttons.

I

PANAMA IN A TAGUA NUTSHELL

Panama, crossroads of the world where the Panama Canal divides a country and two continents. But, Panama is not just a Canal.

Panama consists of a delightfully sophisticated city with a thriving financial/banking center, many great restaurants, and lots of art galleries, museums, theaters and social clubs. Panama also has an interesting and exciting *interior* with beaches, remote tropical islands and a thriving rural agricultural community. The climate is defined by two seasons, dry and rainy. There is little temperature change (See Appendix 1) or length of day change throughout the year. The major tourist attraction is, of course, the Panama Canal, followed by the many parks, with approximately 1,200 varieties of orchids and as many species of birds. Panama also boasts ten percent of the total species of butterflies in the world. The Panama Canal Museum, Miraflores Visitor's Center, Summit Gardens and the Harpy Eagle exhibits are just some of the attractions not to be missed. Traffic is difficult in the city and parking is a challenge in some areas, but there is excellent shopping for all goods and services whether in the *interior*, downtown Panama City or in any one of several modern shopping malls.

Shopping is not limited to just the day-to-day necessities either. There are at least a dozen art galleries to browse and several wonderful locations where native art can be enjoyed. The various Indians of Panama make very fine baskets (*canastas*), tagua-nut carvings, cocobolo-wood carvings and molas. Molas are multi-layers of fabric with intricate designs sewn and embroidered into panels. The Kunas incorporate these panels into their brightly colored blouses for everyday wear. They also sell these panels to the great delight of anyone who acquires one. Just one shopping trip to view molas will explain where the expression *Mola Madness* originates. While molas have long been a part of the native Kuna dress, they are also incorporated into designer clothes for both men and women.

Cocobolo Carving

The official language of Panama is Spanish but other languages are spoken as well. In this very international city, people from more than 40 countries make up the population. You will find social groups and speakers of languages from French to Chinese. The Panamanian people themselves are a delightful mix of descendents of the Spanish explorers, the French

Tagua Nut Carving

Reverse Appliqué Mola

who tried to build a sea level canal, the Americans who succeeded in building the Canal, the West Indians and the Chinese who came to build the railroad or who followed the trade routes, indigenous Indians and a mix of all the expatriates who have lived here for more than the 100 years of Panama's existence.

Three cities comprise the major metropolitan areas of the country:

Panama City, known as Panama, is not only the capital but also the largest of the three major cities in Panama. Located at the southern end of the Canal on the Pacific side, it is also the most populated city. Panama is a cosmopolitan city and a financial center. In addition to its historical monuments and world famous Canal, it boasts excellent restaurants, soaring skyscrapers, and beautiful parks. Those who have lived around the world find Panama the most social community in which they have ever lived. The most popular housing areas in the

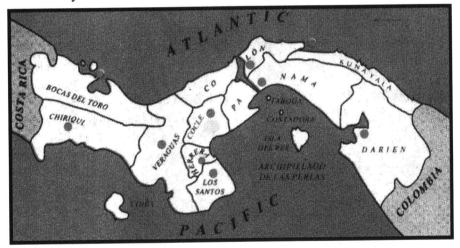

city for expatriates include: Altos de Golf, Punta Paitilla, Punta Pacifica, El Cangrejo, La Cresta, Obarrio, El Dorado, San Francisco, Marbella, Albrook and Costa del Este.

David, in the Province of Chiriquí, is in the western part of the country and is in the heart of Panama's agricultural region. David is the second largest city in Panama, a country town with a pleasant atmosphere. David also has excellent shopping, good restaurants and hotels. The residents of this Province are very proud of their home and quick to identify themselves as being from Chiriquí. The neighboring communities of the Chiriquí Highlands include Boquete, Volcan and Cerro Punta, which have recently been discovered by retirees from around the world.

Colón is situated on the Atlantic side at the entrance to the Canal and is a major shipping port. Currently Colón is also experiencing the beginnings of urban renewal with the development of new hotels and port facilities. It is also the location of the Free Zone. The Free Zone, the second largest free trade zone in the world, with over eight billion dollars in business a year, is open to foreigners and it offers an astounding variety of goods. While the major focus is wholesale, prices for goods and services are lower than in the U.S. and Europe and lower than in many countries in Latin America. Many old families of Panama trace their history to Colón and they still identify themselves as *Colonenses* even though they live and work in Panama City.

Panama, The Land and Its People

Comprised of: Nine provinces, 75 districts or municipalities, 620 *corregimientos* (21 in Panama City), five Kuna comarcas, and one Ngöbe comarca. Districts are governed by *municipios* and are the equivalent of counties. *Corregimientos* are similar to townships and may contain numerous villages or distinctive communities.

Official Name
Republic of Panama

Location
Panama is located in Central America between Costa Rica and Colombia at Latitude 8° 59'N and Longitude 79° 32'W, due south from Miami. Divided by the Panama Canal, it is often thought of as part of Central America north of the Canal and part of South America, to the south of the Canal.

Area
Panama covers an area of 78,200 sq km of which there are 75,990 square kms of land and 2,220 square kms of water and Panama is the narrowest point of the Central American isthmus. Bordered to the north by Costa Rica and Colombia to the south, it is bisected by the Panama Canal and connected by the Bridge of the Americas and the *Centenario*

Bridge. It is shaped like the letter *S* lying on its side and is roughly the size of the state of South Carolina in the U.S. The interesting placement and shape of the country results in the Pacific Ocean being to the South, the Caribbean Sea to the North and the Panama Canal running North and South rather than the expected East and West. In fact upon the completion of a canal transit from the Pacific to the Caribbean you will be further West than when you started! As if this were not confusing enough, the sun appears to rise in the Pacific and set in the Caribbean because of the shape of the isthmus.

Population

The *Contraloria General de la República* reported in July 2006, a nationwide population at 3,285,478, of which about one million live in the capital, Panama City. The *Contraloría* further reports approximately 192 babies are born daily while approximately 40 persons of all ages die per day. This population is comprised of locals and foreigners (*extranjeros*) from around the world including descendents of the Spanish, French, Americans from the United States, Chinese, and West Indians (primarily from Barbados and Jamaica of African origin) who came to work on the railroad and the Canal.

Panama also has seven different indigenous populations including the *Ngöbe-Bugle* (*Guaymi*) of Chiriqui, Bocas del Toro and Veraguas; the *Kunas* of the San Blas; the *Wounaan* and *Embera* of the Darien, comprising 8.7% of the population. Lesser-recognized indigenous peoples included in this statistic are the *Naso* or *Teribe* of Bocas del Toro; the *Bri Bri* also of Bocas del Toro; and the *Bokota* of eastern Bocas del Toro and northwest Veraguas.

The most recent study of DNA (October 2006) by the *Instituto del ADN y del Genoma Humano* of the University of Panama identifies 80% of the population of Panama as what is generally identified in Latin America as *mestizo*. *Mestizo* is the term used to identify the resulting generations from the union of Spanish men and Indigenous women. Further, according to the study, 50% of the genes of *Chiricanos* are indigenous and 61% of those from Herrera and Los Santos are negro.

This scientific study shows a high percentage of negro slaves (West Indians) in the towns of these regions. The racial structure accompanied by the province population in general, results in a mixture of the races as follows: 39.7% Indigenous, 32.9% negros and 27.4% white. This is particularly interesting as it is very different from other Latin countries where there is a significantly smaller component of indigenous. The Spanish exterminated the majority of the ethnic populations of those countries.

Panama has a relatively large middle class. Of the total population, 508,700 live in extreme poverty, primarily in rural and indigenous areas.

Capital

Panama City (referred to as Panama)

Language

Spanish is the official language with about 14% of the population speaking English. English is taught in school and commonly spoken by the upper classes, West Indians and expatriates. Additionally, a number of Indigenous languages are spoken.

Literacy

Education is required up to the sixth grade and 92.6% of the population 15 years of age and over can read and write.

Climate

The climate is tropical, hot, humid and cloudy but temperatures vary with altitude. The rainy season is from April or May until December and is called *invierno* or winter. *Verano,* the summer season, is from December to April and tends to be hotter, windier and less humid. With the beginning of the rainy season in late April, showers are normal in the afternoon every few days. As winter progresses towards July, showers become more frequent (daily) and of longer duration until by November it is raining much of the day and night. Interestingly, it usually stops raining around the first week in December. Occasionally, you will get a light shower in some areas of Panama in the dry season.

Bocas del Toro on the Atlantic coast close to the Costa Rican border is rainier than Panama City. They experience a short dry season in August. Boquete is famous for the *bajareque* (known as *chipichipi* in Guatemala) or constant light drizzle, some times of the year. This weather phenomenon is typical throughout the Chiriqui Highland region. Temperatures are also much cooler at these elevations (above 5,000 feet) and what is humid in the city becomes damp and cold in Boquete, Volcan and Cerro Punta. Volcan's rainy climate results in more rainbows in a week than you will see elsewhere in a lifetime.

Portobelo on the Atlantic coast is considered one of the wettest places in the world, with some rainfall up to 260 days a year. December marks the beginning of the Christmas winds (northeast trades) which blow across the country until the rainy season resumes in April. (See Appendix 1.)

Temperatures

The biggest variance in temperature is between daytime and night, which can be as much as 18 degrees. The average daytime temperature at sea level is 87 degrees F and nighttime 74 degrees F. At higher altitudes, including Boquete, Volcan and Cerro Punta temperatures can drop to 50 or 60 degrees F. (See Appendix 1.)

Government

Panama consists of nine provinces and the territory Kuna Yala Comarca (San Blas), as well as two other indigenous *Comarcas*. The provinces are further divided into 67 Districts. The government is a constitutional democracy. The President and two Vice Presidents are elected every five years and are assisted by Cabinet Ministers. (Beginning in 2009 Panama will have only one Vice President.) The branches of the government are the Executive, Legislative and Judicial. The Legislative Assembly is made up of 78 Legislators elected by popular vote to serve five-year terms. (Beginning in 2009, this will change to 71 seats in the Legislature.) The legal system is based on the Roman civil law system.

Panama is a friendly, welcoming country. Current immigration laws make tourism easy. U.S. tourists are currently issued a 90-day tourist card, which is renewable for 90 days. A number of different residential visas are available for those wishing to live in Panama on a permanent basis. (See Chapter II)

Religion

The majority of the people are Roman Catholic (85%), although there are many other religious groups represented (15% Protestant) and there is complete freedom of worship. Both Muslims and Jews are evident in the population.

Currency

The U.S. dollar is used as the legal currency in Panama as of the 1904 monetary treaty. The *balboa* is the symbolic national currency but bank notes are not issued in *balboas*. Panama does issue its own coins (minted in the U.S.), which are equal in size and shape to the comparable U.S. coins and totally interchangeable in Panama (not in the U.S.) U.S. bills are available in $1, $2, $5, $10, $20, $50 and $100 denominations. Coins, whether U.S. or Panama, are available in denominations of one cent or *centésimo* (commonly called *centavo*), the nickel or *real*, the ten cent/dime, twenty-five cent/quarter or *cinco reales*, and fifty-cent pieces called a *peso*. You will also find one-dollar coins in use in the interior. Fifty and one- hundred-dollar bills can be difficult to exchange at times.

Flag

The Panamanian flag is red, white and blue and is divided into four sections. From left to right on top is a white rectangle with a blue star in the middle and a red rectangle. Below is a blue rectangle and a white rectangle with a red star in the middle. The current national flag was confirmed by Law 48 of 1925 and ratified by Law 28 on March 28, 1941. The blue and red represent the Conservative and Liberal Parties; the white is for peace; the blue star is for the purity and honesty of the life of the country; the red star is for the authority and law in the country.

National Holidays

Date	Holiday
January 1	New Year's Day
January 9	Martyrs' Day
Day before Ash Wednesday*	Carnival Tuesday*
Friday before Easter Sunday*	Good Friday*
May 1	Labor Day
November 2	All Soul's Day
November 3	Independence from Colombia
November 4	Flag Day
November 10	First Call for Independence
November 28	Independence from Spain
December 8	Mother's Day
December 25	Christmas Day

*Dates change according to the Christian Calendar

The current flag is a slight modification of the original 1903 Flag designed by Manuel Amador, son of the first President of the Republic, and made by his mother Maria Ossa de Amador. Only the arrangement of the colors and stars on the flag was changed. The original flag is on display at the History Museum.

National Motto
Pro Mundi Beneficio (for the benefit of the world)

National Flower
Flor del Espíritu Santo Orchid

National Tree
Panama Tree (Sterculiaceae)

National Bird
Harpy Eagle

National Dress
La Pollera

National Anthem (Isthmian Hymn)
Written by Jeronimo de la Ossa and musical score composed by Santos Jorge.

Time
The entire country of Panama is on Eastern Standard Time all year. This is the same as New York or Miami, when Standard Time is in effect in the U.S., and Chicago and Houston during Daylight Savings Time: GMT less five hours.

Safety Issues
Personal safety is generally not an issue in Panama and it has traditionally been considered the safest country in the region. However, as with any large metropolitan city, there are areas of the city considered to be "high crime or dangerous" and are to be avoided especially at night. Some of these areas include El Chorrillo, San Miguelito, Curundu, La Central, and Río Abajo. With the recent increase of casinos in and around the El Cangrejo area (from Via España to Calle Eusebio A. Morales) has come additional crime and prostitution.

Additionally, remote areas including Darien, Madden Dam and Playa Veracruz should be approached with caution. This is especially true in the city of Colon.

Car break-ins, theft, and petty crime are common in Panama and Colon. With the increasing population, in recent years Panama has seen an increase in crime including kidnappings, house break-ins and shootings. Many of these appear to be targeted, "inside-jobs" and in general are carried out by someone who knows the potential victim and his habits. In general, the most common crimes an expatriate may face are jewelry and purse snatching when in areas where you look like a tourist and are wearing jewelry. Do not look like a tourist! Panamanians usually do not wear tennis shoes (unless playing tennis), belly packs, shorts (except at the beach, resorts or on Saturday), tank tops, or t-shirts with messages). (See Appendix 2 for the latest crime statistics and further information on this topic.)

The tourist police on their bicycles are visible all over the city in addition to the regular police.

Economy

Panama's economy is based on a well-developed services sector that accounts for three-fourths of the GDP. The primary one of these is the operation of the Panama Canal, followed by the Colon Free Zone, tourism, banking, insurance, container ports and flagship registry. The slump experienced in the Colon Free Zone and agricultural exports following the withdrawal of the U.S. military forces ended in 2004-2005 led by export-oriented services and a construction boom stimulated by tax incentives. The government has implemented tax reforms, as well as social security reforms, and backs regional trade agreements and development of tourism. Unemployment remains high at about 9.8%.

Major Imports & Exports

Traditional export products from Panama include bananas, shrimp, oil, sugar, coffee, electricity and some miscellaneous products including clothing and chocolate.

Non-traditional exports include fish, cigars, tuna, melons, medicines, meats and others.

Traditional imports include corn, medicines, petroleum products and others.

Kuna Yala, San Blas

The Archipelago of San Blas consists of more than 360 islands stretching along the northern Caribbean coast of Panama toward Colombia. Known as *Kuna Yala* by the indigenous tribe that occupies these islands and part of the mainland, this territory is under the jurisdiction of Panama but has independent control of day-to-day operations. They also have representation in the Panama Legislature. The flag for their homeland, *Republic of Tule*, as it is known, is red-yellow-red and black. The *Kunas* are thought to be the second smallest people in the world after the Pygmies of Africa. They are the creators of the incredible molas as part of the women's traditional dress as well as being a commercial success. They have a well-established farming system on the mainland, which allows them to be self-supporting as well as cash crops of coconuts, which they raise on the islands and sell to Colombia.

Recommended Reading

Understanding the culture and history of a country makes for a more pleasant living experience. The following list is meant to be a guide to starting your education and building your Panama book list:

The Path Between The Seas, The Creation of the Panama Canal 1870-1914, David McCullough, Touchstone Simon & Schuster, 1977, ISBN 0-671-24409-4. The classic introduction to Panama and the Canal that built a country.

Panama, William Friar, Moon Handbooks, Avalon Travel Publishing, 2005, ISBN-10:1-56691-579-1. The most up-to-date authoritative tourist guidebook to Panama.

Panama's Canal, What Happens When the United States Gives a Small Country What it Wants, Mark Falcoff, The American Enterprise Institute, 1998, ISBN 084474030-6. A current look at the challenges of former colonial and dependent countries as they come of age on their own.

Getting to Know the General, Graham Greene, Simon and Schuster, 1984, ISBN 0-671-54160-9. Omar Torrijos as seen through the eyes of the author.

Adventures in Nature – Panama, William Friar, Avalon Travel, 2001, ISBN 1-56691-240-7. Panama's only eco-tourism guidebook.

Portrait of the Panama Canal, From Construction to the 21st Century, William Friar, Graphic Arts Center Publishing, 2001, ISBN 1-55868-477-8.

Panama, Scott Doggett, *Lonely Planet* Publications, 1004, ISBN 0-86442-566-X, Guidebook.

Getting to Know Panama, Michele Labrut, Focus Publication, 1993, ISBN 958-95276-4-7.

The Directory of Important Bird Areas in Panama, Bird Life International, the Panama Audubon Society, United States Forest Service, 2006.

The Tailor of Panama, John le Carre, Ballantine Books, 1996, ISBN 0-345-42043-8. New York Times Best Selling Novel about the British Intelligence in Panama.

Señor Saint, Leslie Charteris, Macfadden-Bartell Book, 1968, Library of Congress Number 58-13275. A novel about love, larceny and discovering the golden frogs in Panama.

Panama, Eric Zencey, A Berkley Book, 1995, ISBN 0-425-15602-8. A mystery novel from the days of the French attempt at building the canal.

Red, White and Blue Paradise, Herbert and Mary Knapp, Harcourt Brace Jovanovich, Publishers, 1984, ISBN 0-15-176135-3. Husband and wife schoolteachers give a candid view of life in the Canal Zone.

A Captain's Guide to Transiting the Panama Canal in a Small Vessel, David W. Wilson, Tantoes, S.A., 1999, ISBN 9962-51-031-7. The definitive guide to transiting the canal.

The Art of Being Kuna, UCLA Fowler Museum of Cultural History, 1995, ISBN 0-93-074160-9. Definitive scholarly study of the Kuna Indians of San Blas with great illustrations.

The Sage, Robert Apold, ProQuill Ink, Imprenta Universal Books, 2005, ISBN 9962-02-723-3. A believable treasure hunt across the Isthmus of Panama and the Canal.

Don't Kill the Cow Too Quick, An Englishman's Adventures in Panama, Malcolm Henderson, Universe, Inc., 2004, ISBN 0-595-31949-1. A retiree's experiences in Bocas del Toro.

Naturalists on the Isthmus of Panama, A Hundred Years of Natural History on the Biological Bridge of the Americas, Stanley Heckadon-Moreno, Smithsonian Tropical Research Institute Panama 2004, Spanish edition, 1998, ISBN 9962-8901-0-1, English edition 2004, ISBN 9962-614-07-4.

Divorcing the Dictator, America's Bungled Affair with Noriega, Frederick Kemp, G. P. Putnam Son's Publishing, 1990 ISBN 0-399-13517. Wall Street Journal Reporter explains the Noreiga years.

What is a Mola?, Willie K Friar, Boulder, Colorado, 2000, ISBN 9962-8810-0-5. The Kunas of Panama and their fabulous hand stitched artwork.

Portobelo Chronicles, Patricia A. McGehee, Republic of Panama, 1994, One sailor's study of other "nobodies" who have arrived in Panama by ship since 1502.

In the Time of the Tyrants: Panama, 1968-1989, R. M. Koster and Guillermo Sanchez Borbon. An account of the Noriega years.

Blubba Transits the Panama Canal, Willie K. Friar, Boulder Colorado, 1999, ISBN 9962-8810-2-1. A tale of a whale and a whale of a tale! A children's story designed to explain how the Panama Canal operates.

A Guide to the Birds of Panama, Robert S. Ridgely and John A. Gwynne, Jr., Princeton. ISBN 9962-614-04-X. The authority on birds and bird watching in Panama.

"Autopista Magazine", Jaime Claramunt, La Prensa, April 2002, No. 122, Page 2. Study of driving habits in Panama.

Baskets of the Wounaan and Embera Indians from the Darien Rainforest in Panama, Margo M. Callaghan, HPL Enterprises Incorporated, Sun Lakes, Arizona 2002.

Guarding the Crossroads, Security and Defense of the Panama Canal, Charles Morris Brooks, Imprelibros S.A., 1st Edition November 2003, ISBN 9962-8862-0-1. Former Panama Canal Commission executive recounts his career involving security and defense of the Panama Canal.

The Jungle Whispers, Kenneth W. Vinton, Robert Hale Limited, 1958. The "hair-raising adventures of one of the few white men who really know(s) the horrors and beauties of the Panamanian jungle."

Spies, Crooks and Others Along the Way, Sandra T. Snyder, Universal Books, Tantoes, S.A., 2005, ISBN 9962-02-849-3. The author and Panama authority answers that oft asked personal question, "what brought you to Panama?" The answer, of course, is "a sailboat." While that is how they came to Panama, and the book addresses their sailing adventures, Spies, Crooks and Others Along the Way, is not about sailing but about the people they met along the way.

Boquete, Valley of the Eternal Rainbow, Milagros Sanchez Pinzon, Culturama Educational Weekly, Impresos Modernos, S.A., 2006, ISBN 996-8816-6-8.

Código de Trabajo, Labor Code, Jaime J. Jovane and Jose Martin Rodriguez, Editorial Nuevo Forum, S.A., 1a Edicion, 1996.

The Panama Cruising Guide, A complete Sailors guide to the Isthmus of Panama, Second Edition, Eric Bauhaus, Sailors Publications, S.A., ISBN 9962-02-829-9

The Panama Guide, A Cruising Guide to the Isthmus Of Panama, Nancy Schwalbe Zydler and Tom Zydler, Seaworthy Publications, Brookfield, Wisconsin, 1996 and newer editions, ISBN 0 9639-566-3-9

Portobelo Guide, The Ancient Cannons Tell their Story, Michel Lecumberry, Texango Publications, 2005, ISBN 2-9522170-4-1. In French and in English.

SanBlas, Molas and Kuna Traditions, Michel Lecumberry, Texango Publications, 2004, ISBN 2-9522170-0-9.

Questions and Answers About the Panama Canal, Willie K. Friar, Boulder Colorado, 2001, ISBN 9962-8810-0-5.

Cat Up The Tree

&

Other Emergencies*

Fire Department/ *Bomberos*
Panama: Tel.: 103, 225-1570/225-6797
Bocas Del Toro: Tel.: 103
Boquete: Tel.: 103, 720-1224 (Ambulance also)

Police/ *Policia*
Panama: Tel.: 104, 232-5577
Bocas del Toro: Tel.: 104   757-9271
Boquete: Police Tel.: 104, 720-1222/2145
Colón: Tel.: 441-4197
David: Tel.: 776-8125

Traffic Police Panama
Tel.: 232-5614 or 232-6845

Emergencies Service
SINAPROC (Servicio Nacional de Protección Civil)
For assistance in case of national disasters: hurricanes, flooding, storms, etc also drownings.
Tel.: *335 or 316-0080
They go all over country.

Medical Emergencies/*Urgencias Panama*
Hospital Nacional: Tel.: 207-8100
                ER: Tel.: 207-8110
                Ambulance: Te.: 207-8111
Centro Médico Paitilla: Tel.: 265-8800
                ER: Tel.: 265-8888

Clínica San Fernando: Tel.: 278-6300
                ER: Tel.: 229-2004, 229-1606
Santo Tomas: Tel.: 227-4122/227-4095
San Miguel Arcangel: Tel.: 230-2830
Hospital Punta Pacífica: Tel.: 204-8000
                ER: Tel.: 204-8111
Hospital del Niño: Tel.: 225-1547
                ER: Tel.: 225-1583
Caja de Seguro Social: Tel.: 264-1739
(eligible Panamanians Only)

Colón:
Hospital de Coco Solo: Tel.: 449-3347
                ER: Tel.: 449-3319
David:
Hospital Centro Médico Mae Lewis:
                Tel.: 775-4616,
                6617-9881 (24 hours)

Bocas:
Hospital emergency: Tel.: 102
Ambulance: Tel.: 757-9814

Ambulance /*Ambulancia*

Panama:
Alerta: Tel.: 188, 800-0911, 269-9778
SEMM: Tel.: 264-1122
Seguro Social: Tel.: 229-1133

Boquete: Tel.: 103, 720-1224

Red Cross/*Cruz Roja*

Tel.: 315-1388; www.panama.cruzroja.org

Tow Truck/ *Gruas*

Panamá:
Gruas Salerno, S.A.: Tel.: 221-8877, 222-0444,
         224-4726, 221-2457
Panagruas: Tel.: 229-2240, 800-4742
Don Gruas- A.A.: Tel.: 232-8603
Móvil Gruas: Tel.: 221-0022/221-0012/617-2200

Coronado, San Carlos, Chame:
Gruas Vitito: Tel.: 240-8016, 6613-2487

Colón:
Gruas de Colón: Tel.: 442-1509

Gran Terminal Nacional
Bus: Tel.: 232-5803

Airports/Aeropuertos
Tocumen International Panama: Tel.: 238-4322
Domestic/General Aviation Airport Panama:
               Marcos A. Gelabert
             Tel.: 315-1622
Regional Airlines:
Bocas International Airport: Tel.: 757-9208
Aeroperlas-Bocas: Tel.: 757-9341
Turismo Aero: Tel.: 757-9841

Port Authority: Tel.: 757-9447

* Panama plans to implement the **911** emergency call system in 2007.

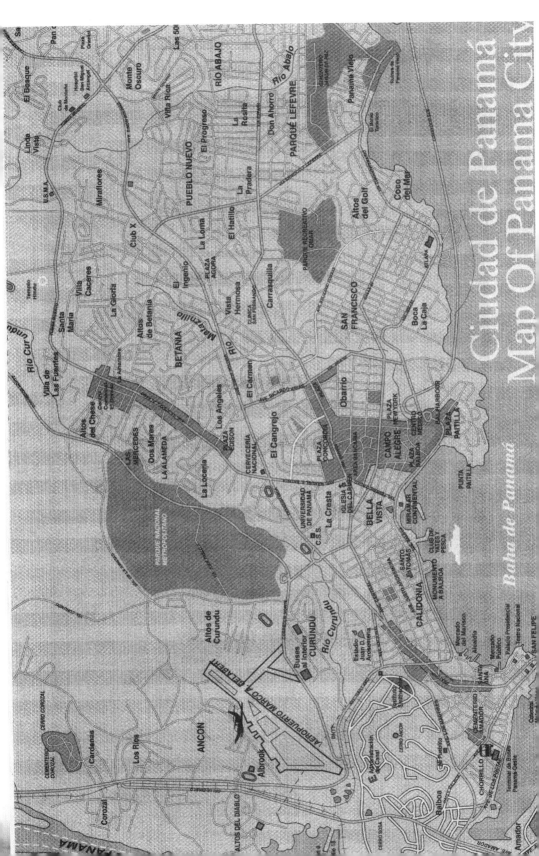

Ciudad de Panamá
Map Of Panama City

Bahía de Panamá

Tocumen Airport

This modern, newly remodeled terminal offers a wide selection of duty free shops for your shopping pleasure as you enter or leave the country. Everything from designer clothes, luggage, perfumes, books, Panama handicrafts and jewelry can be purchased.

Since everyone has to arrive early to complete the check in process, plan to stop in the café for breakfast or just a cup of coffee before your flight boards.

Shoe shines are available near the stairs.

II

ARRIVING WITH FAMILY, KIDS AND PETS

Travel Tips - Arrival

Passengers arriving by air enter Panama at the newly remodeled Tocumen International Airport on the outskirts of the city. What once was a 60 to 90 minute drive into the city has been reduced to 20 minutes with the opening of the *Corredor Sur* four-lane toll-highway. If you are fortunate enough to land in Panama on one of the many flights arriving after six in the evening, you will have the opportunity to view the city along this lighted causeway as it crosses the edge of the bay with the city in the foreground. The first sight of the city is the impressive, high-rises of Punta Pacífica and Punta Paitilla.

Arriving passengers can take advantage of the duty free shops before proceeding to immigration and customs. At immigration you will find from three to four lines identified for Panamanian citizens and residents, which includes *pensionados/jubilados* (retirees). There is a separate line for tourists. Unless you are a Panamanian national or have a special residence status, you will need to wait in the tourist line. No one here speaks English but as long as you have your tourist card or Panamanian ID *(cédula)*, or residential visa *(carnet)*, and passport, plus your completed customs declaration you will have no problem. Tourist cards should be obtained from the airline for $5 before departure from your home country. If not, the card can be purchased in the airport upon your arrival. The immigration agent will direct you as the location changes from time to time. It is best to purchase it before your arrival in Panama. Then just present your papers when your turn comes at the immigration window and wait patiently while they are inspected and stamped.

Beyond immigration, you will find the baggage claim area and customs. Free luggage carts are available for your use at this point. Once you have claimed your baggage, proceed to the customs gates. Here you will be asked if you have anything to declare and will be instructed to put all bags through a screening machine for inspection before proceeding on your way. Luggage carts are not permitted beyond this point but you can either hire a porter, or carry or pull your own luggage. Exit through the double doors and proceed into the main arrival area. Any friends, family or tourist service planning to meet you will be in this area. Here you will also find kiosks for rental cars and taxis as well as welcome salons for Hotels El Panama and Sheraton Hotel and Resort Panama. Taxi rates into the city for single passengers are $25. The official dispatcher at the curbside can arrange shared taxis. However, you can make arrangements ahead of time to be met by a private driver and this will cost about $20. Two such contacts are located in the Panama-on-Line box at the end of the Chapter. Confirm with your driver whether *Corredor* tolls (about $2.40) are included in the quoted rate.

If you are arriving with significant amounts of cash, particularly business people headed to the Free Zone to complete transactions, you may want to make arrangements in advance for an escort into the city. It is not unheard of for business arrivals carrying large sums of money to be hijacked en route to the city.

Departure

Arrange for your taxi the day before your departure. This will cost $20 unless you have an extra large number of bags or more than two passengers for the taxi. A van will cost about $30.

The return trip to the airport will take about 20 minutes on the *Corredor Sur*. Allow additional time if you will be traveling during the evening rush hour (4:00-6:00 p.m.).

Departure tax is $20 per person ($10 for *jubilados/*retirees) and is included in your ticket price. Once you have checked-in, you may proceed to immigration at the entrance to the Gate area. Present your completed Departure card and passport. Your carry-on baggage will be screened here and then you can proceed to the duty-free area and your departure gate.

Visas & Work Permits

There are several types of Visas available and the purpose of your stay in Panama will determine which type is appropriate for you. Citizens from Antigua, Aruba, Australia, Bahamas, Barbados, Barbuda, Belize, Bermuda, Brazil, Canada, Curacao, Greece, Grenada, Guyana, Iceland, Jamaica, Japan, Malta, Mexico, Monaco, Nevis, New Zealand, Norway, Paraguay, Saint Lucia, Sao Tome, South Korea, St. Kitts, St. Vincent & the Grenadines, United States, Vatican, and Western Samoa entering the country must have a tourist visa that will permit his or her stay in the country for up to 90 days. Once in the country, you can apply to change your immigration status (from tourist to any other immigration status). Visit the official web site at www.migracion.gob.pa.

Some countries have agreements with Panama that eliminates the necessity for a visa or tourist card. These include: Argentina, Austria, Belgium, Bolivia, Chile, Colombia, Costa Rica, El Salvador, Finland, France, Greece, Guatemala, Holland, Honduras, Hungary, Israel, Italy, Japan, Nicaragua, Poland, Portugal, Singapore, Spain, Switzerland, United Kingdom, and Uruguay, and most European Union countries. There are also some nationalities that, in order to enter the country, need a previously approved Visa from the Immigration Department in Panama. These include India, China, and Russia, among several others.

The following countries require a visa stamped by the consul of Panama in their country, after submitting proof of financial solvency: Chad, Dominican Republic, Ecuador, Egypt, the Philippines, Peru and Thailand.

Visa Categories

Once you have entered Panama, or even before arriving in the country, you can apply for various types of Visa at the Panama

Imigration office according to the purpose of your visit or stay. There are two main types of Visas:

A.   Temporary Visitor Visas. These Visas give you the right to stay in the country for a predetermined period of time. There are various kinds of Visas within this classification, the following being the most relevant and commonly used:

1. Special Temporary Visa (International Executive)
2. Free Zone Executive
3. Technician or expert
4. Student
5. Scientific or cultural mission
6. Medical treatment.

B.   Immigrant Visas.   These Visas give you the right to permanently reside in the country after a certain number of years have elapsed. There are also various kinds of Visas within this classification, the following being the most relevant and commonly used:

1. Investor
2. Spouse of a national
3. Dependent of a national
4. Forestry Investor
5. Export Processing Zone Executive
6. Labor Department resolution.

There are also Visas for Retirees (tourist *pensionado y rentista retirado)*. Depending on the Visa you intend to apply for, the requirements that you must comply with vary. All of them require various documents from your home country as well as those to be obtained from Panama. Documents coming from abroad must be translated and authenticated by the Panamanian consul at the place of origin or with the Apostille seal. The details printed here and specific requirements may change from time to time and your attorney can advise you.

The following are some common requirements you must comply with for all types of Visas:

1. Power of Attorney granted to a Panamanian law firm or individual lawyer
2. Certificate of Medical Health issued within three months of

application (obtained from a local professional)
3. Passport and copy of passport with at least six months validity (first page with identifying information and page showing last entry to Panama)
4. Four passport photos
5. Police record report from your home country
6. Birth/Marriage certificates (in case of family)
7. Affidavit of Personal Background Data in a special Immigration Form.

Residency Requirements

Permanent Residency is granted to foreigners:
1. Investing $40,000 in a Panama non-retail business and effectively employing three Panamanians
2. Holding a $200,000 CD time deposit (*plazo fijo*) account in a Panama bank for at least two years.
3. Owning a house for $80,000, a time deposit for at least two years in the amount of at least $120,000 and by providing evidence of the source and amount of income used to cover the applicant's general expenses
4. Married to a Panamanian spouse, subject to an interview to verify if it is a bona fide marriage.

Work Permit Requirements

Any individual entering the country and planning to work for compensation in Panama needs to obtain a Work Permit from the Ministry of Labor and Labor Development for which he or she will need, at a minimum, the following:
1. Power of Attorney granted to the Panamanian law firm or individual lawyer
2. Certification of status issued by the Immigration Office
3. Letter from the company describing the work and salary
4. Four photos
5. Copy of your passport

6. Certificate of Incorporation of the employer company
7. Authenticated copy of the Commercial License of the company
8. Certificates from the Public Registry of the employer company
9. Work Contract (for one-year maximum which will become enforceable once the work permit is granted)
10. Original and copy of the payroll.

Not all Visas require Work Permits; those described in A2, and A3 above require one.

Once you have all your documents your attorney will apply for the Visa at the Immigration Office. With a copy of the application including the seal of the Immigration Office, he will then apply for the Work Permit at the ministry of labor. A provisional permit is granted for up to three months while the authorities perform an investigation. Once the Ministry of Labor issues a resolution granting the work permit, this resolution is presented to the Immigration Office, which will then issue the temporary Visa for one year.

While this procedure may seem fairly straightforward, there can be numerous delays along the road to approval. Documents are carefully inspected and often have to be resubmitted either because they have been lost or are not acceptable. Similarly you need to carefully check and verify every document you receive to catch errors, typos and omissions. The very minimum time required to get the process started is three months and many months may pass as the process moves along. It is not unusual to have the process take a year or more to complete depending on the type of Visa and your attorney. In selecting an attorney, choose one that specializes in immigration and has had many successful Visa applications in the last year. With the change of government every five years, some attorneys find they cannot get paperwork processed as easily as they may have under the previous administration. When you are new to the country and applying for any Visa, do your homework in selecting your representative. It will be expensive starting over with a different attorney.

Recommendations for a Speedy Approval

1. *Pensionado* Visa:

   Pension for Life Letter specifically stating what job title or position the applicant held with the company as well as length of time the company has been in business. Shell corporations without any assets created for the sole purpose of issuing a Pension for Life Letter for the applicant are not acceptable.

2. Self-Economic Solvency Visa:

   The real property being purchased to satisfy this Visa requirement can no longer have a Mortgage. In other words, you cannot put 10% down on a $200,000 property while financing the rest to satisfy this Visa requirement.

3. Married to a Panamanian Visa:

   Stricter standards are being implemented in the interview process for this type of Visa. A thorough investigation, including very personal questions, will determine if the applicant is really living with the Panamanian spouse. The Ministry of Labor is conducting visits to the home of the spouse before issuing a Work Permit as Spouse of a Panamanian.

4. Business Investment Visa:

   This Visa requires that the applicant earn a significantly high salary in the Company.

Pets (*Mascotas*) are Part of the Family

There are two generally accepted methods of travel for your pet, in-cabin or as cargo. Many airlines allow small pets to travel in the passenger cabin in a pet carrier placed under the seat. The newer-style, soft pet carriers look just like luggage and are very comfortable for the small (under 15 pounds) dog or cat. However, the pet must have a reservation and a ticket as only one pet is usually allowed in the cabin at a time. Larger pets can be shipped in the special cargo section provided for that purpose. Again they must have a reservation and a ticket. During the U.S. summer months, June through August, many airlines will not allow pets to travel in the cargo section. Make your travel plans accordingly.

Regulations for various pets differ from country to country. Panama allows most domestic animals but restricts agricultural animals from South America. They do require some documents including a health certificate from the vet saying your cat or dog is in good health and it must be stamped by the U.S. Department of Agriculture (or the corresponding institution in your country of origin). In addition, the animal must have a rabies shot within one year of travel. Panama has a 30-day home quarantine for newly arriving pets. Bringing pets into Panama or taking them out is relatively easy. Exact procedures as of 2006 for bringing in or taking out a household pet follow. If all this seems complicated, Golden Frog (*Rana Dorada Movil Intl.*) and Jose Saenz will handle the paperwork and process for a fee. Email: Bocasfrog@yahoo.com or jose@goldenfrog.net; http://www.goldenfrog.net. For further information contact: *Direccion de Salud Animal del Ministerio de Desarrollo Agropecuario*/Animal Health Minister at 266-2303 or Email: dinasal@cwpanama.net.

Pets Coming into Panama

In the Home Country: No more than ten days before your flight, get a pet health certificate from a local veterinarian saying the animal is in good health and has had a rabies shot within the year. The vet should have the necessary standard three-part form. The form must then be stamped by the Department of Agriculture. Take the form to the Panama Consulate closest to you for processing. There will be fees for each of these services.

In Panama: In the meantime, if you have an agent or a relocation firm in Panama, send the following information to them so that they can prepare for your pet's arrival. One week before arrival in Panama your agent must request a "Permission for Home Quarantine". This requires a letter written to the Minister of Health including: owner's full name, owner's passport number, pet's name, type and breed of animal, sex, age, weight of the animal, last address of the pet, and where it will be residing in Panama. Include arrival information for the pet including airline, date and time of arrival.

With this information the agent will notify the official vets for MIDA and the Health Minister of the arrival of the pet. He will then schedule a vet to meet the plane and take custody of the pet for the night, if the pet arrives after normal business hours (8 a.m. to 4 p.m. daily).

Upon arrival at the airport go to the Banco Nacional branch bank in the airport and pay:

$21.00 to MIDA,

$130.00 to the Minister of Health (*Ministerio de Salud Control de Alimentos y Vigilancia Veterinaria*).

Pets Leaving Panama

Pet departure is another occasion when it may be more convenient for you to use an agent who knows the system, speaks Spanish and can handle these details for you.

Ten days before leaving get a pet health certificate from a local veterinarian saying the animal is in good health and has had rabies shot within the year. You will need the following information to process the pet's exit papers:

Full name of owner, owner's passport number, pet name, type and breed, weight, age, sex, and the vet health certificate.

Go to the *Ministerio de Salud* to have the form registered and pay a $10 fee for the registration. The process will require your going to several offices but can be accomplished sometimes in one day. If there is no one available to sign the certificate at the time you go to process the form, you may have to leave it and return the next day to pick it up.

If the pet will be traveling with you in the cabin, you can skip this next step. Schedule transportation for the pet, if it is large enough to require a van (about $30), and arrive at the cargo terminal for weighing and processing three hours before the flight is scheduled to depart. There will be another fee for the pet based on the weight.

Household Goods

The type of visa you hold will determine how and what household goods you will be entitled to bring to Panama. *Jubilados,* legal residents, and returning Panamanian nationals are entitled to import used household goods totaling $10,000, one time. Regardless of which type, you **must have your visa status** before you can import anything. If you have already attained your *Carnet de Retirado (Pensionado/Jubilado* Visa) or other Visa status you will not need further documents. Otherwise, at the time your attorney files the official documentation for your Visa with the Immigration Office, he will request a *Certificado de Recibo de Documentos en Migración* (Immigration Office Documents Reception Certificate). This verifies that the Immigration Office has received your documents and that they are being processed. If you do not have legal residential status, you will be required to pay import duties and taxes on the goods you import.

In addition to the above, you will also need a notarized copy of your passport including the page with your photo and the page with your last entrance to Panama entered; the original Bill of Lading, Air Way Bill or Express Release; original packing list without prices and bank certification of account in the name of the retiree living in Panama. Visa types other than *Jubilado* may require additional documents which your attorney or moving company representative can explain.

In the event that your place of residence is not ready when your household goods arrive, the moving company can arrange to store them for you or you can make arrangements to store them yourself. Several storage (*depósitos*) facilities exist.

Automobiles

Shipping a car to Panama is relatively easy. Seaboard Marine, Ltd. can ship out of Miami direct to the Port of Cristobal. They will complete a bill of lading and charge for the freight.

The automobile can come in the container with your household goods or be shipped separately. Prior to the car's arrival you will need to receive a valuation from the customs agent in Panama and pay the required taxes and fees. This is a percentage based on the value of the car, which the Agent looks up in a book similar to the *Kelley's Blue Book* for determining the value. Once the car arrives in Colon, it must be delivered to bonded storage in Panama City. It is possible for you to take possession at this point and deliver the car to Panama City bond yourself. The paperwork processing after this takes about a month.

You will need all the relevant documents on the car including registration and bill of sale. Taxes will depend on your visa status. Some visas allow the importation of a car at little or no duty but you will still **have a minimum sales tax (5% ITBM)** obligation. Once in Panamá, you will need to obtain a *Permiso de Entrada* from the port, and another form from the *Organismo Internacional Regional de Sanidad Agropecuaria* (fumigation certificate), costing $3. Along with a copy of the car's Certificate of Title, Seaboard will prepare a Letter of Intent for the U.S. Customs Service Export Station. When the car arrives you will pay another fee to Transbal, S.A. and receive a release document (*Sírvase Entregar Las Siguientes Unidades*). The Customs Agent, or *Agente Corredor de Aduanas*, importation document will reflect the fees paid. There are many agents who can perform this function.

Keep in mind that when in the future you sell the car, there will be tax liability. If you sell it to another *jubilado,* government employee or embassy employee entitled to the exemption, you and they will avoid the tax. Otherwise, the tax will have to be paid before the car can be re-registered. The value for purposes of this tax does not always reflect actual value. You are responsible and may pay as much in tax at this point as you would have if you had paid it at the original time of import or purchase. In some cases you may find it to your advantage to pay the duty initially rather than delay.

Legal Information Assistance:

*Alvaro Aguilar -
LOMBARDI CAMBRA & AGUILAR
Attorneys at Law
Incorporation and Management of Companies, Trusts and
Foundations, Immigration,
Real Estate, Tax, E-Commerce and
Intellectual Property Law.

Mobile: +507 6638-8707 Fax: +507 270-2521 / 340-6446
Tel: +507 66159926 / 340-6444 / 6449
Email: aaguilar @ nysbar.com Y!Messenger/Skype
aguilara_5389
Airmail address: P.O.Box 0831-01110,
Panama 0831, Panama
Courier address: Aquilino de la Guardia St. Ocean Business
Plaza, 12th Floor, Panama City, Panama
http://www.alvaroaguilar.net

Market Entry Consultancy for Panama

BSC Panama Consultancy, S.A.
Paul Smith, Corporate Consultant
Facilitating corporate business investor's entry into Panama.

Email: psmith@cwp.net.pa
Tel.: 507-264-3240
Apdo 832-1561
World Trade Center, Panama

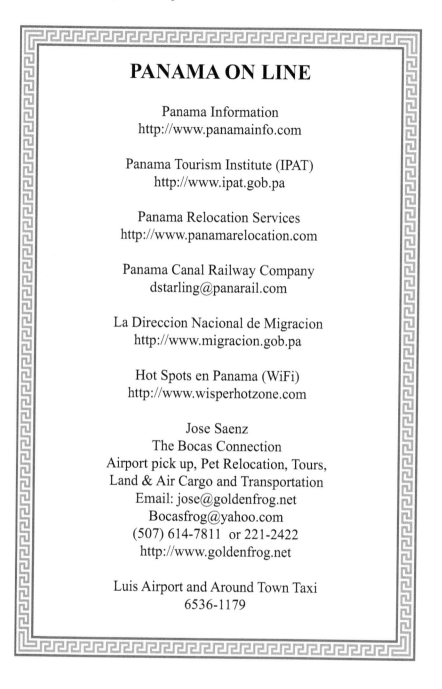

PANAMA ON LINE

Panama Information
http://www.panamainfo.com

Panama Tourism Institute (IPAT)
http://www.ipat.gob.pa

Panama Relocation Services
http://www.panamarelocation.com

Panama Canal Railway Company
dstarling@panarail.com

La Direccion Nacional de Migracion
http://www.migracion.gob.pa

Hot Spots en Panama (WiFi)
http://www.wisperhotzone.com

Jose Saenz
The Bocas Connection
Airport pick up, Pet Relocation, Tours,
Land & Air Cargo and Transportation
Email: jose@goldenfrog.net
Bocasfrog@yahoo.com
(507) 614-7811 or 221-2422
http://www.goldenfrog.net

Luis Airport and Around Town Taxi
6536-1179

Using the Panama Telephone Directory

An interesting difference in language between English and Spanish is that the modifiers, in English come first, but come second in Spanish. For example, you would say a blue bag in English but *bolsa azul* (bag blue) in Spanish.

When it comes to telephone listings the type of business comes first, some times with many unimportant helping words which often determines how a business is listed. For example, the tailor shop *La Fortuna* is listed as *Almacén La Fortuna*. This translates roughly to Store The Fortuna.

If you are looking for a specific school in the yellow pages you will have to search under *escuelas*, *academias*, *colegios*, *universidades*, rather than under the one heading School as in English. Even in the individual listing, the appropriate word for that school may be the first word listed in the name making it more complicated to locate the one you are trying to find. Thus, the School of the United States, *Escuela Estados Unidos de América* is listed under *E* and the *Colegio San Agustin Panamá* is listed under *C*.

Restaurants may have *Restaurante* preceding the actual name or be listed by *La* or *El* (equivalent of The, in English).

III

THE GREAT COMMUNICATOR

You have arrived in Panama and now you wonder how you will keep in touch with your friends and family back home and how you will communicate while in Panama.

Telephones

Panama moved into the twenty-first century when the telephone system was privatized and a British phone company, Cable & Wireless, took over. Where it once took many weeks to get a telephone, now it takes only a few days or a week to get new service connected in the city and major communities. If there is an existing phone in your new house or apartment it is fairly easy to get the service changed into your name and avoid the necessity of disconnecting and reconnecting.

Telephone service comes in several plans starting with limited calling at a basic rate of a few dollars to unlimited calling for $54.95 a month. Rates for businesses are higher. Cable & Wireless rates ($.15/ minute) to the U.S. are cheaper than ATT for long distance. However, there are several companies specializing in long-distance service that start at five cents a minute to the States. Check the front pages 30-33 of the Cable & Wireless Telephone Directory for a complete listing of national and international telecommunication carriers.

Cable & Wireless requires a deposit to open an account but it is refundable should you discontinue service, providing you **produce the original deposit receipt**. As of 2006 the deposit for Panamanian nationals was $40 and $100 for non-Panamanians. *Jubilado*/retiree discounts only apply to **basic** service plans.

Today there are pay telephones conveniently located around town and around the country and they work with phone cards. Phone cards are sold at grocery stores, pharmacies, the phone company, and by street vendors.

Everyone in Panama seems to have a cell phone and they are quick and easy to get. Where it takes a week for a regular phone, you can be connected with a cell phone in a matter of hours. Movistar is the major provider for cell phones but they are also available through Cable & Wireless. There are numerous plans available starting with the phone card system and going up to hundreds of minutes of usage per month. Short-term users may find pre-paid services more convenient than opening an account. Cable & Wireless and Movistar cards are widely available for these systems.

All but the simplest plans include taking messages, call waiting, caller ID, games, address book, camera, radio, instant messaging and automatic dialing. While you can buy your own phone, many plans include the phone. Cell phones are one of the most common things you will see in Panama. In a restaurant, for example, there will often be one on the table for every person present. Since they get so much use, many contracts for service include an annual equipment update. Do keep in mind that it is illegal to drive and talk on the phone and there is a $50 fine if you get caught. Cell phone numbers consist of four digits beginning with 6, followed by four numbers for a total of eight.

The Country code for Panama is "507". When dialing international from Panama, precede the phone number with the code 00 plus the country code. For example to the U.S. from Panama use 001. When calling Panama from the U.S. or Canada, precede the phone number with 011, then 507 and the local phone number. Other countries have international dialing codes preceding the 507-country code for Panama. (See page 68 of this chapter and the Cable & Wireless Telephone Directory for a complete list.)

Everyone is On Line

The possibilities for being email literate are extensive. Internet cafes are conveniently located in most neighborhoods throughout the city, including some McDonalds, and you will also find them in areas as remote as Boquete, Volcan and El Valle. Hotspots or WiFi friendly locations also exist countrywide. In fact, everyone is connected these days. *The World Factbook* reports that there were 7,013 Internet hosts and 300,000 Internet users in Panama in 2005. In order to connect, you can use your current telephone line (ADSL with Cable & Wireless), go through CableOnda or take advantage of the new wireless service. Fees for the services vary and there are differing opinions on which provide the best and fastest Internet service. Check them all out and decide which plan works best for you and your family and your location. Select carefully, however, as many plans require one-year, non-refundable contracts.

Getting Mail

While Panama does not currently have door-to-door delivery of mail, it does have an extensive post office system countrywide. Cities in Panama are divided into districts or barrios and each one has a local post office where you can rent various size boxes.

Rental rates range from $20 per year for a personal box (*apartado*) to $36 for a business. There are additional charges for changing the lock on a new box, adding other names to the box and there is a special rate for retirees. Box fees are due and payable between January 15 and March 15 yearly and are not prorated. In 2005 Panama updated the *apartado* numbering system so that it is consistent throughout the country. Your box number will consist of 9 digits. (See Postal Codes)

Mail service is generally reliable and inexpensive for regular mail. The cost of an airmail letter to the U.S. or Mexico is 35 cents and 45 cents to Europe. You can expedite your mail by paying the fast rate of 85 cents. There are many reasons, however, that make it desirable to use a mail forwarding service for incoming mail from the U.S., speed of delivery and reliability being only two of them. These services are more reliable for packages of any kind as the providers will handle customs and assure delivery. Mail forwarding services also deliver the mail door-to-door. Currently this kind of service is available through Miami Express, Mail Box Etc or Air Box Express (*Aerocasillas*). These companies offer a U.S. post office address and delivery to Panama daily. Mail sent out of Panama via the Panama post office goes reasonably quickly and reliably but these mail forwarding services will also handle outgoing mail for a fee. Look for these services throughout the country. For domestic mail, private courier services such as Chavale, S.A. are fast and relatively inexpensive for getting packages and even larger items to even the remotest locations. For bulk mail in Panama consider Easy Mail.

A third option for mail service exists on a limited basis for U.S. diplomats, and retired military in Panama. A special post office at the U.S. Consulate operates for these eligible people.

Courier Services

For those documents and packages that need fast, special handling whether coming to you in Panama or being sent anywhere in the world, there are numerous courier services available including UPS, FedEx, and DHL.

Magazines

An extensive selection of local and international magazines is available at many outlets including *Farmacia Arrocha*, *Gran Morrison*, Exedra Books, *Hombre de la Mancha* and major hotel newsstands. Additionally, various newspapers include a variety of magazines for their subscription customers. (See below)

Panama Postal Codes

Postal Codes now consist of the area code (4-digits) plus your personal box number (5-digits). For example:

El Dorado—0819-05452 or a box in Bouquete 0413-00017

Volcan 0424

Boquete 0413

David 0426

Potrerillos Arriba 0434

Panama 1, 3, and 5- 0816, Panama 2- 0811, Panama 4- 0815, Panama 6- 0818, Panama 6A- 0819, Panama 7- 0823, Panama 8- 0827, Panama 9- 0830, Panama 9A- 0834, Panama 10- 0835, Panama 11- 0859, Panama 12- 0838, Panama 13- 0839, Panama 14 -closed, Panama 15- 0850, USMA Closed 0820

Punta Paitilla 0831, World Trade Center (WTC) 0832, Plaza Panama 0833

Universidad 0824

Balboa, Ancon 0843

Villa Lucre 0860

Paraiso 0844

Arraijan 1003

Vista Alegre 1005

Capira 1007

Bejuco 1013

Chame 1011

La Chorrera 1015

San Carlos 1017

El Valle 1001

Colón (Calle 9A) 0301, Colón (Zona Libre) 0302

Gatun 0308

Sabanitas 0312

Gamboa 0801

Chepo 0807

Newspapers

Panama boasts three standard daily newspapers in Spanish that are available for home delivery on a daily basis. There are also four tabloids. The dailies vary by editorial dictates but carry many wire service international articles as well as local news, and the usual feature sections. Panama newspapers have a hometown feel with numerous human-interest stories, society pages, comics, horoscope, and local interest articles. They feature sophisticated formatting, include color photos and include a variety of magazine inserts of special interest.

Panama Newspapers

La Prensa, daily and Sunday includes inserts on a regular basis such as: *Ellas, Autopista* and *Mundo Social* to name only three of about 20 magazines. It features a *Wall Street Journal Americas* edition daily and a *New York Times* Sunday edition (in Spanish). It has a weekly financial and business insert *Martes Financiero.*

Panama-America, daily and Sunday. Comparable to *La Prensa* in scope and content but differing in editorial slant.

La Estrella, daily and Sunday.

La Crítica and *El Siglo,* dailies covering local news of Panama including all the accidents and police blotter complete with explicit photos.

Mi Diario, daily and Sunday.

Tiempos del Mundo, weekly

Capital Financiero, weekly business, finance and economics

Noticias Bajareque Times, free monthly publication aimed at the Chiriquí Province community. English and Spanish. Available in limited locations in Panama City. Also available on line.

Valle de la Luna, David, monthly publication in Spanish.

Bocas Breeze, Bocas del Toro, free monthly newspaper in English available in Bocas and selected locations in Panama,and on line.

El Visitante/The Visitor tourist paper in Spanish and English published twice monthly and available at hotels, various businesses or direct from the publisher. Also available on line.

Embassy Services
(Check with your embassy. Not all offer these services.)

*Citizen registration
*General information on Panama
*Orientation on Panamanian immigration procedures
*Issue new or replacement passports (Appendix 12 and 13)
*Information on home country tax obligations and provide tax
  forms
*Assistance to pensioners and retirees (U.S. Social Security office)
*Diplomatic pouch
*Registration of birth of a child (Appendix 12)
*Advice about consumer problems
*Register to vote
*Consular Notices through a Warden System
*Private mail service
*Notary services for documents to be used in the U.S.

Panama Eagle, in Panama City in English (monthly)
Boletin/Bulletin, Free Zone News in English and Spanish
El Faro, Panama Canal News
Panama News, online commentary in English.
Autorapido—weekly supplement listing autos for sale and lease.
On line at http://www.autorapido.com

International Newspapers

A number of international papers are also available at newsstands and pharmacies in Panama City including:

Wall Street Journal, Miami Herald, and USA Today. Miami Herald International is printed on La Prensa's presses and widely distributed throughout the Republic.

Television

Panama has three sources of television service, CableOnda, Direct TV and the limited reception possible from an antenna. CableOnda offers a variety of plans at different prices and currently there are about 90 channels possible. Direct TV offers about 80 channels and not exactly the same mix of channels. Their selection includes numerous music channels and more movies. Either system offers lots of broadcasts from Panama, Spain, Mexico, BBC, Germany, Venezuela, France, Japan and the U.S. While local and international news programs are "live" many broadcast programs are delayed. The *new season*, for example, may start several months later than in the U.S. If you should miss a program that you especially wanted to see – do not worry because it will often be re-broadcast at least once and often multiple times. This includes seasonal series that may be run from beginning to end more than once during the year. Some programs may also be repeated for no obvious reason at any time. Many stations broadcast in English or are available in multiple language choices through the use of the SAP (second audio program) feature on newer televisions.

In making your selection for service, consider channel variety and number as well as your physical location. In some areas one system may work better than another, especially during heavy rainfall when the signal may be interrupted.

Radio

Panama has numerous radio stations offering talk radio, classical, easy listening and popular music. Rush hour traffic and accidents reports are also a regular feature.

AM Radio Stations

610 Talk, Sports and CNN news
650 AM Radio *Mía Cadena Nacional*
710 AM Talk, Sports
900 AM Talk, Sports
1160 AM Radio Metropolis
1430 AM Radio Kids

FM Radio Stations

88.1 FM Radio 10 *Joven* (Kids)
88.5 FM classical and easy listening
89 FM Stereo
91.3 FM *Principales*
91.5 FM *Oxigeno,* more music less words
92.1 FM Super Estación
92.9 FM *Tropical*
93.5 FM. Sunday, 7 p.m. thru 9 p.m., blues, classical, comedy and news in English. http://www.on-the-radio.com Broadcast to U.S., Canada, Great Britain
93.7 FM Radio Peninsula
94.5 FM Radio *Caracol*
95.9 FM Romance
96.7 FM Power
97.9 FM *Mi Radio*
98.9 FM Easy Rock in English in Panama with frequencies to Colón and its beaches
101.5 FM Financial News and easy listening
102.5 FM Corazón
103.5 FM Boquete.   Noon Saturday (repeated 9:00 p.m.

Wednesday)—*Window to Panama* English broadcast of items of interest about Panamá to the U.S. and Boquete

    4:00 p.m. Saturday—Spanglish
    http://www.window2panama.com/streaming.html, 24/7
    103.9 FM Radio 1000
    104.7 FM Stereo *Suave*
    106.1 FM *Sol*
    107.3 FM Omega Stereo, *El Hit Parade*

Libraries

Cultural differences have until recently prevented the growth of lending libraries and bookstores. In recent years several bookstores have opened and there are books available in Spanish, English and some other languages. Currently there are 58 public libraries throughout the country including the newest in Bocas del Toro. In Panama City the *Biblioteca Nacional Ernesto J. Castillero* (National Library) is the largest. In 2002 a donation from the Japanese permitted the acquisition of audiovisual material for 15 of the libraries in the system. A community-based group in Bocas del Toro also created a Children's library in that area.

In addition, many clubs and social groups maintain small libraries with a large variety of used books in English as well as other languages. These include: Who's New Club, 223-0562; and British Aid Society, 276-6331. These groups maintain their libraries primarily for their client/membership but are not opposed to others using the system. The British Aid Society sells the paperback books for about one dollar, which goes to fund their charity work. All of these groups accept book donations. (See Chapter IV for bookstores.)

Embassies

Foreigners can take advantage of the opportunity to register with their home embassy. The benefit in doing so includes the possibility of being included on a Warden's list for email information updates on topics ranging from voter registration to security alerts worldwide. In an emergency a family member outside the country may be able to locate you through the embassy registry.

In addition to representing their country's interests in Panama, embassies can offer advice and support to their citizens in many different areas. The embassy, however, is not a travel agency, loan service or law firm and the assistance provided is limited.

Calling made easy

Panama Country Code: 011   Area Code: 507

(Country code and area codes are not required for calling within Panama)

Cellular phone numbers are eight digits, beginning with a 6

Country codes for calling other countries:

U.S.: 001	Canada: 001	Greece: 30
Venezuela: 58	Great Britain: 44	Peru: 51
Switzerland: 46	France: 33	Holland: 3
Mexico: 52	Nicaragua: 505	Spain: 34
Puerto Rico: 1787		

See the green pages of the Cable & Wireless Telephone Directory for a Complete Listing

PANAMA ON LINE

Capital
Business news, finance and economics
http://www.capital@capital.com.pa

Tiempos del Mundo
http://www.tdm.com

Latin Trade
http://www.latintrade.com

Mundo Social
mundsocial@cwp.net.pa

Business Panama
http://www.panamacham.com

La Prensa
http://www.prensa.com

Wall Street Journal
http://www.wsj.com

New York Times
http://www.nytimes.com

Cable & Wireless
http://www.cwpanama.com

Boletín/Bulletin
http://www.bulletinpa.com
Email: elboletin@cwpanama.net

PANAMA ON LINE

Noticias Valle de La Luna
http://www.valleluna.org

Noticias Bajareque Times
http://www.bajarequetimes.com

Bocas Breeze
http://www.thebocasbreeze.com

Mail Boxes Etc
Mbe_boquete@cwpanama.net

Fletes Chavale, S.A.
Chavale5ta@cwpanama.net

Aerocasillas/Mail Box Express
Panama, Boquete, David, Coronado, Bocas del Torro
http://www.airbox.com.pa

Movistar Telefónica
304-7500
304-7000

Bocas Direct
The Business Directory
http://www.bocasdirect.com
Bocasdirect@aol.com
6605-2083

Easy Mail S.A.
http://www.easymail.com.pa

Panama Chocolate

Bocas del Toro is one of the world's best growing regions for Chocolate (Cacao) all be it very small. Green Acres Farms grows, processes and is the source for chocolate for restaurants and shops in Bocas and in the City. They even have a cookbook with recipes for wonderful Chocolate treats.

Remember, *Save the Rainforest, Eat More Chocolate.*

Baysian

The *Baysian* dialect is unique to Panama's melting pot born during the Canal construction era. Enjoy the fun music of Shorty and Slim as they tell the stories in this colorful vocabulary that can describe something exactly right, although you never thought of it that way.

Panama Coffee

Panama growers produce some of the finest highland coffees available in beans (*semilla*) or ground (*molido*). Because it is grown in the high altitudes of Chiriqui it is naturally low in caffeine.

IV

CULTURE SHOCK

Welcome to Panama!

Panama is a sophisticated city in many ways and a delightful place to live. It is much more formal and conservative in dress and attitude than the U.S, Canada or many other western countries. Remember this when you are packing to move to Panama. While you will not need your winter coat, you will need dress clothes—suits, tuxedo, cocktail and evening dress– and generally *city* clothes. Save your shorts and casual clothes for Saturdays, the beach, and the country.

Patience and politeness are rewarded and appreciated. The *People's Guide to Mexico* introduces the section on Guatemala with these words: "Many travelers mistakenly assume that Guatemala is just a smaller version of Mexico…it is very different." Not all Spanish-speaking countries are alike. Keep these words in mind as you begin to discover Panama – it is not Mexico, the U.S. or England or France or Colombia or the country you came from. In Panama life moves at a slower pace–except when driving–than most developed countries. While in Panama the siesta is a thing of the past, lunch–time, from 12:00 to 2:00, creates a mid-day traffic jam as those who can do so head home and those who cannot go home go out to do errands and eat lunch.

Courtesy

Similar to the tradition in Italy, courtesy requires you greet everyone in the room when arriving at a private gathering, entering an elevator or a small office or business. In fact, when in doubt greet the room in general with a *buenos días* (good morning), *buenas tardes* (good afternoon), *buenas noches* (good evening) as may be appropriate. The *beso* is an air kiss at or near the cheek, that is the greeting of choice among friends and relatives whether men, women or children. (Note: men do not kiss other men.) The warmer the kiss, the closer the relationship between the kissers. Although the *abrazo* (little hug) common in Mexico is not generally done here, there is a variation that locals may not even realize they do. It involves putting the two hands on the other person's upper arms or wrists when exchanging the air kiss. When meeting someone for the first time a gentle handshake is appropriate but the two-handed handshake and air kiss are appropriate thereafter.

Titles

Titles are important and are always used when addressing people in a formal situation. While you may be accustomed to using the title of Doctor with your family physician, in Panama you will address your teacher as *Profesor* or *Maestro*, an Engineer as *Ingeniero* and Attorney or Physical Therapist as *Licenciado*. Using the title is a sign of respect and not to do so is considered rude. Anyone with the equivalent of a Bachelor's degree from a University is entitled to be addressed as *Licenciado* and will usually use the designation *Lic.* before their name. The designation of feminine or masculine common in the Spanish language is also used here as *Dr.* is masculine and *Dra.* is feminine.

Special Understanding

In Western Culture work is valued. Long hours at the office, assuming more and more responsibility, making tough decisions and being able to do things oneself is respected and admired. Similarly, relaxing on the weekend involves cutting the grass, washing the car or putting up the screens. But, remember this is Panama and Latin Culture has a different set of rules. The more work you can delegate, especially manual labor, the more you are esteemed. This helps to explain why the maid may not take a message, the gardener does not clean up the sidewalk, and everyone drops trash everywhere outside his or her own property. Traditionally decisions were made in committees, although this is changing. Even so, employees in general defer decision making to a higher level. Washing your car will degrade you in the eyes of those observing the action. Thus, everyone strives to have a maid, a nanny or two, a gardener, car-wash boy, or driver.

Panamanians are a warm and friendly people, anxious to help. They will ask a favor and they will not be surprised or offended if you ask favors of them. However, ask a favor once, owe a favor forever. This dilemma comes in two types. Often an employee will ask for a favor, perhaps an advance on salary, or extra cash for some "unforeseen" expense. If you are able to assist one time, the employee will assume he can continue to ask for other favors. Secondly, you might ask a friend for a favor of a social, not work-related, type. If granted, the friend will then feel justified to ask you for comparable and multiple favors in the future. Be careful what you ask for so as not to abuse the system or be taken advantage of in the process.

Entertaining and Special Occasions

Entertaining is formal in the city but more relaxed in the country or at the beach on weekends. However, even at the beach your hosts will most likely either have staff at these homes or bring their city staff with them. Regardless, of where you are being entertained, no one will expect you to pick up your dishes or make your bed.

Birthdays are very important. Everyone will help you celebrate your birthday and in fact they will be quite upset with you if you deny them this delightful happening. Celebrating birthdays gives your friends an opportunity to demonstrate how much they care for you whether with a telephone call, card, flowers or simple gift. For the co-workers at the office it provides a welcome diversion from the daily tasks as everyone shares cake and coffee and an opportunity to wish you well. Keep a list of birthdays for the people important to you and help them celebrate. Children's birthdays are addressed below and in Chapter VI.

Mother's Day is the most important occasion in Panama. Several years ago there was a movement to adjust holidays to create more three-day weekends. No one had any objection to celebrating something on a Monday or a Friday in order to provide a long weekend, until it came to the outrageous idea of moving Mother's Day from the established date of December 8. This is such a revered Catholic holiday that not even the incentive of more time off would persuade the Panamanians to change the date. Remember mom with cards, flowers, candy or dinner out.

Weddings are covered in Chapter XI.

Gift Giving

Panamanians are great givers of gifts. It is not unusual to receive a little gift when someone comes to your house for dinner or for just a glass of wine.

Whether it is a wedding or a birthday or any other occasion, recycling is also part of the system. It is especially prevalent for birthdays as the children's parties can easily involve 50-100 children. That many gifts for one or even two children all at one time would be overwhelming. While many parents, put some aside for presentation later in the year, more common is the practice of passing on those gifts at the next birthday the children are invited to attend. Not just birthdays, wedding gifts that just do not suit the new couple, are used for gifts to other friends at their weddings, or as Christmas or birthday presents. My father used to love to tell the story about a box of Whitman Sampler Chocolates that he and his brother passed back and forth at Christmas for about five years. It was a family joke and perhaps the epitome of recycling. However, since living in Panama I once made the mistake of giving the children of a friend a gift for Christmas that the mother did not see me deliver. The children opened it, put it aside and clearly it was later retrieved by the parent and put in the recycle category. The next Christmas it was given back to me as a gift! She clearly had not figured out who gave it to the children and made the mistake of giving it back to the original giver. The next time I gave it as a gift it did not come back.

Time

Western and Eastern cultures alike put great value on time. To Latins, time has a different meaning, like traffic lights, it is a suggestion rather than the rule. Therefore, when inviting your Latin friends to an event or party give them a time 30-45 minutes earlier than your gringo friends. That way everyone should arrive at about the same time.

Meal Times

Dining in Panama is a delightful experience whether at the home of friends or at any of the dozens of good restaurants. Breakfast tends to be a light affair, in general, often consisting of coffee and a cheese sandwich or empanada. Lunch is at 1:00 and is usually the big meal of the day consisting of meat, plantain, rice and dessert. Rice and plantain are two essentials in the Panamanian diet and cooking rice is considered an art form. Dinner is usually sometime after 7:30 p.m. See Appendix 4 Local Cuisine and Appendix 10 Restaurants for my personal favorites. It is polite to wish *buen provecho* (good appetite) to your tablemates.

Bargaining, Negotiating, Discounts

While less common than in Mexico or Guatemala, the fine art of bargaining does exist in Panama. There are all sorts of opportunities for a discount (*descuento*) if you just ask. **Legal resident retirees** are entitled by law to a variety of discounts and if you are fortunate to have this status either as a Panamanian national or *extranjero* with a special visa, ask at the pharmacy, the doctor or hospital, restaurant or airline counter. (See Appendix 3 Benefits for Retirees. Do not ask if you are not a legal resident. Restrictions apply.) Keep in mind that these discounts are a cost of doing business for the local merchant. Do you really need to ask for a discount on a meal under $10?

On a more informal basis, ask for a discount when purchasing native handicrafts especially if you buy in quantity. While a major clothing store, supermarket, liquor store or hardware is less likely to bargain in the traditional sense, they, too, will offer special prices for good customers making large purchases.

Learning Spanish

While it is possible to live in Panama and not speak Spanish, you will have a more interesting experience, varied life style and more opportunities if you learn the language. Language schools, private tutors, conversation groups and the various universities are resources. Many language schools are distributed throughout the downtown area as well as the interior making it convenient to attend. Classes at these schools and universities are based on skill level and are often offered early in the morning or after working hours. Classes are by the semester or course (generally 4-6 weeks). There are also classes available for children to study English or Spanish during the Panama summer months (January to March). Private tutors will come to your home or office and charge by the hour. The going rate is between $20 and $25 per hour.

Panamanians appreciate your efforts to speak the language and will be patient, friendly and helpful. Use what you know. Besides, the more you practice the more your skills will improve. The Who's New Club offers conversation groups in several languages for women, and other social groups afford opportunities to further your practice. Additionally, reading the local paper will not only keep you up-to-date on local happenings but also improve your language skills. Television *novelas* (soap operas) are another good source of training for your ear.

Language Schools

Spanish Learning Center
El Cangrejo
Tel.: 214-4914

University of Panama
El Cangrejo or Vía La Amistad
Tel.: 263-6133

Spanish Panama. Com
Building Anita, Main floor, El Cangrejo
Tel.: 213-3121, 6697-3863
http://ww.w.spanishpanama.com
Email: info@spanishpanama.com

Berlitz
Ave. Balboa and Calle A. Ruiz
Plaza Balboa Bay, Marbella
http://www.berlitz.com
Email: info@berlitz.edu.pa

Spanish by the Sea
Bocas del Toro, Isla Colón
Tel/Fax : 507-757-9518
http://www.SpanishbytheSea.com

Spanish by the River, Boquete
http://www.spanishbytheriver.com
Email: Info@spanishbythesea.com
Tel.: 507-720-3456

ILISA Spanish Language Schools
Tel.: 1-800-454-7248 (toll free)
Tel.: 011 (507) 317-1011 (Panama City)
Email: thorwald@ilsa.com
http://www.ilisa.com

ELS Language Center
Calle 54
Obarrio
Tel.: 264-0924

Learn Spanish in Boquete
http://www.HablaYaPanama.com
Tel.: 507-720-1294

Private Tutors

Daniella Stransky
Punta Paitilla
Portuguese, Spanish, French
Tel.: 264-8772, 6615-1663

Sandra Snyder
La Cresta
English
Tel.: 264-0567
Email: stspanama@pobox.com

Noris Collazos
Las Cumbres
English
Tel.: 239-3885

Language Tips

There is no better way to learn a language than to be totally immersed in it and the culture. Studying in Panama while living here provides many opportunities to both listen and practice what you are learning. Even the most limited television selection will include numerous programs in Spanish or with Spanish subtitles. Listening to the radio while driving around town is another opportunity to sharpen your skills. Buy a newspaper daily and, using your dictionary, you will not only keep up with the current events of the day but also hone your reading skills. Take every opportunity to practice what you have learned. Spanish speaking people in general and Panamanians specifically are patient with foreign speakers and are pleased when you make the effort to use their language.

One last suggestion, when about to enter a situation in which you need to speak Spanish (at the bank, doctor's office, gas station, etc.) think through how the conversation or question and answer exchange would go in English. Often, the same general format will be followed in this new situation. For example: at the doctor's office you are going to be asked your name, address, phone number, date of birth, age, ailment, etc. You can anticipate these questions (in Spanish) and prepare your answers (in Spanish) ahead of time thus, improving your communication skills.

Below is a list of suggested Spanish Language books to help you. At a minimum buy the *501 Verbs* and a good dictionary.

Spanish and English have a common heritage in Latin and, as a result, there are some 2000 cognates or words that are basically the same in spelling, pronunciation and meaning in both languages. One technique to try when attempting Spanish, is use the biggest words you know and by changing the ending of the English word you will be speaking Spanish. This sort of works as in the following examples:

Spanish	English	Spanish	English
-mente	-ly	absolutamente	absolutely
-dad	-ty	necesidad	necessity
-cion	-tion	condición	condition
v	b	automóvil	automobile
f	ph	frase	phrase

Big Words Equivalent Examples

Administration	administración
Anniversary	aniversario
Anonymous	anónimo
Anticipate	anticipar
Approximate	aproximar
Circumstance	circunstancia

Concentration	concentración
Edifice/building	edificio
Grand	grande
Hospital	hospital
Refinement	refinamiento
Representation	representación

However, be aware that there are also false cognates, words that sound like their English equivalent but have very different meanings, as in:

Embarazada to mean embarassed. *Embarazada* actually means pregnant!

Studying French or Chinese

Panama has such a diverse population that you will find classes and tutors in a variety of languages in addition to English and Spanish. The *Alianza Francesa* offers classes in French language, culture, film and social events for Francophiles and friends.

La Alianza Francesa
Email: alliance@cableonda.net
223-7376 or 223-5972

The Chinese Cultural Center in El Dorado offers a variety of classes including Chinese cooking and Mandarin.

http://www.ocac.gov.tw/overseaseng
Email: ccchp@ccchp-isys.edu.pa
236-0255

German Cultural Center, *Centro Cultural Aleman,* offers courses in German at all levels.

http://www.centroculturalaleman.com,
Email: centroaleman@udi.edu, 225-1926.

Culture & Language

So you speak a little Spanish? Panama, like all other Spanish-speaking countries, has its own jargon, colloquialisms and special ways of saying things. It may be a *banda* in Mexico but it is a *cinturón* in Guatemala and a *correa* (belt) in Panama. Mexican Spanish is often *colorful* but in contrast you will find Panamanians speak a very proper and polite Spanish. Words learned in Mexico in daily use are never used in Panama. You will hear *chuleta*, which does not mean pork chop, used in a moment of exasperation. Spanglish is very common, however. The presence of the large American population has had more influence than just the Canal. You will hear *garaje* (garage) instead of *bodega, parking* instead of *estacionamiento, walking closet* for walk-in closet, bacon instead of *tocino, mitin* for meeting, and e-mail, just to mention a few examples.

Some fun words you will encounter include:

Push button—push button (motel for secret rendezvous)

Bochinche—gossip, a favorite pastime

Bajareque—drizzle rain common in Boquete

Diablo rojo—Red Devil or Panama bus

Wachiman—watchman/security guard

Tranque—traffic pile-ups

En camino—in the street, anytime you are not home

Más o menos—more or less

Tocayos—people with the same name

Muy especial—describes a person who is difficult

Viejos verdes—old men (gringos) with green (money) known to gather in Bocas del Toro and casinos in the City

Panamanians drop the last letters of words. A good example of this is differentiating between twelve thirty and two thirty. Sounds simple—in English. However, in Spanish *doce y media* (12:30) and *dos y media* (2:30) both sound like *doughy media*. If you are making a reservation for lunch, an appointment with the doctor or just confirming the time to meet with a friend, it can be very confusing.

Superstitions

There are lots of expressions, proverbs and superstitions that are common to Panama and taking a Spanish class will expose you to these insights into Panamanian thinking. One of these superstitions is about ironing. Your maid will tell you to only iron at night (it is cooler) and "when you are ironing do not get near anything cold (including air conditioning) or open the refrigerator door as you are sure to contract arthritis"! Use this one to your benefit if you do your own ironing. You can tell your husband that he will have to take you out to dinner after a day of doing the family ironing, as it was not possible to open the refrigerator to take out anything for dinner!

New Year's Good Luck

Originally the idea of a Spanish king in a year with an excellent grape harvest, it has become tradition in Panama and other Latin countries to eat 12 grapes as the clock strikes 12 midnight on New Year's Eve. One grape per strike of the clock is the custom but if there is no clock to guide you, just eat them at your leisure at the midnight hour.

Proverbs and Expressions

Many of the proverbs and expressions are similar to those used in English but there are many unique ones.

Mas vale pájaro en mano que cien volando. (A bird in the hand is better than 100 flying.)

Mas vale tarde que nunca. (Better late than never.)

When saying good by to friends, "Big Kiss" (*beso grande*) is a common farewell.

Juega vivo

Juega vivo is translated as the game of life, but in Panama it means more as interpreted by the locals: "play it smart", "take any unfair advantage to get what you want". "Ignore all the rules, do what you need to get what you want." "Play fast and loose with the rules." "The rules are for the other guy, not me." This goes a long way to explain attitudes in Panama in general whether driving a car, dealing with government, standing in line or doing business.

Do's and Don'ts

Do say *Buenos Días, Buenas Tardes, Buenas Noches*. Do not say *Hola* (Hi) except to close friends, children and animals.

Do air kiss the cheek. Do not give hand-crunching handshakes.

Do greet everyone when entering or leaving a room.

Do give your Panamanian friends an arrival time 30 to 45 minutes earlier than the rest of your guests. Do not be offended if they still arrive late.

Do have patience when conducting any kind of business whether personal or professional. Do not show impatience or yell.

Do use your horn when driving. Do keep moving in traffic; Do not pull out and stop.

Do be aware of social class. Do not discriminate by color.

Do *Dress* all the time, no matter where you are going. Do not wear tank tops, shorts, or shirts with writing on them except at home or at the beach or weekends.

Do call your friends often. Do not call them on Sunday.

Do not bring drugs, use drugs or get caught with any amount of illegal drugs. Panama has a zero tolerance policy.

Do not wear your hat inside, especially at the table.

Do not leave your dog's droppings where they fall.

Do not talk loudly in public places.

Rabiblanca

Panama is similar to many other Latin countries in that it historically identifies its heritage with a group of founding families. The rabiblancas are the descendants of ten elite families that form the social structure of the country. They are also the core members of the Union Club.

Big Fish in a Small Pond

Two key things to keep in mind in Panama: Everyone is related to everyone. That is why it is important to know to whom you are speaking and never speak ill of anyone. Because Panama is such a small country, a small town, you can be a big fish in a small pond. It is assumed that you as an *extranjero* must be one or two social levels above what you actually would be in your home country. Otherwise, how could you hold the position that you do or be able to travel and live abroad as you do? Remember Panamanians are social conscious.

Coming to Panama? Think City!

When you come to Panama, plan to **DRESS**. In Panama City, the dress is very formal considering the climate. Business dress for men is suit and tie, or long-sleeve shirt and slacks, and comparably appropriate dress for the ladies. Many offices require uniforms, which may be a dress shirt and tie for men and a coordinated skirt and blouse or suit for the ladies. Regular daytime wear for the ladies is what is called the *Panama Lady Dress*. It is a two-piece suit, short sleeved and like a suit but worn without an additional blouse. These should be of lightweight fabrics, in general, but buildings are over air-conditioned so dress for cold weather inside! A shawl is always handy. Either pants or skirts are acceptable for women. The Panama Lady Dress will take you to the office, to lunch, to tea, even out in the evening depending on the style and fabric. There are many events during the year for black tie, cocktail dresses and long gowns. Weddings, in particular, are formal affairs.

Remember, you will be treated according to how you look and dress. Good grooming is essential. In the States a mechanic would not think twice about going to the store in his work clothes, but in Panama any worker will shower and change to nice clothes before leaving his or her place of work. If you are going to do business at a government or business office, dress accordingly. If you are going shopping downtown, dress appropriately. Shorts, tank tops, athletic attire, baseball caps are not appropriate out of context. Many government offices, including those of the Canal administration and immigration will not allow you to enter in shorts. Similarly, remember to remove your hat when you go indoors, especially at a restaurant. If you keep in mind that tennis shoes are for playing tennis; and if your outfit looks like something to wear while washing the car, you probably are not dressed for doing anything but playing tennis or washing the car!

Panamanians, especially the ladies, put great emphasis on beauty. When planning an evening out, a dinner party at home or just regular maintenance, a manicure and pedicure are customary. Some indulge in an all day session including massage, manicure, pedicure, waxing, hairstyle, facial and makeup as part of the requirements. These services are readily available and at reasonable prices so enjoy the custom.

Being well groomed for the men is equally important. Panamanians consider beards in the same vein as a mask. In fact, masks in public are illegal—you are trying to hide. If you are accustomed to wearing a beard you may want to rethink the practice, especially until after you complete all legal processes required for immigration. A moustache, well trimmed, is not considered offensive.

While dress is more formal in the city, the general idea of presentable dress in public is equally as important in the small towns of the interior. To the foreigner, the dress in these towns may seem casual, but the locals will still be careful about dress when visiting important offices or just going "downtown" to shop. You should follow their example.

Panama has many good restaurants of all types and you can have afternoon high tea in several different places. In Panama's nicer restaurants you will find men in a sport coat and no tie, or long-sleeve shirt and slacks. Shorts are never appropriate.

Since Panama is very international, you will find a group or a club of every description to fit your interests. With all there is to see and do in Panama, there is no opportunity for you to get bored and lots of opportunities to dress up!

On weekends, however, Panamanians head for the beaches or mountains and the dress shifts accordingly. Beach and resort wear are expected at Coronado, Gorgona, Contadora, Decameron or any of the many beaches or islands on both coasts. In El Valle jeans and a casual shirt are in vogue. If you do find yourself in the City on Saturday, tailored shorts, sport shirt and deck shoes are acceptable for men around town in the daytime. And, around the house there is nothing more comfortable than the *Guaymi* dress. This is the traditional dress for the women of a group of Indians of Chiriqui and Bocas del Toro. This colorful, loose cotton dress is perfect for informal entertaining or lounging around the house.

Everything you want or need is available in Panama and at good quality including the necessary umbrellas. There are many stores for evening gowns and everything else. However, prices are higher than in the U.S. Dry cleaning is less expensive than in the U.S, and is readily available but the quality is *variable.*

Life in the Tropics. Remember, clothes must be cleaned between wearing or they will mold. Storage in plastic bags should be avoided for the same reason. Additionally, leather requires constant care or it will start growing. Shoes need very special attention both because of the tendency to grow mold and the deterioration of the glue. It is not uncommon to have strappy sandals let go on the dance floor. I carry Crazy Glue in my evening bag as I have had this happen on more than one occasion. Heel caps, and similar glued-on parts of shoes as well as the sole in general are not immune to just disintegrating in this climate. The good news is that Panama has lots of shoe stores, offering a wide variety of fun shoes at reasonable prices as well as good shoe repair shops. See Appendix 11 for handy household hints.

Pollera Dress and Folkloric Dancing

One of the most beautiful local traditions involves not only the *folkloric* or typical (*típico*) dancing of Panama but it is done in the exquisite *pollera* dress. These dresses are regional and handmade. Yards and yards of fine white handkerchief linen, hand gathered and embroidered and lace trimmed with handmade petticoats beneath, are just the beginning of the ensemble. Each dress takes a year or more to make and is custom made for each young lady. As if they were not spectacular by themselves, they are then further accessorized with yards of gold necklaces and bracelets. A little pompom or ribbon of contrasting color hangs front and back and determines the color of the satin slippers on the feet to complete the bottom of the outfit. On the head is the crowning touch in an array of either white or multi-color hair decoration known as the *tembleques*. This headdress made of fish scales is often added to over a period of years and is quite elaborate.

The dancers of the *Folkloric Ballet* or traditional dance troupes are delightful to watch as they spin around the floor showing off the dresses to best advantage. In contrast, the male partners are simply dressed in black pants, traditional pleated shirt, hat, and black and white slippers. However, different regions of Panama offer variations in the style of the shirt, generally known as a *guayabera*.

There are also more casual variations of traditional dress called the *basquiña*. This easy to wear linen two-piece dress can be custom made at a reasonable price or purchased ready-made in Central Avenue.

The *pollera* festival is held annually on July 20th in Las Tablas. This is a wonderful opportunity to view the most beautiful display of national attire including the oldest and best of the *polleras*. A similar festival of *polleras* is held in Panama City. http://www.danzaspanama. com

Restaurants

The choice of restaurants is excellent and includes everything from fast food to gourmet. Whether you are looking for something *típico* (traditionally Panamanian) or continental, Panama will not disappoint. One thing Panama does have in common with Mexico is the *churro*. This delightful extruded variation of the donut is popular in Mexico and found in Panama. Keep it in mind next time you want the best cappuccino in town and something delightful to go with it and head for Manolo's in El Cangrejo on Vía Argentina, or in Obarrio.

For a delightful selection of pastas and equally interesting sauces to accompany them at a reasonable price and served in a lovely outdoor café setting, be sure to get to know El Pomodoro Café in the Las Vegas Hotel. When something a little more upscale is on your agenda, reserve a window table on the garden at La Posta. I was sad when Golosinas closed and the wonderful owner, Lourdes, moved to El Valle. However, she has opened *Casa de Lourdes* in a beautiful country setting that is well worth the drive to enjoy. And, whether in the city or Boquete, Machu Picchu creates delicious Peruvian cuisine. (See Appendix 10 for my complete list of Tried and True Restaurants.)

In the past the tip has not been added onto the bill and tipping in restaurants is usually 10%. However, recently many restaurants have started adding this in automatically. Check your bill so you do not tip twice.

No precautions are necessary when dining out, as Panama offers an excellent selection of all types of food at good quality. However, when dining in the old part of town you need to be alert to your surroundings. Do not wear flashy jewelry and do park near the restaurant where you are dining. Most restaurants have a parking attendant who will direct you. For valet parking a dollar tip is customary but less than one dollar is appropriate for a car watcher.

Music

Music and dance are to Panama what Fred and Ginger are to the U.S., only here it is Sammy and Sandra Sandoval, a brother and sister musical team. Salsa is the dance of choice although any Latin beat will start moving the feet and every other body part. It is possible to take dance lessons for any of the popular dances, tango - salsa, cha-cha - so take advantage of the opportunity and dance.

Two other kinds of music are typical to Panama. *Pindín* is what you will hear on the party busses (*chivas parranderas*) rented for an evening of driving around the city, drinking and stopping to dance all over town.

This is a favorite to celebrate birthdays or any other occasion.

Murga is the music of Carnival and national holidays. Lots of horns and drums played loudly with enthusiasm make this local favorite readily recognizable.

Business Customs

Know with whom you are dealing and their family connections. In Panama as many other places, it is not what you know but whom you know. Panamanians follow this advice when meeting new people and do not be surprised if they ask you whom you are related to and who you know. They like to establish how you fit in before they get friendly.

When conducting business, start any meeting with polite conversation. Topics to be covered include the weather, family, the weekend past and weekends planned. The business to be discussed should be the last item on the agenda. While this may seem inefficient by Western standards, it is expected and gets the job done, if a bit later than you are accustomed to experiencing.

Get it in writing. Only contracts written in Spanish are recognized in Panama.

If you come from a country where realtors work weekends and especially hold "open house" on Saturday or Sunday and holidays, you are in for a surprise here. Realtors work Monday through Friday as a rule. However, some realtors are beginning to be available on Saturday mornings and the occasional open house can be found. Model apartments and houses are available especially as the housing market expands.

A check of the officially recognized holidays in Panama will alert you that it might be difficult to get things done sometimes. In general the month of November has enough official and unofficial holidays to make it challenging to get anything accomplished, especially in a government office. February is the carnival month and everything slows down. Do not plan on accomplishing much from the week before Christmas until about the 6th of January and for a week at Easter. Everyone takes off from Thursday till Sunday of *Semana Santa* (Easter Week). As long as you know about these dates and can plan around them, the normal weekends away and long weekends that come throughout the year, you can manage. In fact, go with the flow and plan to enjoy the time away from the office. Otherwise try to avoid needing a mechanic or a doctor during those times.

Weekends Away

Families are important and from Friday afternoon until Monday morning the weekend is for the family. Just ask any Panamanian; "no one is in the city on weekends." They head for the *interior*, which is any part of Panama outside the City. If you are not at the beach house, you are at the country house–or alternate weekends from one to the other. Having a boat adds another option to the weekend plans. One of the most delightful experiences you may be privileged to have is being invited to a friend's cottage in El Valle, beach house at Coronado or Contadora, or Gorgona, or on a sail to Taboga. The Latin love of family and resulting closeness is one of the many wonderful experiences of living in Panama. Adopt the custom of total relaxation on weekends and realize the benefits.

Zonians

The Canal Zone was a ten-mile wide, 50-mile long stretch of land running parallel to the Panama Canal. The United States had jurisdiction over this 500 square-mile area by rights granted it under the 1903 treaty. It was in this area that many of the seventeen military bases in Panama were located and it was in this area that the Canal employees and their families lived and worked and played.

With the implementation of the Panama Canal Treaty October 1, 1979, the Canal Zone came under the jurisdiction of Panama. During the 20-year transition period that followed, U.S. properties and lands, not required for the Canal operation, were gradually turned over to the government of Panama. The total transfer was completed December 31, 1999.

The Canal employees and generally anyone living in the Zone became known as *Zonians*. Many of these people are second, third, fourth, even fifth generation residents of the Canal Zone and Panama. Prior to the signing of the treaty for the turnover of the canal, everything they needed was available in the Zone commissaries or provided for them. They had their own schools, clubs, organizations, services, hospitals, police, fire department and legal system. Many of them married Panamanians and their children became dual nationals.

Many changes occurred after the treaty implementation and the Zone opened up, and more changes have continued since the turn over. Most U.S. Canal employees retired and moved to the U.S. The military bases and their personnel were transferred to the U.S., Puerto Rico, Ecuador and other countries. However, a small number of U.S. citizens who continue to work for the Canal, and some Canal retirees still live in these Canal communities. Others who left initially have found their way back to Panama to live, especially as they approach retirement age. Many of them are descendants of the creators of the Engineering Wonder of the World, The Panama Canal. Read *Red, White and Blue Paradise* for an understanding of life in the hay-day of the Canal Zone. (See Chapter *I*, Recommended Reading.)

Currently the transferred military bases have taken on a new life as desirable housing areas. The transformation of Albrook, for example, has resulted in a delightful residential area. Clayton has both developing residential areas, the *Ciudad de Saber* (City of Knowledge) with numerous schools, the offices of the United Nations, UNICEF, and research facilities.

In more recent years, whole new housing communities have been built in these areas such as Albrook Gardens and most recently, apartment buildings have started to appear in Clayton and Amador Heights.

With the building of the new facility for the U.S. Embassy, Consulate and related facilities in Clayton, new housing developments aimed at the employees of these facilities are under construction. When completed in 2007 the resulting Embassy facility and community may in part be reminiscent of the old Canal Zone.

Useful Language Books
Dictionaries
Diccionario Inglés-Español, Español-Inglés, Edwin B. Williams, Bantam, 1989, ISBN 0-553-26370-6.

The New World Spanish/English Dictionary, Signet Publishing, 1996, ISBN 0451-1816-89.

The Oxford-Duden Pictorial Spanish & English Dictionary, Clarendon Press, Oxford, 1985, ISBN 0-19-869155-6. (Bilingual pictorial dictionary providing English and Spanish names for everyday articles, machines, urban and rural structures and their component parts and materials.)

Simon & Schuster's International Dictionary, Spanish-English, English-Spanish, Second Edition, 1997, MacMillan General Reference, ISBN 0-02-862013-5.

Grammars
Essential Spanish Grammar, Seymour Resnick, Dover Publications, Inc., New York, 1964, Standard Book Number 486-20780-3, Library Congress Catalog Card Number 63-4093.

501 Spanish Verbs, Christopher Kendris, Barron's Educational Series, Inc., 1996, ISBN 0-8120-2602-0.

Hamel's Comprehensive Bilingual Dictionary of Spanish False Cognates, Bilingual Book Press, 1998, ISBN 1-886835-06-3. (Bilingual reference book detailing false cognates, the correct definitions of the false cognates and the correct terms to use.)

La Fuerza de las Palabras, Selecciones del Reader's Digest, México City, D.F., México, 1977, ISBN 847-142180-1. (Very detailed review of Spanish grammar and writing styles. While the styles are somewhat dated, the grammar is one of the most detailed in print.)

Bilingual Reference Books
Dictionary of Proverbs and Sayings, English-Spanish Spanish-English, Berta Alicia Chen, CMC Publishing, Inc., 1998, SBN 9962-810-00-0.

Idiomatic Expressions, Expresiones Idiomáticas, Antonio Carbajo, Editorial Diana, 1997, ISBN 9681-1320-530.

Spanish Course Books

Bravo! At a glance, Tracy D. Terrell, et al., McDougal Little/ Houghton Mifflin, 1993, ISBN 0-8123-8700-7. Nine main units present Spanish in a way that will allow you to talk about topics and situations that are of interest to you and your friends.

Spanish Language, Grammar, Tenses, Uses, Examples, Exercises, Answers, Pablo V. Castellanos S., Antigua, Guatemala, 1987.

A Structural Course in Spanish, David L. Wolfe, et al., The Macmillan Company, New York, 1963.

Think and Talk Advanced Spanish, Berlitz Publishing Company, 1991, ISBN 2-8315-1163-1.

Party Places for Children

McDonald's
Tel.: 270-6700

Kid's Planet
Tel.: 214-7022

Kid's Zone
Tel.: 264-5844

Space Play World
http://ww.spaceplayworld.com
Tel.: 302-2305 Albrook Mall
Tel.: 302-4864 Los Pueblos

Great Party Supply Shopping

GDP
Calle 70 San Francisco and Ave. 3a
Tel.: 270-2444

Machetazo
Via España/Central Avenue, Calidonia
Tel.: 227-3222

Gago Aldea Navideña (Christmas Store)
Costa del Este, Parque Industrial, Calle 2d
Tel.: 271-5226

UPIM
Calle 1ra. El Carmen
Tel.: 263-9694

Galeria de Regalos, S.A.
Calle 50 & Via España Tel.: 300-7065

Looking for Books in Spanish, English, French

Exedra Books
Vía España & Vía Brazil
http://www.exedrabooks.com
Tel.: 264-4252

Gran Morrison
Los Pueblos: 217-7155
Supercentro El Dorado: 2607403/260-5316/260-3995
Vía España: Tel.: 269-2211/223-3286
Vía Transístmica: 261-5871/261-5777/261-5568
http://www.pananet.com/lewis

Hombre de La Mancha
http://www.bookshombredelamancha.com
Email: informacion@bookshombredelamancha.com
Multiplaza, Multicentro, Dorado, Calle 52 Bella Vista,
Albrook Mall, Chiriquí Mall, Cesar Park, Chitré, Aeropuerto
de Albrook, Causeway

Farmacia Arrocha
Tel.: 360-4000
http://www.arrocha.com/farmacia.html
Ricardo J. Alfaro, Los Pueblos, Vía España, Vía Argentina,
Calle 50, Los Andes, Punta Paitilla, Albrook, Costa del Este,
David

Libreria Argosy
Vía España & Argentina
Tel.: 223-5344

PANAMA ON LINE

Canine Carriers
http://www.caninecarrriers.com

Animal Land Pet Movers
http://www.petmovers.com

Balboa Academy
http://www.BalboaAcademy.org

The International School of Panama
http://www.isp.edu.pa

City Club Panama
http://www.cityclubpanama.com

Rand McNally Maps, Guidebooks
http://www.randmcnally.com

Avalon Travel Publications
http://www.travelmatters.com

Florida State University
http://www.fsu.edu/panama

The Oxford School
http://preescolaroxford.com

Almacen La Fortuna
The Tailor of Panama
302-7890/91

Identification Required

Panama law requires that everyone, nationals and *extranjeros* carry a photo ID at all times. This can be in the form of a *cedula* for nationals, *jubilado* visa card (*carnet*) or other similar visa card issued by the Panama government, or a passport.

If you do not want to carry your passport with you, a copy of the page with your personal information and photo plus the page showing your entry to Panama is sufficient.

While your Panama driver's license has a photo and your fingerprint, it is not considered acceptable identification except in instances involving driving.

V

A HOUSE, AN APARTMENT, A HOME

In Panama City and Beyond

Traditionally, city living meant apartment living. Panama City has as many apartments of every size and description as you would find in any major city. Whether you own it or rent it, apartment is the correct word. Although the term condominium is becoming popular, it is not in common use. In recent years more single-family houses and duplexes have become available in a number of neighborhoods and are popular with locals and foreigners alike. There remains one big advantage of apartments over houses, however. It is easier to just lock the door and leave your apartment feeling secure whether you are just traveling to the interior for the weekend or taking an extended vacation.

Panama City is divided into neighborhoods called *barrios*. The most popular in the downtown area for residences include: **Punta Paitilla, Bella Vista, Obarrio, El Cangrejo, El Carmen, La Cresta**, and **Marbella**. A little more suburban are the areas of **El Dorado, Betania, La Alameda, San Francisco, Parque Lefevre, Coco del Mar, Costa**

del Este and **Altos de Golf**. New and an expansion of the Punta Paitilla area is **Punta Pacifica**. Since the turn over of the U.S. military bases in 1999, Panama has been developing and selling the "reverted" areas. Many of these outlying housing areas offer single-family houses as well as duplexes with large yards and surrounding park area. Most recently they have started developing some mid-rise apartments in these areas as well, which include **Amador**, **Albrook**, **Cardenas**, **Clayton**, **Balboa**, **Albrook Gardens** and **Ancon**.

A Room With a View

One of the wonderful advantages of high-rise living is the incredible view. From your window you can look out at the hills, the Canal, the bay or the city. Regardless of where you look, Panama is one of the most beautiful cities in which you will ever live.

Apartment buildings in Panama range from as few as six stories to as many as 40 or more and the range of services and facilities are as diverse. Almost all buildings have 24-hour security, parking, and elevators. Many buildings offer emergency generators, reserve water storage, swimming pool, recreation areas, social areas, spa and/or exercise facilities. It is not uncommon for the facility to include stove, refrigerator, washer and dryer (referred to as *línea blanca or* "white line"), air conditioners or even window treatments. In general housing in Panama has more bathrooms than the typical house in the U.S. They may have a doorman or concierge to offer assistance with packages. At least one has valet parking. They all have some sort of security including controlled entry that is particularly desirable for those who travel extensively or just follow the locals to the country for the weekend. All but the smallest apartments and houses will include a small living area near the kitchen and laundry areas for a live-in maid. The maid's bath is cold water only.

Panama City is currently experiencing a great building frenzy. High-rises are being constructed, planned or talked about in every area of the city. The heights proposed for some of these skyscrapers *(rascacielos)* are in the 70- to 100-story category. All this building becomes a major consideration for the potential buyer or renter when making long-term decisions in this no-zoning environment. What is a beautiful view of the city, the bay or the mountains out your window today may be a solid wall tomorrow. Additionally, the noise and construction pollution are considerations.

Whether you decide to buy, rent or lease, you will also want to investigate what services are included in the maintenance fee or rental rate in addition to the physical apartment. When you rent or lease, your agreement usually includes all maintenance fees, water, trash removal, and propane gas for cooking. Some rental agreements also include a basic cable TV plan. While use of the pool and common areas is included, there is normally an additional charge for use of the social areas, meeting rooms or other expanded use areas available. Many older buildings have lovely built-ins including china rooms, shoe racks, shirt shelves, bookshelves and storage areas.

Rental/lease agreements are an official government document and are standard for all residential properties. Regardless of the term of the agreement, they are cancelable with 30-days written notice (known as a diplomat clause). A security deposit equal to one month's rent is required and it is deposited with a copy of the signed agreement with the Housing Ministry (MIVI). It will be held for the life of the agreement and refunded when the tenant satisfactorily vacates the property.

When deciding where to live in the United States, for example, a family would consider availability and quality of schools in the neighborhood, as well as the commute for the working parents. However, in Panama distances to work are so short and schools tend to be located outside residential areas, making these considerations less applicable to the decision-making process. The decision of where to live is based on type of housing desired and amenities of the neighborhood.

Deciding whether to buy or rent is the next big consideration. The housing market in Panama is not as fluid as it is in other countries. However, buying is relatively easy and there are no restrictions to prevent foreigners from buying property in Panama. (See Appendix 12) A few things to keep in mind, however, when making your decision include: mortgage rates vary with the cost of the property and amount of the down payment; property taxes for newly constructed homes are not applicable for the first fifteen years of ownership which makes new construction more desirable; and, while it is possible to sell a property, it tends to be a slow process. Unless planning on relocating here permanently, most foreigners choose to rent. On a positive note, interest paid on a mortgage is tax deductible from U.S. tax liability.

Over the last two years, the range of prices, amenities and locations has greatly increased while prices in general have remained stable. Apartments thought generally acceptable to *extranjeros* can be purchased starting as low as $65,000 and ranging up to over $300,000. The upper-end apartments fall in the category of whole floor, four or more bedrooms and large square footage. According to an article in *La Prensa,* in many areas occupancy rates run about 60% in existing buildings and new buildings are being started continually. Another report in the June 2006 issue of *Espacios* magazine identifies 26 buildings over 45 stories planned for future construction. Regardless of whether you decide to rent or buy, check out the neighborhood for traffic and planned construction. Zoning laws do not prevent a high-rise going up next to a single-story house or a shopping center being built in the middle of a residential area. If you do decide on a house, barred windows and entrances are as common in houses as in apartments. Many people in houses also use the services of a rent-a-guard.

Consider all quoted prices as negotiable. If you can sign a lease for a longer term than usual you will have a further negotiating advantage on price. (See Appendix 12 for further guidelines when buying property.)

Panamanians love their dogs and apartment living proves no deterrent to having one or more of any size. However, check with your building for any restrictions to be sure. Early mornings and evenings are popular times for everyone (including the maid) to be out walking a dog. However, based on the droppings left on sidewalks, yards and even the street, it appears that *pooper-scoopers* are not in general use in Panama. However, at least one neighborhood, Bella Vista, has provided little kiosks with plastic bags for picking up and disposing of dog droppings.

If you live in a house rather than an apartment, remember a dog is a further safety feature.

The Realtor

Law 6 of July 8, 1999 revised the laws concerning real estate agents and instituted licensing. As a result all realtors must have taken a class, an exam and qualified for a license. Anyone practicing real estate without the license is subject to both steep fines and jail. The multiple-listing concept, however, has not yet arrived in Panama. Realtors tend to *specialize* in certain buildings or areas. House hunting is yet another area where the services of a relocation firm can be invaluable in saving you time and money. By working with their realtors, these firms can arrange to show you a variety of properties based on your instructions that fit your family needs and your budget in the neighborhoods you desire.

Recently a review of books on Panama confirmed that the real estate market is one area where we should advise caution and take our own advice. Real estate agents, realtors, *Bienes Raices*, are a touchy subject. The field in general has been described as a Mafia and it certainly is an area where *juega vivo* is the rule. If you have the good fortune to be working with a relocation firm, their team of realtors, as I have said, have **your** interests at the forefront. If you are investigating on your own, heed my advise of coming to look, renting first and investigating adequately before you decide to buy. Talk to a number of people and get recommendations from locals. Keep in mind in this market of churning real estate that it is unlikely that a Panamanian will buy from a *gringo* who has paid an inflated price, which also further reduces your future resale market. Remember the rule in business always is whom you know. Be sure you know whom you are dealing with.

The Neighborhoods

Downtown Areas

Punta Paitilla has been one of the most popular areas with foreigners; however, recently many new areas have been developed providing opportunities to live all over the city. Punta Paitilla is a little finger of land that extends into the bay and is dominated by high-rise apartment buildings. The proximity to the bay results in exposure in some areas to an objectionable smell, especially at low tide. There are old and new buildings offering a great variety in size and style of apartment. An adequate number of apartments is available either for rent or for sale, however, prices in this area tend to be higher than some other areas. Traffic, which has long been a problem as a result of the high density and limited number of streets in and out of Paitilla, has been exacerbated by the recent development of neighboring Punta Pacifica, as well as the major exit of *Corredor Sur* into the area, not to mention the continued overbuilding in Punta Paitilla itself. There is, however, convenient shopping at the entrance to the neighborhood which is an added attraction. This is also the neighborhood where the Union Club is located next to an attractive and busy park.

Punta Pacífica is an interesting extension community of Punta Paitilla. Built on landfill, it juts out into the Bay of Panama, adding to the spectacular skyline welcoming arrivals from Tocumen along the *Corredor Sur.* In fact, visiting cruise ship passengers are overwhelmed at the skyline of Panama when visiting for the first time. Punta Pacífica, originally planned for single-family houses along the shore with some low rises further inland, has quickly developed into another major area of high-rise apartments offering a wide variety of prices, whether for purchase or rental as well as various amenities. One building boasts assistance with all aspects of relocation for the foreign retirees.

El Cangrejo, an older neighborhood with a great variety of smaller apartment buildings as well as some single-family houses, has recently seen the addition of numerous high-rise buildings. With the added construction, including one major casino, the traffic in this area has greatly increased. The increase in building has also resulted in water pressure problems. However, this charming little area is very reminiscent of San Francisco, California, with little hills, a neighborhood park, convenient shopping, and a variety of restaurants all within walking distance. The community is divided by Vía Argentina, a wide boulevard that is beautifully decorated by the residents for the Christmas holidays.

Obarrio is a neighborhood that has undergone great change as more and more commercial and residential high-rises are being built among some beautiful single-family houses. There are still many streets of single-family houses in this attractive area but with the added construction comes more traffic congestion.

Marbella has many duplexes, low-rise apartments and some single-family houses. This neighborhood is nestled between a number of commercial areas and major through streets.

La Cresta is west of the downtown area, close to the *Corredor Norte* entrance and easily accessible to the main cross-town streets. **La Cresta** means The Crest and this neighborhood climbs the hill from Vía España to overlook the bay and the city. While this is an older neighborhood, it too boasts a number of newer high-rises and also offers a great variety of older low-rises as well. It also has a few remaining elegant, old residences scattered throughout the neighborhood. **La Cresta** residents find the neighborhood very friendly and secluded. All of the multi-level buildings enjoy a favorable temperature difference due to the altitude and enjoy cooling breezes the year round. As evidenced by its residents, La Cresta is a neighborhood ideal for morning exercise with its numerous stairways and meandering hilly streets.

San Francisco and Beyond

The neighborhoods adjacent to **San Francisco** offer a great variety of housing options. Some of the nicest areas for single-family houses are located here and include **Altos del Golf** and **Coco del Mar**. While prices vary, some of the most expensive properties in town are located in this area.

Panama Sample Rental Prices

(September 2006)

	Low Range	Mid Range	High Range
Apartments	$	$	$
2 bedroom	400-600	600-1000	1000-2500
3 bedroom	800-1100	1200-2300	2400-3500
4 bedroom	2000-2500	2500-3500	3500-5000
Houses			
3 bedroom	1200-2000	2000-3000	3000-4000
5 bedroom	2500-3500	3500-4000	4500-6500

The older **San Francisco** area in general offers a wide variety of housing options including multi-family houses, single-family houses and an increasing variety of high-rises. Prices tend to be more economical in this area and density up to this time has been reasonable, (70 new buildings are planned) and as a result traffic in the neighborhoods is somewhat less. Shopping is also convenient with the development of MultiPlaza Mall in neighboring Punta Pacifica.

Costa del Este along the *Corredor Sur* is a newly developed area of single-family houses in gated communities reminiscent of Florida or California or any other suburban development in the United States. These landfill areas are being designed with young families in mind and include parks and play areas for children. Prices and styles of houses vary. However, the *Costas,* as they are collectively referred to, have become very popular with locals and foreign residents alike. High-rise apartments are now being incorporated into the area to particularly attract the "grandparent" set to this area. Strip-malls provide convenient access to grocery, pharmacy, dry cleaners, take-out and other neighborhood shops.

The Transferred Areas
Amador, Clayton, Balboa, Cardenas, Quarry Heights, Ancon Hill, Albrook, Albrook Gardens

With the closing of the seventeen military bases in Panama, 3,815 family housing units were transferred to Panama and the entire area reverted to Panama jurisdiction. Initially, ARI was the government agency responsible for marketing these properties. In 2006 MEF, Ministry of Economy and Finances, assumed this role. While the original military houses are often small and simple by Panama standards, many have been completely remodeled and the neighborhoods have become very popular, especially **Albrook** and **Clayton** with their extensive parkland. Additionally, many new housing areas have been developed including Albrook Gardens consisting of attached houses and several low-rise apartment complexes. With the popularity of these areas has come commercial development offering grocery, pharmacy, banks, gyms and other neighborhood shops. Additionally, the proximity to Albrook Mall with its extensive collection of shops and grocery shopping has made this suburban area very popular.

Other Suburbs

El Dorado, like **San Francisco**, has high-rises scattered throughout the area, rather than concentrated like **Punta Paitilla**. The primary one is the **Pacific Hills** development, atop the highest hill in the area. This complex offers three high-rise buildings and a variety of apartment styles to choose from as well as a large variety of amenities. Currently a fourth and fifth tower are planned and several smaller towers are being developed along the peripheral streets. The surrounding neighborhood is comprised of single family and duplex houses in the **Alameda/Dos Mares** area as well as several lower-rise apartment buildings. This area is continuing to expand and develop.

An Overview

With all this construction come many new options for location, price and housing choice. Where it was once difficult to find four-bedroom houses or apartments, they are now more available. Unfortunately, the lack of zoning enforcement and necessary infrastructure to support this construction creates its own set of problems. Commercial buildings encroach on residential areas and add to the traffic flow problems as well as resulting in over parking on the streets. Many areas suffer from frequent water outages or continual low water pressure. However, many newer buildings do have water tanks or electrical plants for emergency situations. An article in *La Prensa* in September 2006 reported that six new water pumps were being installed in the plant in Chilibre to increase the water production and provide potable water 24 hours a day to areas previously having problems. This new system will provide water to Bethania, La Alameda, Las Mercedes, Hato Pintado, El Crisol, Cerro Viento, Tocumen and various communities of the San Miguelito district.

Another report the same week discussed the concern for increasing electrical requirements for the remainder of 2006 through 2008. Sewage treatment and cleaning up the bay is still in the discussion stage.

One last concern recently raised again in view of the additional mega-high rises planned, involves the fire department. The current equipment is designed for 23 meters or six floors. Additional equipment is being requested to reach 45 meters or 15 floors.

The Interior

Since I wrote my first article for *Business Panama* about the beginning of the Snowbird influx many articles in both national and international publications have been written promoting Panama as the place to spend the winter. Likewise, Panama has caught on as a potential retirement haven. As a result numerous new housing developments have sprung up in the interior.

The *interior* has long been the identification of anything the other side of the Bridge. However, now that there are two bridges, the original Bridge of the Americas and the newly opened, in 2005, *Centenario* Bridge, this region has become known as Panama West. Now access to those *weekend spots* of Coronado, Gorgona and El Valle has never been easier. Additionally, the newcomers to Panama, those coming especially to retire, have discovered the beauty of such locals as **Altos de Maria, Los Sueños, Boquete, Volcan, Cerro Punta** and **Bocas del Toro**.

Bocas del Toro was the first community to receive the influx of Canadians, Americans and Europeans. They caused a mini real estate boom, increased the need for hotels and restaurants and boosted the local economy. Increased tourism was not far behind. This was soon followed by the discovery of **Boquete** with its wonderful climate in the mountains. Whether you are looking for the beaches or the mountains, Panama West is becoming home to many, locals and foreigners alike.

While it will take some time for most of the infrastructure in the interior to catch up with this boom, already the new arrivals are getting involved in the community. They are creating clubs, taking on community service projects and changing the landscape both physically and culturally. They ask about emergency telephone numbers and how the garbage recycling system works, both of which have recently been created. Despite the rapid changes that are happening Panama continues to be a delightful place in which to live, only now there are many more options for Living in Panama.

The Beaches

Coronado, Gorgona and Surrounding Areas

Coronado has long been the beach area of choice with the *rabi blanco* set. This gated community just a little over an hour from the city has in recent years expanded to include a variety of houses, from mini-mansions to cottages and Coronado now has a high-rise apartment building. With the opening of a large modern El Rey supermarket at the main intersection to this community, additional businesses have opened including Pharmacy Coromar, Western Union, Hardware Coromar, Boyd Díaz Optical, Global Bank, Airbox Express, Clínica Médica Medical Labs, the Corowalk Inn, a gas station and several small restaurants.

Chame the last town before **Gorgona** offers an Internet café. Another ten minutes beyond Coronado along the Panamerica Highway is the neighboring town of **Santa Clara** where there is an excellent fish market. Post offices are located in these neighboring towns to service the beach area.

The development of the Coronado area has likewise benefited the communities like **Altos de María** and the neighboring towns and residents of communities as far away as **El Valle** utilize the commercial facilities.

Safety is Always A Concern

Here are some suggestions for ensuring your personal safety in your home:

1. When assuming possession of a new or remodeled property from the contractors, change all outside door locks.

2. Keep garden area surrounding the house fenced and keep multiple dogs in the garden. Dogs should be intimidating, such as German Shepherd or Doberman.

3. Establish a long-term relationship with your domestic help. Know them and their families. Hire the best and strive to keep them for years.

4. For houses and ground floor apartments keep bars on all windows and insure that doors are burglar resistant.

5. Outside door locks should be kept locked at all times, unless you are in the immediate area.

6. Know your neighbors; let them know you and the members of your family. Talk with them about your safety concerns and set up reciprocal security measures.

7. Never leave your house unoccupied.

8. Set "104" on the speed dial on your phone

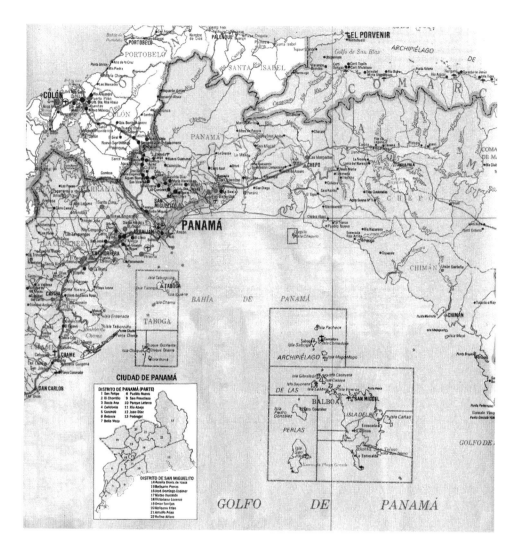

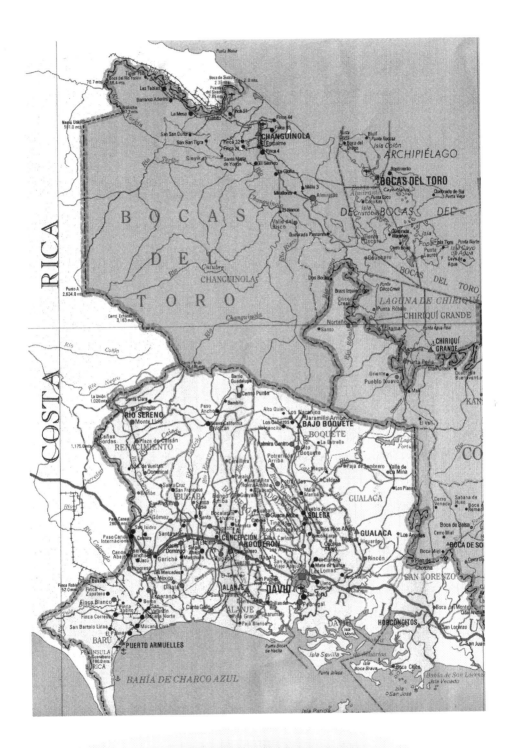

Living in Panama
119

El Valle de Antón has what you need...

Centro Comerical El Valle is your one stop shop for everything from Texaco gasoline to small appliances. This country store is reminiscent of a small *Machetazo* in the city as it has notions, groceries, pharmacy, hardware, newspapers, house wares, school supplies, lawn mowers, doors and more.

Near Mountains

Altos de María is the first little mountain community reached out of Panama City. About thirty minutes from the Bridge of the Americas is the turn off for **Sara** (in the little town of Bejuco) and another twenty or thirty minutes up a winding mountain road is Altos de Maria. Once only a weekend get-a-way, it has now developed into a residential retirement community.

Another 30 to 45 minutes beyond the beach community of Coronado, and higher in the mountains, is the Indian community of **El Valle de Antón.** Nestled in a lovely valley, this popular weekend destination has changed greatly in the last year in terms of expanded groceries, hardware and household goods available. As more retirees discover this pleasant, flat valley, home to many locals on bicycles, and horse back riding along the side streets, more houses have been built and there are more year-around residents.

The Communities of Chiriqui Province

David

Five hours by car along the only road running the length of Panama is the second largest city, **David**. A farming community at sea level, David is the hub for this region. Commercial enterprises are beginning to catch up with demand in the area, as evidenced by the impressive new El Rey Supermarket and Shopping Center at the Boquete Road and Panamerican Highway intersection in David. Additionally, a Do-It-Center, Arrocha Pharmacy and Furniture City are in the same commercial center. This El Rey is one of the biggest in the chain and the selection is impressive with a beautiful display of fruits and vegetables fresh from the local fields. Also in David you will find Super 99, Romeros, and Price Smart. Car dealerships, banks and other commercial services are readily available as well as a regional airport.

Boquete

Boquete is a small valley in the mountains about forty-five-minutes drive from David and has become a popular spot with foreigners. This lovely valley community has a proud heritage of first being *Chiriquí*. Ask a Panamanian where they are from and if from this particular province, they will identify it with particular pride. Chiriquanos are also proud of their agricultural accomplishments including flowers, vegetables and coffee. Boquete itself is known for its business people. Do not confuse the Chiricanos with the indigenous people. These are two very different cultures and peoples living in the same area.

However, this primarily agricultural area has not been profitable for coffee farmers for a number of years and as a result these farmers are selling out for real estate development. Ironically, a few of these new buyers have turned small coffee *fincas* (farms) into boutique coffee operations commanding big prices for a superior quality product.

In downtown Boquete, Centro Bruna, on the main street, is old but well stocked and popular with locals and newcomers alike. The new grocery in town is Romero, more modern in this colonial town, but with less selection than Bruna.

In the last year Boquete has developed incredibly as more goods and services have materialized to meet the increasing market.

As a result of this influx of newcomers, the local economy is up and employment opportunities are good and salaries improved. While real estate prices in downtown Boquete are escalating, they remain reasonable in the countryside and neighboring communities. For example, land costs $400 a meter in town but $50-60 out of town. Prices vary based on the owner and the location. Like the coastal community of Bocas del Toro, however, Boquete is beginning to experience extranjeros buying property at say $20,000 and putting up a little house and reselling to other gringos for $150,000. This has little benefit to the community and prices land out of the reach of locals.

Needless to say, all this activity in the interior is having some questionable effects on the community in general, despite the improved economy. The climate, for example, is becoming warmer, perhaps because of all the construction. While Panama is attractive to foreigners with its no-tax policy, this same policy also creates a burden to the community which receives little funding from the central government.

Boquete in a Tagua Nut Shell:

Banks: CACSA, BNP, Global, Banistmo, Caja de Ahorros and Banco General is coming soon.

Gas Stations: Delta

Building materials: Hopsa

Tourist Info Boquete: http://www.Boquete.org

Language Schools: Spanish by the Sea/Spanish by the River; Habla Yo

Book sources: Local library (very limited), Bookmark Used Books on the Boquete Road

Radio Station, *Window to Panama*, on 105.3 or Skype 12:00; *Spanglish*; both programs are broadcast to this interior mountain region and to the U.S.

Attorneys: Mauad y Mauad; Nixia Guerra; Parduchi

Alcoholics Anonymous and Al-Anon:
   720-2623/5 or 776-3147

Moving companies: Canal Movers; Panama International Packers

Restaurants: Machu Pichu (Peruvian); Bistro; Panamonte, El Rancho (Argentine), Antojitos (Mexican); Palo Alto Restaurant

Video rental shops

Noticias Bajareque Times, English/Spanish newspaper
   6714-4007, http://www.bajarequetimes.com

Clubs and organizations: Tuesday Morning Club, Rotary

Theater – Community Players

Mail Forwarding Services: Daily Mail International Freight Panama, S.A. 720-1864, 223-9351, http://www. Dailymail.org; Aerocasillas/Mail Box Express; MailBoxes Etc. which is also center for FedEx, UPS and DHL

The simple country roads are becoming filled with potholes from all the heavy equipment passing over them to new construction sites. While the newcomers complain about the condition of the roads, they fail to realize that their tax-free status does nothing to contribute to the budget of the area that is responsible for the increased demand for road repair, infrastructure of all kinds including electricity, water, trash removal, health services and even schools.

These new residents come from all over the world and many are bilingual, European, Italian, German, Brazilians, U. S. or Canadian citizens. They add an interesting dynamic to the community and the real estate boom is often foreigner selling to foreigner at greatly inflated prices. As I sit here high atop a ridge overlooking a shallow valley planted in coffee, listening to the thunder in the distance, I can see the appeal of Boquete to many. It is quiet except for the occasional Weed Eater in the distance and the chirping of an incredible variety of birds in the huge tree directly in front of me. The sky is blue and the clouds brilliantly white in contrast. The distant peaks are in sharp relief. The greens are as green as I remember Wisconsin in the summertime but this is definitely the tropics, lush in vegetation and rich in wild flowers. It is also remote.

I can also see why Boquetanians do not want their lovely little community *Disneylanded*. Thus when a plan was proposed that would have been out of step with the local culture and history it was refused.

Recycling

Real Boquete is a program that teaches kids about recycling. The Center is located in town behind Bistro Restaurant. A local Foundation was established to support this program which involves six local schools. The money from the recycling program goes to the schools. There is pick up in some areas or you can take your items to their office. Currently they recycle some paper and plastics and aluminum cans. The schools also collect and benefit from the money earned but the focus is on the benefit to the environment. School children are taken to visit the recycling plant as well as the local dump to better understand the benefits of the program beyond the short term monetary gains.

Volcan/Cerro Punta

Also reached from David, 45 minutes to an hour along another road, in the mountains is **Volcan.** Downtown Volcan serves this region with two hardwares, four supermarkets, several restaurants (including one Greek) and *Banco Nacional de Panama, Banco General* and a post office. *San Benito* Woodshop and *San Benito Ceramica* offer quality products at reasonable prices. Another ten minutes up the mountain is the community of **Cerro Punta** with its beautiful farms.

Bocas del Toro

Bocas del Torro, perhaps the most remote of these newly developing communities, is comprised of a series of islands off the main land. It is reached by several airlines making it only an hour from the city and all the needed goods and services. It is also reachable by road from David to Almirante on the mainland and then ferry to Bocas town on the island of Colon. Water taxis based on Bocas service the various island communities. Several companies provide regular deliveries from Panama City to Bocas of everything from food stuffs, building supplies, books, gardening items and furniture. This a community where English is spoken more than other areas of Panama. Meanwhile, Bocas del Toro realtors churn properties.

Most recently Bocas del Toro has acquired a public library for the province, located in the *Terminal de Transporte de Changuinola*. Open Monday to Friday, 10:00 a.m. to 4:00 p.m.

Once a profitable banana growing area, it is now more known for tourists and for the Smithsonian Research Center.

Not only the weather is different in this area, but the people Bocas attracts and the life style are very different as well. Travel between island communities requires a private boat or water taxi. The locals are typical of the Central American coastal regions with a predominant population of West Indian descent (English speaking) and indigenous peoples. Bocas tends to attract the bohemian, hippies to some, and backpacking set. A local recently referred to the newcomers to Bocas as "Hemingway want-a-be's." Boquete is more upscale by comparison.

Bocas del Toro in a Tagua Nut Shell

Island Communities
Isla Colon, Isla Cristobal, Isla Bastimentos, Isla Carenero

Island Services

Union Fenosa Electric Company	757-9228
Cable & Wireless	123
Direct TV	758-7090
Banco Nacional	757-9230
Global Bank Changuinola	758-5948
Information	102 or 757-9642
Immigration	758-8651
Canadian Embassy	264-9731
U. S. Embassy	207-7000
U. K. Embassy	269-0866

Bocas Breeze http://www.thebocasbreeze.com

Taxi-Water	757-9028
Taxi-Land	6565-2353
Mail Service Bravo Center	757-9229
Courier Service Jose Saenz	6614-7811
Super Gourmet	757-9357

Email: labocaloca@cwpanama.net

Climate

Every region of Panama is different. When I wrote *Living in Panama* initially, my focus was on the City, as the City was where a third of the population lived and the interior was considered a place to go for holidays and weekends. Thus attention to the weather was not important beyond the obvious that Coronado, Gorgona and the beaches were popular in the summer (December to April) and the mountains, El Valle in particular, were the place to go for cooler climes. In general, it was known that in Panama it was either raining, was going to rain or had stopped raining.

Further away to the West for longer trips, but not often for Panamanians, were the agricultural regions of Boquete, Volcan and Cerro Punta in the Chiriqui Province. Bocas del Toro on the Costa Rican border was looked at like so many Caribbean coastal cities of Central America as some place less than desirable and a place most Panamanians had never been. Thus, many newcomers unfamiliar with the region are surprised at the heat and continual rain in Bocas. They are equally unprepared for the *bajareque* in Boquete, known as *chipi chipi* in Guatemala or drizzle in English. It can be damp, cold and depressing for some. The temperatures in general in the mountain regions are cool especially compared with the City. Both **Boquete** and **Bocas del Toro** experience *Veranito del Agosto* (little summer in August) when the weather is very pleasant.

During the dry season the **ash** from burning fields is a particular nuisance. Long, thin, black tendrils of ash blow for miles and land on balconies, window sills, cars and seem to find a way into your house or apartment no matter how tightly the windows and doors are closed. Trying to sweep it away leaves black marks assuring you will welcome the onset of the rainy season.

Cerro Punta, at the highest altitude in the mountain towns seems perpetually in the mist. While it can be beautiful, it can also be cold and wet. Just 10 or 20 minutes down the mountain in Volcan the temperatures are more pleasant but still cool and rainbows abound. (See Appendix 1, Temperatures, Precipitation and Altitudes.)

Bocas del Toro like Portobelo is one of the rainiest places anywhere. I have heard new arrivals to Bocas ask "does it ever stop raining?" The answer, is sometimes. Sometimes as previously mentioned in August there are some rain-free days. Otherwise, it is a hot, humid, rainy, coastal flat series of islands with mangroves—about as opposite to Boquete as you can get weather-wise.

El Valle de Anton offers the most nearly perfect climate the year round.

Building and Buying in Panama

Regardless of what a newcomer says brought him to Panama to live, economics play a part in the move. Everyone expects to live better for less. While that is generally true, there are also compromises to be made. As one gringo I interviewed explained, it is possible to build a house in Panama to U.S. specifications that meet all the customary expectations. However, it will cost more than building the same house in the U.S. This is one more reason to understand the culture here before you start and you will not be disappointed or frustrated.

Keep your expectations realistic as attention to details is generally lacking. Change is expected, however, so you can ask a worker to modify, redo, change anything with no problem. However, as my interviewee explained, pick your battles for quality.

Building costs in Panama as elsewhere have also increased. For example tile that was $4 is now selling for $6 in Boquete. The good news is that labor is available in areas like Boquete as the increase in building has put skilled labor in demand.

Now That You Have Found an Apartment or House

Paperwork and lots of it is the rule in Panama whether it is for immigration, school registration or getting set up in your new home. Plan ahead and make a dozen copies of your passport or *cédula* to start the process for arranging for utilities and services. You will also need copies of your rental agreement.

Final Word to Those that Buy

Until recently most *extranjeros* came here for business and most likely rented - buying was not a consideration. Today many come here with buying in mind and both the location and focus are different from that of the relocating executive. People ask me all the time, "what is the best area in which to live?". My answer to them is that "it depends". It depends on you and your family and your needs, preferences and pocketbook. Some people love the mountains and there are numerous options for them. Others are happiest at the beach. Still others are city people. What ever your preference and regardless of your economic considerations, my advise is the same. Come here and spend some time. Rent an apartment or a house in the area you think you like. You may want to try several areas and take advantage of an aparthotel arrangement in order to experience a variety of locations. Come for a week, a month, the winter season or as long as you can.

Take time to experience the neighborhood and the climate. What are the effects of heat, humidity, mold, pollen, concrete dust, and rain on you and your family? Rainy, overcast weather can be depressing. Panama is a delightful place in which to live but it is not right for everyone. **Rent first.** Be sure you have considered all the relevant factors before making a purchase. Do not be pressured by over helpful realtors. You will live with the property you purchase for a very long time.

Sample Housing Costs

Houses and apartments in Panama traditionally have more bathrooms than U.S. equivalent housing, plus maid's quarters. Most apartments and condos have common areas including social areas, pools, and exercise rooms.

Apartments

Community	# Bedrooms	Price
Punta Pacifica	4	$515.000-$595,000
	3	$274,000-$390,000
	3	$133,000-$164,000
	2	$ 52,500-$ 98,000
El Cangrejo	3	$127,000-$184,000
	3	$ 87,700-$ 93,000
	2	$ 61,000
San Francisco	3	$ 90,000-$121,500
	2	$ 69,500
Obarrio	3	$105,000
Dos Mares	2	$ 75,900
Costa del Este	2	$ 73,500
Albrook	2-3	$ 54,400

Houses

Community	# Bedrooms	Price
Costa del Este	3	$220,000-$295,368
El Dorado	3	$160,000
Coronado	2	$125,100
Las Cumbres	3	$ 59,000-$ 62,500
	2	$ 35,975-$ 40,600

PANAMA ON LINE

A Guide to the Housing Market
http://www/Metropormetro.com

Short –Term Rental Assistance
http://www.panamacasa.com

Hostel/Lodge Villa Marita
El Santuario, Boquete
Email: villamarita@cwpanama.net
http://www.panamainfo.com/marita

Home Tech
Household Appliances
263-9611
http://www.techhousepanana.com
Email: techhouse@cwpanama.net

Panama Now
http://www.loquehaypahoy.com

PANAMA ON LINE

Regus Instant Offices Worldwide
http://www.regus.com

Promises
Promises@movistar.com.pa

Black Tie
Email: blacktie@sinfo.net

BBK Furniture
http://www.ventas@bbkfurniture.com

Republicans Abroad
http://www.republicansabroadpanama.org
http://www.republicansabroad.org

Democrats Abroad
http://www.democratsabroad.org

U. S. Income Tax Preparation
H & R Block@pa.inter.net

Reprosa
The Treasures of Panama
http://www.reprosa.com

Dual Nationals

Children born in Panama to foreign parents are entitled to citizenship of both countries and become known as dual nationals.

Pat Alvarado, children's author, brings you an incredible selection of books just for children in Spanish, English, Chinese and French.

Piggy Press Books
http://www.piggypress.com;
Amazon.com
and Panama local bookstores

VI

LITTLE PEOPLE ISSUES

Children and the family are one of the most important entities in Panama society. Children remain children—they are not forced to become little adults. In fact, in middle and upper class families, children often live at home until age 30.

Birthday celebrations are important for everyone but especially so for children. Parties are big in numbers if not in expense. The little girls come in their best party frocks complete with flowered headbands or barrettes. The little boys come in sport shirts, pants and dress shoes. Many restaurants such as Wendy's, McDonald's, Burger King, children's party places, Kid's Zone and the Union Club offer special spaces just for holding children's birthday parties. Often an entire family of children will be invited to the same party, especially if they are close in age. You will be expected to reciprocate when you have a party for your children.

The School System

Whether they are called school, academies, institutes, *colegios* that include grades K-12 or universities, Panama is fortunate to have a wide selection of private schools from which to choose. It also has a diverse population representing many countries, cultures and religions, which is also reflected in its schools. Panamanian public schools exist throughout the City and in the rural communities. Education through the sixth grade is mandatory. Schools beyond the sixth grade in rural areas often must be reached by traveling long distances. Public schools tend to be very crowded and, in fact, many operate in two sessions per day in order to accommodate the student population. A recent report on public schools found that in 2005 of the 16,604 students that took entrance exams for the University of Panama, 60% failed. A further report found that numerous problems existed including failure of discipline and organization in the public schools. In general, public education is under funded and very poor. As a consequence, families that can afford to do so, send their children to private school.

Private schools in Panama cater to every student need whether your emphasis is academic, multi-lingual, bilingual, religious, all boys, all girls, or international. Tuitions vary as widely as the academic emphasis.

Schools are also further divided by **school-year** schedule. All public schools and the majority of private schools operate on the Panamanian school calendar year that is March to December. Classes begin about the first week in March and end just before Christmas. Students are then free for most of the Panamanian summer (December to April). The International School of Panama, the Balboa Academy and St. Mary's operate on the American school calendar year, which runs from August to mid-June. (This is also the school year in Europe, Canada, Japan and other parts the world.) The **school week** is Monday through Friday and the day begins about 7:30 a.m. and ends about 2:00 p.m. in the private schools. Schedules vary according to specific school and age of students. Public schools are on a similar schedule unless they are operating two shifts, in which case, the second shift may not end before 5:00 or 6:00 p.m. There is a mid-year vacation the last week in July and first week in August.

Interruptions to the school year due to labor or political problems occur in most years and particularly affect public schools. Consequently, the Ministry of Education frequently makes ad hoc changes in the calendar for any given year.

Most private schools include Pre-Kinder to 12th grade. The public **school structure** is further divided into Pre-kinder, Kinder, *primaria* (1st through 6th), *secundaria* (7th through 12th) grades. Some private schools are converting to a further division of the *secundaria* to include middle school (7th and 8th) and high school (9th through 12th grade). **Class size** in private schools range from 25-40 students depending on the age of students and the school. Public schools tend to have much larger classes, ranging from 40-100 students.

Grading in the Panamanian system schools is done every two months. Grades are given at teacher/parent meetings and with written reports four times a year. Grades are 1,2,3,4,5, with 5 being best. In the International School, St. Mary's and Balboa Academy, grading is on the ABCDF system, with A being the highest grade and F being a failing grade. Some universities, such as Florida State University, are on a semester system. Additionally, the Panama system of teaching, whether private or public school, from elementary through University, is by rote or memorization as opposed to teaching *to problem solve* in the American system.

Enrollment requirements for school include:

1. Birth Certificate,

2. Transcript of grades (*Certificado Escolar*),

3. Photos,

4. Health Certificate and

5. Appropriate school application and tests.

Tuition for private schools includes a matriculation or registration fee and a monthly fee. Some schools allow for payment in three or four installments but the majority requires monthly payments. The International School additionally requires a sponsor fee for students whose parents are here with a corporation or embassy.

Public schools also have tuition fees but are much lower than Private Schools.

Uniforms. Students from pre-kinder through twelfth grade are required to wear uniforms established by the individual school. These uniforms may be purchased at the school or at specialty stores for students. Especially in the interior many parent organizations sell the appropriate fabric for the uniforms and then a seamstress makes the uniforms. Pants and skirts are about $10 and shirts or blouses are about $12. Books are purchased either from the school or at a school bookstore. Requirements vary depending on school and school grade but average about $150 per school year.

As you can see there are a number of decisions to be made in selecting schools, budget considerations being only one of many. Another important consideration is peer group, as children growing up in Panama make life-long friends in school who will continue to be important throughout life in business and in society.

Private Schools

Kindergarten – High School

Brader
Maggi Arias de Sánchez
Bianca Ortega, Academic Director
Elementary to 12th grade. 530 Students
Primary language Spanish
Class size about 28
School year March – December

Colegio Episcopal de Panamá
Joyce Green, Director
Tel.: 223-4836
Email: helends@sinfo.net
Kinder to High School
School year – March – December
Class size about 25

Upper grades have only one class at each level
Multilingual – English, Spanish, French, Japanese

Balboa Academy
City of Knowledge, Clayton
Tel.: 211-0035
Jean Lamb, Director
Pre-Kinder- 12, all instruction in English
(The school most like US public schools and accredited by US auditors.) School Year—August –June
http://www.balboaacademyweb.com
Email: jquinn@balboa-academy.org

Crossroads Christian Academy
Corozal
Tel.: 317-9774/6602
Email: cca_panama@hotmail.com

Canadian International School Panama
Calle K, El Cangrejo, Edif. No. 10
Tel.: 264-7699, 223-6010

International School of Panama
Cerro Viento
Tel.: 266-7037
Anthony Horton, Director
http://www.isp.edu.pa
School year—August-June
Pre-Kinder - 12

St. Mary's School
Tel.: 315-0725
Email: StMary-school@larinmail.com

Instituto Alberto Einstein
Vía Israel
Tel.: 270-2266
Established in 1955, is religious-Zionist in philosophy approximate enrollment of 750 students from pre-school through high school

The Oxford School
Urb. Edison Park, Calle 7
Vía Simón Bolívar
Tel: 321-0061, http://www.oxfordpanama.com

Colegio International Oxford
Ave. Fredrico Boyd
Tel.: 265-6422

Escuela Franco Panamanian Luis Pasteur
Calle 74 y Vía Israel, 119
Tel.: 226-8356

Escuela Montessori de Panama
Calle 3, El Coco, Altos del Golf
Tel.: 226-1596

Colegio de La Salle
Calle S J B de la Salle
Tel.: 263-6257

**Colegio de Las Esclavas
del Sagrado Corazón de Jesús**
Clayton
Tel.: 317-0048

Colegio Internacional Maria Inmaculada
Calle Octavio De Icaza, La Alameda
Tel.: 260-0855

Colegio Internacional Sek Panama
Carretera Nuevo Club de Golf
Tel.: 220-2046

Colegio Isaac Rabin
Clayton, 156
Tel.: 317-0060

Colegio Javier
Calle 4 Perejil, 7-100
Tel.: 269-4222

Colegio Real de Panama
Calle 66, San Francisco
Tel.: 270-3348

Colegio San Agustin
Costa del Este
http://www.colegiosanagustinpanama.com
Tel.: 271-4590, Email: csapanam@cwpanama.net
Preschool through high school, bilingual

Academia Interamericana de Panama
Costa del Este
Tel.: 271-0012

Instituto Italiano Enrico Fermi
Calle 72, Paitilla
Tel.: 226-2002

Instituto Panamericano
Las Sabanas, Vía España
Tel.: 222-0302

Escuela Interamericana de Panama
Carretera al Nuevo Club de Golf, Cerro Viento
Tel.: 266-7037

Colegio Internacional Saint George de Panama
Cerro Viento
Tel.:220-4585
http://www.stgeorge.edu.pa

Escuela Montessori de Panama
Santa Elena y Via Porras
Tel.:226-2116
http://www.montessoridepanama.com

Instituto Guadalupano
Boquete
Bilingual, Grades 1-12

Procorial PO 12
Boquete
K-9 and adding an additional grade each year till grade 12

Universities

Universidad de Panama
Main Campus Panama City 263-6133
Harmodio Arias M. Curundu 232-8410
http://www.up.ac.pa

Universidad Católica Santa Maria la Antigua (USMA)
Colon 441-4932, Los Santos 966-9111, Chiriqui 775-3284
El Dorado 230-8323, http://www.usma.ac.pa

Florida State University Panama
La Boca, Balboa, Ancon
Tel.: 314-0367
http://www.fsu.edu/panama
Bachelor's Degree
English Language program

University of Louisville Panama
Calle 45, Bella Vista
Tel.: 264-0777
http://www.louisville.com.pa; www.louisville.ed

Universidad Interamericana
Laureate International Universities
http://www.uip.edu.pa, www.logisiticaad.com
Tel.: 261-4305

Universidad Americana
http://www.uam.ac.pa
Panama, Tel.: 213-1967/1214; Chorrera, Tel.: 244/7809/1765

Universidad Latina de Panama
http://www.ulatina.ac.pa

School Bus Service

Bus service is available through the private schools at a monthly charge. Public school children use the local buses at a reduced rate. Many parents choose to deliver and pick up children, sometimes in carpools, creating further *tranques* especially in the downtown areas.

Extra-Curricular Activities

Panama offers a wide variety of activities for children after school including community soccer, baseball, basketball, swimming, karate and private lessons in dance and music.

Dance Schools

Pointe
Calle 72, San Francisco
Ballet, Tap and Jazz
Tel.: 270-2678

Steps
Calle 74 at Ave 3B South
San Francisco

Escuela de Danzas
Teresa Mann
Calle 70 #82, San Francisco
Tel.: 226-2337

Academia de Danza y Yoga Developpe
Lara Petrosky de Saint Malo
Ballet for Children
Punta Pacifica
Tel.: 215-3536 or 613-7775
Email: Developpedance@yahoo.com

La Academia de Danza Ileana de Sola Josefina / Nicoletti
Girls from 3 years of age
El Cangrejo, Edif. Emily, detrás del Parque
Vía Argentina
Tel.: 223-0046

<u>Folkloric Dance</u>

Academia de Expresiones Artisticas
Elisa de Céspedes

María Céspedes
Tel.: 317-9049

Classes are held at the Panama Hotel on Saturdays and are grouped by ages:

Children 4-16 are divided in classes held at 11:00 a.m.-12 noon, 12 noon-1:00 p.m., and 1:00-2:00 p.m.

Adults 17+ are held from 2:00-6:00 p.m.

Traveling with Children

Until recently children were not issued a Panamanian Identification Card (*Cédula*) before age 18. Currently, however, many schools charge $5.00 per student to provide a child *cédula*. Check with your particular school for details.

Children traveling to and from Panama present some unique problems with equally unique solutions. Children two weeks old and older need their own passport. Children of foreign parents born in Panama may be eligible for both a Panamanian passport and a passport of their home country. Check with your respective embassy for requirements and details. (Appendix 15, List of Embassies. Details for U.S. citizens are below.)

Children traveling with only one parent will need permission from the other parent. This can be accomplished with a letter from the non-accompanying parent granting permission for the child to travel with the other parent. A copy of the parent's passport should be attached and the letter may or may not need to be notarized. (Panama notaries charge $5. The airlines seldom actually ask to see the letter.)

A New Baby

<u>Reports of Birth Abroad</u>
Children being registered as U.S. citizens must be brought to the Consulate by the U.S. citizen parent along with the following original

documents to secure a first passport, a Consular Report of Birth Abroad (similar to a birth certificate) and a Social Security number:

1. Child's Panamanian birth certificate, (a complete record on legal size paper with revenue stamps) is obtained at the Civil Registry.

2. Evidence of parent's U.S. citizenship. This may be in the form of original U.S. birth certificates, U.S. passports, Certificates of Citizenship, or Naturalization Certificates. Military IDs are NOT proof of U.S. citizenship.

3. Parents' marriage certificate.

4. Evidence of dissolutions of previous marriages. If either parent has been previously married, submit original divorce decrees or death certificates.

5. If only one parent is a U.S. citizen (and was not employed by the U.S. government at the time the baby was born), contact the U.S embassy for further requirements.

6. Evidence of U.S. Government employment at the time of the child's birth in Panama (if applicable). Evidence should consist of a letter on letterhead, which gives dates of employment and date of arrival in Panama (and departure, if applicable).

Fee and issuance: The registration fee is $65.00 and a passport may be issued at the same time for an additional $82.00 for a total of $147. (Additional requirements must be met if the child is conceived out-of-wedlock. See details at http://hongkong.usconsulate.gov/consular/acs/birth.htm).

Curfew for Minors

Since October 16, 1995 a curfew for minors (under 18 years of age) has been in effect throughout Panama City. Under the law, students attending night classes must have a *carnet* issued by the school, or if employed, a certificate of employment must be obtained. The curfew was approved by the Office of the Mayor, the National Police, and the various *corregidores* in an effort to minimize violence and delinquency in the City.

Minors who are picked up for a curfew violation are subject to detention at a police station until they are released into the custody of their parents. Parents may be fined up to $50.00 for the violation.

Curfew Hours:

Sunday through Thursday .... 9:00 p.m.
Friday and Saturday .... 11:00 p.m.

Publications for Children

Encouraging children to read became an active campaign in recent years and consequently numerous daily and weekly publications have materialized. Some are included with daily newspapers like *La Prensa* and *PanamaAmerica,* as well as available for purchase at newsstands.

Nannies

While it is a convenience to be able to utilize the services of a nanny while living in Panama, it does have consequences. For many people a nanny is a live-in babysitter who can watch the children while parents have an evening out, be there when children come home from school when both parents work and generally be an additional person to watch out for the children. However, the gap is wide in education, culture, and expectations between the usual nanny in Panama and the *extranjero* family. Keep this in mind when setting limits for your own children and when observing the behavior of their friends.

Tooth Bunny

Just like the tooth fairy in many other countries, the tooth bunny is the bringer of money to those good little children that lose a baby tooth in Panama. Put it under your pillow when you go to bed and the tooth bunny will replace the tooth with money.

PANAMA ON LINE

Universidad Católica Santa Maria La Antigua
USMA
http://www.usma.ac.pa

Consejo del Sector Privado
Para la Asistencia Educacional
COSPAE
Email: instdeingles@cableonda.net

Kids Zone
Interactive play for Children
8 months to 3 years
Email: babysteps8@hotmail.com

Global Nomads Association
http://www.gng.org

U. S. State Department – Services
http://www.travel.state.gov/

Moving with Children
http://www.usps.gov/moversnet/

Mis Comicaturas (my comics)
http://www.aprendoweb.com

PANAMA ON LINE

Alianza Francesa
Learn French
Email: alliance@cableonda.net
223-7376

Explora
Fundación Centro de Ciencias y Arte
http://www.explorapanama.orgarticledetailenglish.

Virtual Jewish History Tour in Panama
http://www.jewishvirtuallibrary.org/jsource/vjw/Panama.html

In Panama the locals say...

Power is determined by how many people you can inconvenience.

If it were not for poor planning, there would be no planning at all.

There are two kinds of cars: those that have been in accidents and those that will be.

Every business in Panama has had an episode of being embezzled or will have – either by relatives or employees.

Panamanians are serious about only two things—the lottery and Carnival.

VII

GETTING CONNECTED

Moving to a new country provides lots of opportunities for learning new ways to do old things. This chapter will give you some guidance in handling the day-to-day activities of **Living in Panama**.

Just a few things you need to know so you will not get burned

Panama and many other Spanish-speaking countries have found a creative solution to using bathroom fixtures made in the English-speaking world. If you are accustomed to the hot water faucet saying H for hot and the cold-water faucet being labeled C for cold, you will find these reversed in many cases. In Spanish hot is *caliente*, also with a C. Expect the faucet labeled C to be hot and the H faucet to be cold (H for *helado*/ice).

Normally, the faucets will be in the accustomed positions of hot on the left and cold on the right – but not always. Check first, especially before stepping into the shower. Additionally, do not be surprised if the maid's bath has only a cold-water faucet.

In general most hardware and fittings are on the English or U.S system of measurements, as are weights and measures, though the metric system is also in use.

In all but the largest stores and shops it is still the custom to go through multiple stations in order to pay for a purchase and receive the item. Do not be surprised if a salesperson writes up your order and passes you and a sales slip to another person who will "ring up the sale" and collect your money. Then you will be given yet another slip of paper and passed to another counter to receive your purchase. There will be time spent at each location to verify information on the slip and assure you get the correct package. If you wish gift wrapping you will be sent to another station with another slip. Most stores provide free gift wrapping and do a beautiful job.

Utilities

In recent years many of the utilities in Panama have been privatized to the great benefit of the community. Telephone service is one example, which was discussed in Chapter III. Television service alternatives were also discussed in Chapter III.

A Spanish company, Union Fenosa, provides electricity for most of the city. In the interior it is provided by EDEMET. Electricity service for a residence requires a deposit of $110 and can be made by cash, check or credit card. Be sure to keep your original receipt for deposit in order to get a refund at the time you discontinue service. Electrical output is 110-volt alternating current, 60 cycles per second, the same as in the U.S. However, adapters for some European electrical products are available.

Gas, water, trash, and sewer service are usually included in the monthly rental rates on apartments but are billed and paid for separately on other housing units. Stoves and some water heaters are gas-fired which is a convenient energy source. Propane gas is available from two companies, Tropigas or Panagas. These companies deliver for large users or you can take your container to their facility for filling. Fittings for these tanks are not interchangeable.

Telephone service countrywide is provided by Cable & Wireless for your domestic and international calling. Additionally, numerous specialty services offer international calling at friendly rates. Cellular (mobile) phone service is available through Movistar and Cable & Wireless. There is a telephone and calling plan to suit the needs of everyone. Public telephones are conveniently located all over the country and city and as far away as the Darién and Kuna Yala. Most of these phones work with calling cards, which can be conveniently purchased, at grocery stores, pharmacies, on the street and a variety of other locations.

Paying Bills

While Panama now has reasonably good service when it comes to electricity, telephone, water, and television, paying the bills is a bit more complicated. Service providers can mail their bills to your post office box or have them delivered to your door. Delivery to your residence assures timely receipt of the bill, as the local mail service is variable in reliability. Bills may be paid in any of the following ways:

1. Paid in person by cash or check at the office of the provider.

2. Paid in cash at El Rey or Super 99 Supermarkets or some Banks.

3. Paid online by direct transfer from your account through Banco General or Banistmo. Several other banks plan on providing this service in the future.

However, **Do Not** mail your payments to the company through the local post office, as it is too slow.

The simplest of these choices is paying online from the convenience of your home computer. However, most people still go to one of the above choices and pay bills in person in cash (or send their maid or messenger). If you choose this method, avoid waiting until the last moment to pay the bill and you will not have to stand in a long line. Cable-Onda on Calle 50 now has more parking which has eliminated the long lines waiting to get into the parking lot. However, it too, is more convenient to pay online from your bank account with some banks. Giving the providers your credit card information so that they can automatically deduct your monthly bill from your account can lead to problems if your credit card number is compromised. Be extra careful with your credit cards.

Household Help

Maids, nannies, gardeners, drivers and ironing ladies are common in Panama. Help here is inexpensive, if variable, and everyone has at least a maid, perhaps several. Families with children have nannies, especially as most women work outside the home or are busy with their social activities. Many people have a driver who also may do errands and jobs around the house.

There is a story about a man who faced a dilemma when he caught a large fish. The fish was so big that it seemed as likely that the man would be pulled from the boat into the water and taken away by the fish, as that he would land the fish on the deck of the boat. As he struggled to land his fish, he thought to himself, "Does he have me or do I have him?" That is the same dilemma faced by those in Panama with domestic help. While the daily or monthly outlay is small, the additional fees and obligations incurred are potentially lifelong and expensive.

After you have had an employee for a number of years they begin to think of you as a *patrón* or protector. As a result it is typical of employees to ask for loans, assistance with money for their family members whether to build them a house, furnish their house, provide school clothes and books for their children, or provide medical care and medicines for family members.

Employees of all kinds are employed for 12 months (including a one month vacation) and paid for 13 months. They are required to be enrolled in the *Planilla* that provides for their social security that includes medical care and retirement benefits. The longer you have an employee work for you the more you will owe in benefits. The employment laws are very favorable to the employee and as a result, the employee is generally eligible for severance pay regardless of whether is being fired for cause or quitting.

Employers are expected to provide uniforms and house shoes. If you have a maid daily, she will need at least three uniforms, two for regular work and one for use when you are entertaining. Occasional day help may or may not wear uniforms. Most employers do not allow shorts. You will need a written agreement including a three-month trial period after which time you can cancel the agreement at no further expense. You may also wish to require a medical certificate stating the employee is not pregnant in order to avoid further expense. Once an employee has passed the trial period, however, he or she must be enrolled in Social Security. The employee can make the necessary payments to the plan for his portion and yours but must bring you the receipts. Payment is based on a percentage of pay. Carefully keep track of all payments, vacation and leave time as well as lateness or disciplinary actions.

You can hire a day maid for between $10 and $12 per day. A full-time, live-in maid will cost between $150 to $200 per month. Requirements for payments for full-time domestic employees are specific and complicated. The Panama *Codigo de Trabajo*, Labor Code, is available (in Spanish) for purchase at Gran Morrison or Exedra Books and is a wise investment for those with full-time help.

A Panamanian friend gives this advice concerning domestic help:

1. Know who you are hiring; get references and check them.
2. Hire the best people you can find.
3. Hire them with the idea of keeping them employed for a long time.
4. Treat employees in a professional manner, **not** like a member of the family.
5. Do not overpay your help. *Extranjeros* have a tendency to want to *help* and improve the financial situation of those they feel less well off than themselves. You do your employees a better service by being aware of local customs and rates and following those established norms.
6. Keep written records of every thing you pay, days taken off for sick, holiday or vacation time.

When you entertain it is easy and inexpensive to hire waiters and bartenders to help for the evening. There are also numerous excellent caterers to choose from, many of whom can also supply waiters for your event. Many restaurants also offer take-out of a single item or an entire meal for a group and deliver.

A final word of caution: most household burglaries are committed by someone with a connection to you, an employee or former employee.

Pet Care and Feeding (*Mascotas*)

<u>Veterinarians</u>

There are numerous excellent vets in Panama, many who specialize in small animals. A lesser number speak English. In general they perform the same services and provide the same pet supplies you will find in your home country. A routine visit to the vet will cost between $10 and $25 depending on the vet and whether you go to him or he makes a house call. For example, rabies shots for a cat cost $19. Some vets and vet clinics are on call 24-hours including weekends and holidays.

Yes, they make house calls and it is not unusual for your vet to call you at home to follow-up on your sick pet.

Pet food and supplies including kitty litter are also readily available at all the major grocery chains, Arrocha, Melo Pet stores, Novey Hardware and other similar stores. This is equally true in the interior including Boquete and El Valle.

Caution: Cats love to play with the geckos (little lizards) common in Panama. These little animals have *breakaway tails, which* help to insure their escape when caught by the cat or other animal and also provide entertainment for the cat as the tails continue to wiggle once detached. However, **they are poisonous if swallowed**. While your cat may not die from eating one gecko or tail, the poison accumulates in the body and over a period of time continued ingestion will prove fatal.

Dogs can encounter a similar danger by swallowing **frogs**. Some varieties are **instantly poisonous**.

For pet needs check the yellow pages under *Veterinarios.*

Animal Kennels and Care

When you plan your vacation or weekend away, do not forget to plan for your pet. There are several kennel possibilities in Panama. One of them offers outside run areas for the dogs. Prices range from $5–$12 per day and all allow you to bring your own food. Some recommend you bring your own cage as well. A bed and breakfast for pets and people is located in La Cresta. They offer pleasant accommodations for your pet, with a reservation, and personalized service for a reasonable daily fee.

Looking for a Pet

Fundacion Humanitas is a group of concerned citizens that keep track of animals of all kinds that are available for adoption. Members of this group take in strays and attempt to place them in good homes. If you wish to provide a home for an animal or make a monetary donation, email: humanitasppamor@yahoo.com or call Daniella at 264-8772. Dr. Samudio of Animals & Pets and Dr. Kurt Menzel, who has a private clinic in San Francisco (226-4436), staff the program.

Boquete residents have organized a spay and neuter clinic two to three times per year. Spay Panama in Panama City is a non-profit organization that provides low cost neutering services. They offer the services of three volunteer veterinarians on request by a community with sufficient need to warrant their visit. The fee for service is $10.

Do not abandon your pet to the streets of Panama when you decide to move.

Shopping Customs

It is easy to live in Panama. You can find all the goods and services you need at a cost more or less equal to the United States, Costa Rica or Mexico, for example. (See Appendix 5 Cost of Living.) Shopping in Panama is also a social outing. Particularly **unlike** the U.S., people dress up to go to the supermarket because they will encounter friends and acquaintances in every aisle. Not only are there three major grocery chains in Panama City and additional ones in the interior to pick from, but there are numerous specialty shops as well. Some grocery stores are open 24 hours a day. They offer both local and imported assorted foods for every taste and need from kosher to Chinese. Not only will you find many of the brands and items from the U.S., but also Panama grocers import from Greece, France, Peru, Costa Rica, and elsewhere.

While quality and availability are excellent in general, this is especially true when it comes to the wonderful selection of locally grown fruits and vegetables. Fresh tomatoes, papayas, strawberries, passion fruit, grapefruit, pineapple, melons and dozens of other choices are available the year around. The grocery stores here are at a standard you would expect back home and; in addition, Panama offers the added advantage of the fresh fish market, public vegetable market, Chinese market and warehouse shopping.

The old fashioned pharmacy, while it still exists in neighborhoods, has been replaced by the mega-pharmacy offering everything from the traditional medications and first-aid supplies to house wares, school and office supplies, magazines, cosmetics, costume jewelry and Christmas decorations. Check the newspaper for listings of which pharmacies are open 24 hours on rotation. Additionally, the major grocery stores also have a pharmacy department.

The best places to shop for clothing, appliances, or household goods, are specialty stores for these items. The department stores have clothing, toys, house wares and linens but generally not appliances. Discount warehouse (Price Smart and Mega Depot) stores are conveniently located in several areas of the city as well as the interior. There are several large hardware chains as well as numerous neighborhood hardware stores.

The shopping mall has arrived in Panama. **El Dorado** mall, the original, continues to serve this suburban community with a variety of boutique shops, as well as major anchor stores: El Rey, Super 99, Gran Morrison, Dante's as well as an adjacent Felix B. Maduro.

Two additional malls in the downtown are conveniently located. **Multicentro Paitilla** has a movie theater and four floors of boutique shops and a large casino. **MultiPlaza Pacific Mall** adjacent to Punta Pacifica provides convenient shopping with all the major and many smaller shops found anywhere in Panama. This is a U.S. style mega-mall with everything from Maduro's to Stevens, Do-It-Center, Timberland, Liz Claiborne, Naturalizer, Ann Taylor, Cinnabun, Sony, Casio and many other familiar names. Additionally they offer Riba Smith Supermarket, movie theaters and several restaurants.

On the opposite side of town, **Albrook Mall** provides convenient shopping for those traveling from the interior by bus or air as well as for the communities of Albrook, Clayton, Cardenas and Balboa. Here you will find Super 99, movie theaters, a variety of restaurant and fast food outlets, Conways and numerous boutique shops.

Further out in the suburbs, **Los Andes** and **Los Pueblos Malls** offer bargain shopping. In David the **Mall Chiriqui** serves the needs of the surrounding communities of Boquete, Volcan and Cerro Punta with restaurants, movies, clothing stores, banks, pharmacies and more.

An alternative to shopping for clothing is the use of a dressmaker. Panama offers an excellent variety of dressmakers and tailors. Some have small shops in their home, or will come to your home to sew and do fittings. Many of these dressmakers can copy your existing favorites or design new things for you. There are also excellent tailor shops (*sastrerias*) for men's suits, tuxedos and shirts. You can provide your own material, select from the inventory in the larger shops or have the dressmaker buy what is required. Rates vary but an average dressmaker will work for $25 a day or charge by the item about $7 for a skirt and $20 for a dress. A custom suit will cost about $300 depending on design and fabric.

Panama also boasts a number of primo fashion designers of world class. Consider one of these when next you need a special outfit at reasonable cost for a custom creation of high quality.

One of the reasons Panama is such a convenient place to live when it comes to acquiring goods and services is that Panama imports from around the world. This provides for not only an incredible selection of goods but also a variety of qualities and prices. Many importers buy in container-load quantities that may create very favorable prices to the consumer. However, attention to the quality of the item is a must when buying whether it is fabric, tires, automobiles, large appliances, small appliances or electronic equipment. Determining the impact of buying discontinued goods, seconds or last year's model needs to be a part of your decision process in making a purchase. It will be further to your advantage to check out pricing options for purchase through the Internet before making large purchases locally as not all imports result in favorable pricing to the consumer. Additionally, counterfeit goods are prevalent in everything from handbags and watches to deodorants.

Línea Blanca or white line refers to major kitchen appliances normally found in an apartment or house. This includes refrigerator, stove and washer, sometimes dryer. A great variety of U.S. and Japanese makes and models are readily available in a variety of price ranges. Gas stoves are the norm in Panama as opposed to electric. If you purchase a new stove or bring yours with you it will need to be converted from natural gas to propane. Local appliance dealers do this routinely at no additional charge at the time of purchase and installation. The adapters are readily available for your existing stove. Make it a routine to have your stove checked and the flame adjusted annually.

Fortunately, there are excellent repair services available for a variety of appliances from televisions to refrigerators and at a reasonable price.

Grocery Stores

Supermercados Rey.
Via Espana, Calle 50, El Dorado, Coronado, Albrook, David, Colon, 18 locations in all plus Mr. Precio, mini-marts in the interior, and deliveries from many locations
Punto de Oro (point card for gifts)
http:/www.puntodeoro.com, customer service: 270-5535

Super 99
Punta Pacifica, El Dorado, San Francisco, Albrook

Super Kosher, S.A.
Punta Paitilla

Riba Smith, S.A.
Bella Vista, Transistmica, MultiPlaza Pacific
Mercadeo@rimith.com
http://www.rimith.com
Personal shopping and home delivery

Mini-Super Bal Harbor
(the Chinese market)
Bal Harbor Shopping Center, Punta Paitilla

SuperXtra
Arraijan, San Miguelito, Los Pueblos, Juan Diaz, 24 de Diciembre,
Ojo de Agua, Chorrera
http://www.superXtra.com

Centro Comercial el Valle
Main Street, El Valle de Anton
One stop shopping for pharmacy, groceries, hardware, electric tools,
car batteries and Texaco gas

Romero's
David, Boquete, Volcan, Tel.: 775.2131 / 775-6950

Centro Bruñas
David, Boquete

Supermercado Barú
David

Berard Supermarket
Volcan

La Boca Loca Super Gourmet
Main Street
Bocas del Toro
Tel.: 507/757-9357

Pharmacies

Farmacias Arrocha
Punta Paitilla, Calle 50, El Dorado, El Cangrejo, Albrook, Costa del Este, David

Farmacia Metro X
El Dorado, Obario, Calle 50, Betania, Paitilla

Farmax
Plaza Edison, Marbella

Farmacia Paitilla Hospital
Consultorio Medicos Paitilla

Hardware Stores

Novey
Avenida Central, Ricardo J. Alfaro, Via Cincuentenario, El Dorado

Do It Center
El Dorado, Rio Abajo, Los Pueblos, MultiPlaza, David
http://www.doitpanama.com
info@doitpanama.com

Discovery Center
Via España y Calle 5ta, Rio Abajo
Email: semfyl@cwpanama.net
221-7948 (my personal favorite)

Ferrateria Empresas Fink
Volcan

Ferrateria Miki
Volcan.

Consult the local telephone directory when you are in need of goods or services; and you will be pleasantly surprised at the many products and services available in such a small country.

All-Round Store

Machetazo is the all-round, shopper's friend. This local store offers groceries, house wares, fabrics, hardware, cards and party goods, pharmacy and cosmetics, candy and flowers, just to name a few. Keep it in mind when you are planning a party or looking for hard-to-find items at a reasonable price. Located in Avenida Central, Santa Ana, Calidonia, San Miguelito, Tocumen, Arraijan, Chitre, Santiago, and Penonome. Email: Impmach@machetazo.com

Street Vendors

All around town at major intersections you will find the street vendor. While sitting in your car waiting for your turn to move through the intersection, you can purchase the day's supply of plantain, fresh pineapple, mangos, peppers, tomatoes or whatever fruit or vegetable is in season. This convenient sales approach eliminates the necessity of stopping at a store, parking and getting out of your car when it is raining or you are short on time. The price is a convenient $1 a bag for whatever is being sold.

These enterprising vendors can also help you with various accessories for your cell phone, from calling cards to leather covers to hands-free talking gadgets. They may have the latest set of tools, calendars, sunglasses, perfumes, flowers, weight loss devices or the daily newspaper. Something you recently saw advertised on TV for $19.95 will be sold on the street for $15 or less if you negotiate.

All Kinds of Rentals

It is possible to rent formal wear for both men and women from gowns to tuxedos. Rentals of all sorts of supplies for dinner parties including chairs, tables, table cloths, chair covers, glasses and plates are also available. One supplier has all sorts of garden party covers from simple awnings to air-conditioned tents.

While you await delivery of your household goods, you can rent a bed, a room of furniture or an entire household to make your temporary accommodations comfortable.

Recycling

There is one area where progress is further ahead in the interior than in the city and that is recycling. As mentioned in the discussion of Boquete, a recycling program is underway. In the city, Riba Smith provides bins for recycling newspapers and periodically for clothing items. *Casita de Mausi*, home for recovering cancer patients, also recycles newspapers.

However, in general the recycling system in the city goes something like this: You put your trash in the containers provided by your apartment or house and immediately the employees of your building sort through it for *good stuff*. What seems like trash, or a worn out appliance to you is usable to someone else. After this first sort, the trash is ready for pick up by your respective local trash company. At this time, it goes through a second sort for *good stuff*. Again, when your discards finally reach the local dump, there are scavengers who will further sort through it for usable stuff. Thus a sort of informal recycling goes on all the time.

Sanchiz, Siebrasse & Asociados, S.A.
Strategic Management and
Communications Counseling Services
Since 1982
http://www.ssa-publicrelations.com
Email: info@ssapanama.com

Repair Resources

Panasonic Latin America, S.A.
Servicio al Cliente
http://www.panasonic.com.pa
229-2294

Tech & House
Novatron
Appliance Service
263-9611
http://www.techhousepanama.com
Email: techhouse@cwpanama.net

Emilio's Movil Shop
317-1537
6672-7305
Beeper 811

Zapateria Agusomar
Shoe repair
El Dorado Mall

El Rey Supermercado
Watch Repair
Via Espana or El Dorado

Plateria Florentina
Silver repairs and replating
226-3703

Cromados Panama, S.A.
Chrome Repairs and Replating
224-9727

Panama Government Offices

Stop the Violence/Sexual Abuse
800-0014 or 147
Free and confidential

MIDA
Ministerio de Desarrollo Agropecuario
507-0600
http://www.mida.gob.pa

Defensoria del Pueblo
Central 500-9800/9801

Law 29 Defensa de la Competencia
For cash refunds on returned articles
http://www.clicac.gob.pa

General Department of Revenue of the Economy and Finance Ministry
207-7753
Email:dgireclamos@mef.gob.pa
http://www.dgi.gob.pa

Autoridad Nacional del Ambiente (ANAM)
500-0855

National Police
Central Telephone Ancon 511-7000
Information and Investigation 511-9308/09/10
Dept. Transit Operations 511-7389 or 511-7390

Panama Government Offices

Ministerio Publico/Public Ministry
Edificio AVESA 505-3200
Edificio U.R.S.M. 507-3300
http://www.ministeriopublico.gov.pa

Gobierno Nacional/National Government
Direccion General 507-6876
Sub Direccion General 507-6867
Direccion Administrativa 507–6841
Direccion de Desarrollo Social y Cultura
507-6840
Oficina de Relaciones Publicas 507-6851
Unidad de Informatica 507-6837

Autoridad de Proteccion al Consumidor y Defensa de la
Competencia/Consumer Protection Authority and Competition
Defense Agency
Central office 510-1313
Client Line 510-1300
http://www.authoridaddelconsumidor.gob.pa

Administracion de la Zona Libre de Colon/Free Zone Colon
Administration
475-9500, 475-9501/02

Superintendencia de Bancos de Panama/Superintendent of Banks
506-7800, 506-7900

PANAMA ON LINE

Hotel Bambito Resort (Volcan)
http://www.hotelbambito.com

Gran Hotel Nacional
David, Chiriqui
http://www.panamainfo.com/granhotelnacional

Alquileres de Agasajos
Party Rentals
269-3621
Glasses, plates, silverware, party goods

La Cresta de Oro
Bed and Breakfast for People and Pets
info@lacrestadeoro.com

Angel's in the Kitchen
Specialty Cookies and Cakes
Angiebakx@yahoo.com
223-0562

SOS
Translation Services
serviofi@cwpanama.net

Information 24-7
http://www.boquete.org

PANAMA ON LINE

Sheraton Hotel and Resort Panama
http://www.starwoodhotels.com/sheraton
Movistar
http://www.movistar.com

Four Points Sheraton
http://www.Hotel.sheratonpanama.com

Marriott
Email: mhrs.ptypa.dom@marriott.com

The Bristol
Email: yvergara@thebristol.com

Coronado Hotel & Resort
http://www.coronadoresort.com

Gamboa Rainforest Resort
Email: reservation@gamboaresort.com

Grupo Taca
http://www.taca.com

Aeroperlas
http://www.aeroperlas.com

Aventura y Cultura
http://www.pesantez-tours.com

PANAMA ON LINE

Costa Blanca Royal Decameron Resort
http://www.decameron.com

Crystal Suites Hotel
http://www.crystalsuites.com

MultiPlaza Pacific Mall
http://www.gruporoble.com

Cats & Dogs Care Center
6613-5895
Email: sandrarios@cwpanama.net

La Fortuna
La Sastreria de Panama
Taylor of Panama
Casa Matríz, Via Espana
302-7890
Aquilino de La Guarda & Ave. Balboa
302-7893
Email: ventas@lafortunapanama.com

www. Listings

Check the Panama yellow pages Web Site Section
for an incredible list of Internet sites.

VIII

Planes, Trains, Buses, Ferries and Automobiles

IN TOWN AND IN THE COUNTRY

Cars and SUVs

All the things you need to know about having an automobile!

Fifteen minutes on the streets of Panama City and you will know that you are not driving in Omaha! The development of the infrastructure, including number and size of streets, has not been able to keep up with the increasing traffic requirements of this bustling City. As a result, the density of the traffic and the creativity of Panamanian drivers are intimidating. Like the U.S., Canada, and Central America you drive to the right. Seat belts are required and you must wait for the police to arrive in the case of an accident. However, if you adopt a slow and cautious driving style you will find drivers, particularly taxi drivers, passing you on the left or right. Driving requires your full concentration; talking on the cell phone is not only illegal but also dangerous. Try to get the feel for the tempo of the traffic to fit in without becoming too aggressive. Traffic laws are very flexibly observed. If you need to cross four lanes of traffic, be ready to go, indicate your intentions, wait for a little opening and start across. As long as you do not delay anyone too much they will let you slide right through. Do not be timid and do try to keep moving. Although most Panamanians drive as though they are in the only car on the road, they do anticipate that you will need to merge into traffic and a space will open up for you.

Use of the horn. Everyone uses it pretty freely with a light tap to wake up the driver ahead or to encourage the slow driver to move along, a blast to chastise a driver who is doing something unusually stupid, and for taxis, two taps to alert potential passengers or shapely women of their presence. The traffic lanes are very narrow and hitting the rear view mirror of the car in the next lane is not uncommon. While you are trying to merge to the next lane it is impossible to be watching in all directions at once so drivers around you will tap the horn to warn other drivers when they are getting too close.

Motorcycles. Be constantly on the alert for motorcycles. They will create their own lane between two lanes, shoot in and out of traffic and squeeze in where there is no place to squeeze. Unbelievably, there are not too many motorcycle accidents.

Accidents. A recent newspaper report of traffic accidents in general in the City cited an average of 26 accidents per day on Avenida Central/Via España. With the increase in more freeway-driving, more serious injury accidents are becoming a concern. The driving techniques used in the city at low speed do not translate well at high speed. These include continual lane changes, merging into very small spaces and driving too close to the car ahead. Be particularly cautious when driving at the beginning of the rainy season, as streets tend to be slippery. It is not unusual to experience hydroplaning in these conditions on the freeways known as *Corredor Norte* and *Corredor Sur.*

The rainy season poses its own set of problems as it can rain so hard at times as to cause a *white out* where it is impossible to see, or flood the streets making driving difficult and dangerous. Watch out for missing manhole covers, as they are fairly common. While these may have been removed for economic gain by the remover (sold for scrap metal), they are just as likely to have been displaced by fast moving rainwater. It might even be useful to remember where the covers are normally in your regular driving route; when the streets are flooded, it is a particularly bad time to get a wheel stuck in a manhole! Remember, there are two kinds of cars here, the ones with dents and the ones that will have dents. The good news is that bodywork is inexpensive in Panama, since it is a volume business. Be careful! If you do have an accident, call the police, call your insurance agent, get witnesses and keep them at the scene till the police arrive, and confirm the written police report. Take photos if you can. (Many cell phones have a camera.)

Automobiles are reasonable to finance and or buy, which means there are too many of them on the existing streets and this goes double

---

In case of accident the following emergency numbers will be of assistance:

Transito-Emisora/Highway Police—232-6845 identify the problem; give location, request police and ambulance if needed.

Alerta: 800-0911, Ambulance, for medical emergency

Policia Nacional/National police: 104

Bomberos/Fire Department: 103

Tow Truck: Mr. Grua 188, Gruas Salerno 221-8877

---

for taxis. In 2000 there were 452,026 vehicles in circulation. That number has increased to approximately 558,553 (300,000 in Panama City) as of June 2006. As of June 2006 there were 110 traffic lights (*semáforos*) in operation and a study is being made to install another 180 new lights, which will also have a system for central control. With the recent increase of building projects all over the city, traffic has become even more congested requiring new solutions to the resulting problems.

Car insurance is also reasonable but the majority (75-80%) of drivers **do not** have it. Many insurers offer on-the-spot assistance should you have an accident. They will provide you with an emergency number in case of accident and a company representative will arrive to assist you at the scene of the accident and help you through the reporting and legal processes.

Parking. While parking at home is less of a problem than parking in general, as spaces are included with high-rise apartments and with houses, it is becoming more difficult. Many neighborhoods now have cars parked in every available space in the streets as more families have multiple drivers and multiple cars. Parking in downtown areas is very congested. The advent of the shopping mall has not only created a pleasant shopping experience but these malls provide parking that is inexpensive or free. In both shopping centers and downtown, you will find the *parking assistant*. They will help you find a space, help you into it, watch your car, and help you on your way out, all for twenty-five cents. For a few dollars they will also wash your car. The new shopping malls have more sophisticated car wash operations but still offer a quick wash for a few dollars.

In Panama, you sometimes feel as if you have stepped back in time to a friendlier era. Pulling into a gas station is one of those times. **Gas stations** are full service, helpful places that wash your windshield, check everything under the hood, and put air in your tires, while you sit and relax. A small tip ($1 or less) will also get you a smile from the attendant. Panama only offers 91 or 95 octane unleaded gas or diesel. Prices go up and down with the current market but are generally cheaper than other countries and shortages seldom happen. With the increasing gas prices, some taxis have converted to propane.

Test Drive Sunday. When you are new to Panama and the driving system, taking a Sunday drive is recommended. Traffic is less and you will be able to take time to get acquainted with the one-way streets and other idiosyncrasies of driving in Panama. If driving still intimidates you, take a taxi or hire a driver. The good news is car jacking, theft and vandalism are not common.

Life in the Tropics. As mentioned in other sections herein, the climate can be tough on your home, your body, your hair, and no less on your car. Tires, windshield wipers and batteries last about a year in this climate. Plan to replace them more often than you are accustomed to doing elsewhere. Similarly, you will use your air conditioner every time you drive if you live at sea level. As a consequence, air conditioning parts wear out long before the rest of the car. Expect to replace condensers and evaporators as well as regularly recharge the system. Be sure your system is recharged with either R-12 or R-134A and not with HC-12A (hydrocarbon with butane and propane.)

Car Registration

Annual car registration and inspection are required in Panama. Registrations expire one year from the date of original registration as indicated on the sticker on your license plate. In the month required for your car's renewal you will need to follow this two-step procedure:

Take the Title Certificate (*Registro de Propiedad Vehicular*) and registration, and *Certificado de Inspección Vehicular* issued by the *Autoridad del Tránsito y Transporte Terrestre* to any inspection station, for the *Revisado*. These inspection stations display the sign, *revisados*, and can be found all over town at gas stations, muffler shops, tire shops, etc. The car inspection will cost $19.00 (includes tax) per vehicle. You will also need to make any required repairs. They will then take a digital photo of your car for the records.

Next, take your title, registration, inspection certificate and $28.00 per vehicle to the appropriate vehicle registration office that is determined by the number on your license plate. As of 2005, all license plates are actually issued at the main office for the City. You can still pay for the process at any of the various offices but you will still have to go to the main office to receive the plates. Generally, it is less time consuming to just do the whole process at the main office. If in doubt as to which office you should go to for the registration, ask the people doing the inspection. In fact, some inspection stations offer an additional service for $10 of obtaining the license plates for you (well worth the cost).

As this step can take some time, you need to either plan to stand in line and be patient or use the services of someone to do this. Fortunately, there are many *runners* who will take care of this process for a fee of $10 to $15. Ask your neighbors or work associates for a reliable referral. As with the payment of all other bills in Panama, you will find the lines shorter if you pay as soon as the renewal is due rather than waiting until the last days. (Note: If you have more than one vehicle with the same month of expiration you can do this process for all vehicles at the same time. You do have to produce each vehicle for the required photo. All payments are in cash.)

Driver's License

In a survey conducted by the editors of *Autopista Magazine*, 50 drivers in Panama were tested in parallel parking and city driving. Participants included young and old, men and women and taxi drivers. The overall conclusion of the three evaluators was that "Panamanians do not know how to drive"! Only one person in the group could parallel park on the first try and only 20% were able to park after various attempts. When driving in general "most did not even know how to hold the steering wheel". The worst participant was a "taxi driver who thought he knew it all". He was "unable to follow instructions, did not use his direction signals, passed a stop sign without even being aware it existed and when needed tromped on the brakes with all his might". Clearly these driving practices explain, "why we have so many dented cars in Panama". It was the conclusion of the conductors of the study that "we need stricter practices and enforcement of the driver's license issuing process in order to improve our drivers."

In the meantime, the *Autoridad de Tránsito y Transporte Terrestre (ATTT)* will be happy to issue a Driver's License or *Licencia de Conducir*. In order to obtain your first license you will need your passport, immigration visa, your home country driver's license, blood type and $20.50. (No test required.) You no longer need the previously required blood test and glucose tolerance test unless you are applying for a commercial license. If you are renewing your existing Panama license, you will only need that license, a copy of your *cédula* or immigration visa and the $20.50 fee. Take the above documents to the ATTT office driver's license bureau where they will take your photo and ink your thumb for a print on the reverse of your license. The License is issued for the length of time remaining on your current visa or four years, whichever is less. You are required to obtain a driver's license if you are driving in the country, other than as a tourist, for more than one month.

Tourists may drive with their 90-day tourist card and the driving license of their home country. Be sure to have your passport or a copy of the identification page and entrance page of your passport with you when driving. Should you decide to apply for a Panama license while here as a tourist, remember the license will only be issued for the length of time on your tourist card (90-days maximum) but will cost only $5.50.

The Albrook office is open Monday thru Friday, 9:00 –5:00 p.m. and is convenient for applicants from the City and those visiting from the interior as well. The Pedregal office is open Monday thru Friday 7:30-5:00 and Saturday from 9:00 a.m. –12:00 noon.

If you do not have a license from your home country and are applying for the first time, or are under 16 years of age there are additional requirements including classroom instruction, written test of 100 questions and driving test. Additionally, if you are over 70 years of age you will need a Medical Certificate from a Panama doctor. For further information see the ATTT web site at: http//www.transito.gob.pa. and www.transito.gob.pa/cuestionario.htm.

Pedestrians

Pedestrians come in two kinds in Panama. The locals walk the same way they drive—with little or no regard for the traffic around them. As a driver, expect pedestrians to step off the curb at intersections without checking for oncoming or turning traffic. Expect pedestrians, bicyclists, and vendors to move in traffic lanes.

Extranjero pedestrians, who may think they are street-wise when crossing streets, are equally in danger. Motorists do not necessarily honor designated crosswalks. Do not step out into a crosswalk assuming everyone will stop. Be alert to the traffic around you when walking. It sometimes seems like pedestrians are fair game.

An interesting observation: grocery shoppers *drive* their grocery carts much the same way they drive their cars.

Once You Are on the Road

Complying with Traffic Laws

Every vehicle is required to have a copy of the *Manual for Driving in Panama* (available at Arrocha Pharmacy), a first-aid kit and a flashlight. From time to time you will encounter roadblocks in which the local police check for these items, as well as valid driver's licenses or current registration. The manual is in Spanish, which may slow you down when it comes to reading it from cover to cover. However, if you do not read it you will be even with the average Panamanian.

Commercial vehicles are required to carry reflective triangles for use at accidents or roadside repair sites.

Panamanians are nothing if not flexible when it comes to driving. Once during the Carnival festivities when the rerouting of traffic made it difficult to get across town, some inventive driver drove the wrong way on a one-way street past the hospital and started a trend for the day. No one got upset and there were no accidents. The next day when the festivities ended, the traffic pattern returned to normal. Similar solutions to traffic situations occur when there are accidents and use of a one way street, the wrong way, will solve the detour need.

There are at least two streets in Panama that are *backwards* all the time but it makes perfect sense that they be so. Between *Via España* and *Calle Tres (*which becomes *Cincuenta*), there is a one-block stretch, also called *Calle Tres that* is two-way. *Calle Tres* is not only two-way for this block, but the **lanes are reversed.** This makes perfect sense as it makes for ease of turning left from both directions by having the lanes reversed. There are signs posted to warn drivers of this change in pattern. This same logic is in place on a little cross street in the Hollywood/

Curundu area between the two main one-way streets through the area. Again, this makes for ease of turning left onto the streets involved.

During the peak commute hours, Balboa Avenue changes direction for its traffic lanes in order to carry the increased traffic coming into the city in the morning. Watch for notices of lane switches on other streets in the city as well. Large yellow signs showing the lanes, directions in effect and the times of operation are clearly posted.

As of this writing, plans are again being discussed for extending the *Corredor Sur* from Paitilla to the Causeway to ease the traffic load on Balboa Avenue. This would be constructed offshore much like the seven-mile stretch from Atlapa Convention Center to *Costa del Este*.

Driving in the interior of Panama is much more civilized in general. Buses use pullouts and are more likely to stay in their own lane. Drivers in general are more courteous. However long stretches of two-lane road where it is difficult to safely pass, lack of guardrails, excessive speed, potholes and other obstacles can contribute to accidents.

Dealing with Traffic Police

Panama traffic police have two functions. They direct traffic at intersections and look for offenses for which they can write a ticket. At an intersection controlled by a policeman, he may spot you on your cell phone or notice that your car registration is out of date and pull you over for a ticket. Often a policeman or a group of policemen will be standing at various locations looking for violations such as illegal left-hand turns. (There are very few legal left-hand turns in Panama.) In any of these instances you can sometimes talk your way out of a ticket or you can graciously accept the ticket (*boleta*) and pay the fine. **Do not offer bribes.** Tickets are paid at the local *Tránsito y Transporte Terrestre* office close to where the ticket was issued. This is another instance where you will go from window to window. First you present your ticket and take a seat. Next you are called to confirm the ticket and the amount to be paid. Last you actually pay the ticket. Each transaction takes place at a different window. You can also pay at any *Caja de Ahorros*. For a complete list of fines and places to pay check: http://www.transito.gob.pa

The other ticket you may encounter is for parking overtime. Be sure to put your quarter in the parking meter every time and keep track of your hour. Parking meter ticket writers do an excellent job for Panama. The cost of the ticket is determined by the amount of time you are over from the time of the writing of the ticket. They quickly hit the maximum fine of $5.00 so it is worthwhile to pay immediately. You have 30 days to pay tickets in general but all outstanding tickets and fines must be paid before you can obtain annual registration for your car.

When driving in the interior, you will encounter another kind of policeman, the motorcycle cop. He is usually parked along the road between towns, under overpasses or at the outskirts of the town. These policemen have radar and radios and are looking for speeders. Be alert to posted speed limit signs and obey them.

Getting Around Town and Around the Country

Recently there was an article in a local paper explaining new routes through the old sections of Panama City. With the article was a very detailed map showing exactly how the new routes ran through the area. What was missing were any street names or even indications of north or south on the map. This is not surprising; even if there had been street names most people would not have recognized them. Directions for driving, finding businesses and residences in Panama are given by landmarks. Except for the major cross streets, *Via España, Calle Cincuenta, Balboa Avenue, Federico Boyd, Avenida Brazil,* and the *Corredors,* few people know the names of the streets.

Typical directions would go something like this: I live in Paitilla. Drive up Balboa Avenue past where the Gran Morrison used to be and turn right where the Super 99 used to be. Go past Bal Harbour Shopping Center on the left and continue on up the hill, past the park to the third building on the left. Addresses are given by building name and there are hardly any address numbers as are common in other places in the world. Typical landmarks for giving directions are McDonald's, Taxi (the name of a store that used to be across from Panama's World Trade Center), and various banks. Almost every major neighborhood has a

McDonald's or a bank that will get you oriented. Newcomers have trouble with this system.

One other little idiosyncrasy that is typical in Milan, Italy, also occurs in Panama; and Balboa Avenue will serve for the illustration. Balboa Avenue runs from the fish market to the McDonald's in Punta Paitilla where it becomes Via Israel. It continues as Via Israel past the MultiPlaza Mall until the sharp turn at the Atlapa Convention Center where it becomes *Cincuentenario*. A similar change of street names by area occurs with both Via Espana that becomes Central Avenue and with Federico Boyd. Federico Boyd is also known as Ricardo J. Alfaro and runs between Avenue Balboa and Via Espana where it changes to Avenue Manuel E. Batista until it crosses Transistmica where it again becomes Avenue Ricardo J. Alfaro and Tumba Muerto. Commonly people will refer to this street in the first section as Federico Boyd and all the rest of it as Tumba Muerto.

New plans for improving and expanding streets in Panama include changing the names of many streets as a first step.

Keeping Your Car Running

Getting car parts in Panama can be a long, slow process, especially at the dealer. If you are thinking of purchasing a new or used car consider one that is common locally. Japanese imports, for example, are popular and parts tend to be more readily available. However, ordering the parts yourself for your necessary repairs will save you time for sure and probably money in the long run. **Napa on Line** (http://www.napaonline.com) is as close as your computer offering parts for an incredible number of makes and models regardless of year. I have ordered a new radiator for my 1992 Lexus and received it in five days using one of the mail forwarding services. The same is true of shock absorbers, various gaskets and replacement belts.

Taking a Taxi

Taxis in Panama are clean, safe and inexpensive. They are also supposed to be bright yellow as of 2006. The taxi fares are calculated by movement between zones. Each time you move to another zone or neighborhood the rate increases twenty-five cents. You can go around town for $1.00 to $1.50 depending on how far you travel or the number in your party. Rates to outlying areas are slightly higher, for example: a taxi from downtown to the Causeway will cost $5. In 2006 *La Autoridad de Tránsito y Transporte Terrestre (*ATTT) analyzed the situation and expanded the Zone system to six Zones. Starting in Zone 1 and traveling east, each zone increased by 25 cents. The maximum tariff for one person going from Zone 1 to 6, with this system was $2.25. Usually you do not tip taxi drivers. It is safe to hail a taxi on the street but it is better if you can call for a radio taxi to your home, office or hotel.

SET (tourist) taxis from hotels operate on a different, much higher rate (not more than $3.25 within the City). To avoid paying the higher fees, call and order a taxi or just step out of the hotel and walk to the corner and hail any passing taxi.

Taking the Train

The new train route follows the old 47-mile Trans-Isthmian Panama Railroad but the similarities end there. This new, state-of-the-art railroad boasts beautifully appointed cars with designer lighting, computer desks and hook-ups, comfortable seating and even an observation car. Crossing the isthmus from Albrook Station on the Pacific side to Colon on the Atlantic side, the train passes through jungle, along the Gatun Lake, along the Canal and covers the 47 miles in one hour and five minutes.

Passenger trains depart from Panama City (Albrook) Monday through Friday at 7:15 a.m., returning from Colon at 5:15 p.m. Each car can accommodate up to 50 people. The train is available for private parties as well. Fares as of August 2006 were $38 roundtrip, $22 one way, with 50% discount for kids and 30% discount for retirees. Current information on schedules and fares, as well as special excursions, can be obtained at http://www.info.panarail.com.

The train provides a safe, easy, comfortable way to commute to Colon regardless of the weather.

Taking the Bus

Buses in Panama are almost as plentiful as taxis but they come in a larger variety, some with very colorful paint jobs. There are local buses, buses to the interior and international buses. It is not recommended that the foreign visitor use the local city buses. In general, they are not particularly comfortable, not air-conditioned and they are very crowded. A taxi is a better choice. However, if you do use the bus, the local fare is twenty-five cents and you pay as you exit.

Even if you do not want to ride one, you will surely want to take time to look at them. Affectionately known as *Diablo Rojos* (red devils), Panama buses are famous. As is common in many Latin countries what we know as school buses in the U.S. are typical city buses here, only they are not bright yellow although they sure are bright. Bus painting is an art and the artists will decorate the buses with scenes from the interior, the canal, the jungle, or the mountains. The back door usually has a portrait of the driver's wife, girlfriend, children or favorite performing artist. There may be names painted in a banner below the windows along the side of the bus that may be the names of girlfriends or family members. Many buses are currently being painted as moving advertisements. Thus you may encounter a bag of M&M's, a tennis shoe, a soda can or other complete product represented by the bus. In 2006 Panamanian bus painters participated in the biennial Liverpool England International Bus Art Exposition.

Panama buses are owned by independent operators and are competing for many of the same passengers and routes. The drivers are focused on getting to the next bus stop ahead of any other bus. To this end they will cut in and out of traffic, stop long before the official bus stop to pick up passengers, stop in traffic lanes other than the curb lane or designated pullout lane for buses. They tie up traffic and add to the congestion. You need to be alert to the movements of buses all the time when driving in Panama, particularly when driving alongside one that wants to take over your lane. The police spend many hours standing in the bus lane preventing buses from moving in other lanes and preventing them from stopping other than at the designated locations. However, the minute the police leave, the buses resume their creative practices.

Buses of all sizes and styles provide service from the City to the interior including: Arraiján, the Central Provinces, Chorrera, Capira, Changuinola, El Valle, Colon, and David. Bus fares vary from as little as $5-6 for the closer provinces to $24 to Changuinola, the most distant destination. *Jubilados*, retirees, are entitled to a 30% discount. You must present your *cédula* or *jubilado* identification card.

A visit to the new *Gran Terminal Nacional* at Albrook is worth-

---

Taxi Rates in Panama City as of Feb. 2007

Zone 1 starts at Av. De Los Poetas and Zones move across the city in the direction of Tocumen Airport:

Zone	Rate
1	1.00
2	1.25
3	1.50
4	1.75
5	2.00
6	2.25

Taxi rates in the Interior as of Dec. 2006
Chitre, David, Las Tablas and Penonome

Basic rate: $.65-.95 depending on the City
Rate between zones: $.15-.25 additional 2 km.
Extra Passengers: $ .15
Late Night rate: $.15 additional
Ordered taxi as opposed to picking up in the Street:
 $.10 additional

---

while even if you do not need to take a bus. It boasts numerous shops including local handicrafts, hardware, jewelry and bakeries. The terminal is an impressive, modern operation and buses are among the transportation systems that operate on a strict timetable. It also has a very convenient MGJ office to pay traffic tickets or obtain your driver's license. It is adjacent to the Albrook Mall.

International buses, that is buses headed for San Jose, Costa Rica and beyond to Mexico, are modern, air conditioned, offer movies and have a steward. If you want to plan an excursion and leave the driving to someone else, this is the way to do it. The cost is about $50 round trip to Costa Rica, $80 Nicaragua, and Guatemala $182. Buses leave daily from the Albrook Terminal. Call Panaline at 227-8648 or Ticabus at 314-6385 for information and reservations.

Ferry to the Islands

Panama boasts hundreds of islands and a number of them are accessible by ferry. When you are ready to get away for the week or the weekend, a ferry to Contadora or Taboga are two possibilities. Taboga is just an hour away by ferry and perfect for a day at the beach. For longer getaways, consider Contadora.

Expreso Del Pacifico
Tel.: 261-0350/229-1639/229-1742
Muelle (Pier) 18, Tel.: 232-6687
Email: willifu@cableonda.net

Taboga
Monday – Friday

Depart Pier 18	6:00	8:30	1:45	3:00
Return	7:00	9:45	3:45	

Saturday and Sunday

Depart Pier 18	8:30	10:15	3:00	5:00
Return	9:15	2:00	4:00	6:00

Offers packages to **Contadora** upon request

For additional information contact: Calypso Queen, 226-1991; or Canal & Bay tours, 314-1349.

Canal Transit

The Panama Lady sails at 7:30 a.m. Check their web site or call for dates of departure. Tel.: 225-8491, 225-6566, 225-8489, Viajes Jazmin, http://www.prensa.com

Kuna Yala/San Blas Islands

San Blas Sailing Charters

Tel..: 232-7598
Email: bchemier@cableonda.net,
http://www.SanBlasSailing.com

Las Perlas Sailing

Henri Corrand, Tel.: 264-8223
Email: hcorrand@excite.com

Airlines and Airports

El Aeropuerto Internacional de Tocúmen, Panama (PTY) is newly remodeled and expanded, offering international flights daily with American Airlines, Avianca, Aire, Continental Airlines, Copa Airlines, Cubana, Grupo Taca, Iberia, Lan Chile, Lloyd Aero Boliviano, Aeroflot, Delta and Air Madrid. http://www.tocumenpanama.aero

Marcos A. Gelabert Airport offers daily domestic air transport from Albrook. Domestic carriers include: Aeroperlas, Air Panama and Turismoaereo. Additionally, there are charter flights available to any of Panama's 150 airstrips.

Helicopter service is also available from:

Helipan: Tel.: 315-0452 or Helix, Tel.: 264-5155.

AOPA (Aircraft Owners and Pilot Association) Alfredo Fonseca Mora, Email: afonsmor@cwpanama.net

Albrook Flight School: Aeropuerto Marcos A. Gelabert, Tel.: 232-7349

Panama Skydive: Tel: 226-0320

Panama Skydiving Center: Tel: 322-0369

PANAMA ON LINE

Panama Surfing
http://www.riomarsurf.com

Platinum Fitness Center Albrook
315-0645

Sport Tec Fitness Center
269-5010

DHL Worldwide Express
http://www.dhl.com

Solutions Abroad
http://www.solutionsabroad.com

Greenwich Time
http://greenwichmeantime.com

Center for Disease Control and Prevention
(CDC Travel Information)
http://www.cdc.gov/travel/camerica.htm

International Special Reports
http://www.Internationalspecialreports.com

Panama Canal Authority
http://www.acp.gob.pa

New, Used and Automobile Leasing Weekly
http://www.autorapido.com

Panama:

Space Age Technology in a Third World Environment and Charm…

Listen for the melodic call of the Pan Flute in the early morning in your neighborhood and take advantage of the magic of the local knife sharpener. For a few dollars this gentlemen can renew the edge on your scissors or knives through the ancient sharpening wheel mounted on his bicycle.

A FINANCIAL CENTER

Money

The Balboa and the U.S. Dollar

They are one and the same except for the name. Panama has been joined by an increasing number of countries in the world that uses the U.S. Dollar as its currency (Liberia, Ecuador, and El Salvador, too). While Panama does not print its own bills, it does have the U.S. Mint make Balboa denominated coins. These coins are about the same size and value as the equivalent U.S. coins and are totally interchangeable in Panama. They work in slot machines, coin washers and parking meters. See Chapter I for a complete explanation of coins in Panama.

Banking

Panama is a world financial center. In fact, it has some 84 banks representing financial institutions from around the world as well as local banking institutions. Of these, 40 have general licenses, 37 are international, 5 have representative offices and two are state owned banks. A variety of other special purpose banks also exist including mortgage lending, credit card, off shore and virtual. In the words of one banker, "if you expect your money in legal currency, look for a bank to do business with that is the old fashioned bricks-and-mortar variety". In general, banking here works just as it does in any major U.S. city. Banking hours are generally Monday through Friday from 8:00 a.m. until 3:00 p.m., with some banks offering Saturday services. However, due in part to the concern for money laundering and in an effort at transparency, there are some idiosyncrasies to banking in Panama that you need to know.

Opening a Bank Account

Banking rules are formal here. Banks need to "know their customers" and as a result will ask a lot of questions in writing, including what is the purpose of the account, how much you plan to deposit each month, and what is the source of incoming deposits. They will ask who you will write checks to and for how much.

A checking account is called a *cuenta corriente* and a savings account is called *cuenta de ahorros*. In order to open either a personal savings or checking account, you need references from two of your current banks and sometimes one additional personal reference. If you only have one bank, a reference from another financial institution can be used. These letters must be written in or translated into Spanish. If they are from a foreign institution they must be authenticated with Apostille or by the Panama Consul. You will need your passport or *cédula* and copies of these documents. In addition to the initial deposit and signature cards, you will also need a copy of your current electrical bill.

In order to open a business account you will need all of the above documents including signature cards and copies of identification for the President, Secretary and Treasurer of the company (*Extranjeros* will need two photo ID's but Panamanians only need their *Cédula.*) In addition, you will need a copy of an *Acta* (letter signed by the Secretary of the Board authorizing the opening of the account), copy of the last paid *Tasa Unica Anual a las Sociedades Anónimas,* copy of your papers of incorporation, copy of the *Registro Comercial Tipo,* the name of your attorney, and *Autorización para Recabar y Suministrar Información* (permission for the bank to receive credit information).

Be sure to sign the signature cards **exactly** the way you will do so on checks. Banking is very sophisticated in Panama and your signature will be matched to your signature card by computer at the time a check is presented for payment. The slightest variation will invalidate the check. It will take from a week to ten days to actually open the account once all the documents are submitted.

Husbands and wives should also consider opening accounts as *Joint with Right of Survivorship*. This should read Jane Doe **OR** John Doe, not **AND.** In case of death of one of the parties, the account will remain active in the name of the surviving spouse.

Checks can be written in Spanish or English. Be sure to write out the year completely, i.e. 2007 not '07. Also note that dates written in numerals are in a different order than in the U.S., with the order being day, month and year rather than month, day, year. Checks are taxed ten cents each, which may be charged at the time of purchase of checks or at the time of use. When charged in advance, at the purchase of checks, the bank receives the tax sooner than when it is charged as each check is presented for payment.

Money Transfers

Wire transfers to and from your account can be made to banks around the world. Most banks in Panama charge a fee, which may be either a flat rate or percentage of the transfer for this service and banks in the U.S. charge a fee of $10 on the same transaction. Fees for transfers are negotiable especially if they occur frequently as a regular part of your business operations.

An alternative to a wire transfer is use of a check drawn on the bank from your home country that will take from seven to 21 days to clear. Another alternative is a cash advance on a credit card or withdrawal on a debit card.

ATM
Automatic Teller Machines (ATM's) are available at banks, in grocery stores, and are freestanding in convenient locations like the airport. They work just like the ones you know in your home country (in English or Spanish) except that they dispense U.S. dollars. At a bank ATM you can make payments, deposits and withdrawals of cash, which is generally paid out in twenty-dollar bills. Not all ATM's charge fees on your account.

Credit and Debit Cards
Visa and MasterCard credit cards are in common use in Panama. You can use the ones issued from your home country bank or apply for local cards through your Panama bank or financial institution. American Express cards are usable in some locations but are not as common as Visa and MasterCard. If you want cash and do not want to use the ATM, you can complete a credit card transaction in the bank. This generally requires approval by a bank officer and proper identification along with your credit card.

Most grocery and department stores also have debit card capability at the check out register as well as accepting credit cards.

Other Financial Institutions
In Panama you will find offices for Merrill Lynch International and the *La Bolsa de Valores de Panama* (stock market) which currently includes: Wall Street Securities, S.A.; Tower Securities, Inc.; Banistmo Brokers, Inc.; Citivalores, S.A.; B. G. Investment Co., Inc.; Lafise Valores de Panama, S.A.; Global Valores, S.A.; HSBC Securities (Panama), S.A.; BAC Valores (Panama) Inc.; Banco Nacional de Panama; Panamericana de Valores, S.A.; Credicorp Securities, Inc.

Major Banks in Panama

Banco General (very conservative, offers mortgages)
http://www.bgeneral.com
Tel.: 800-5000

Banistmo (purchased by HSBC in 2007)
http://www.banistmo.com
Tel.: 800-1717

Banco Continental (solid, well run)
http://www.bcontinental.com
Tel.: 215-7000

Banco Nacional de Panamá
http://www.banconal.com.pa
Tel.: 505-2000

Scotiabank (large, offers home mortgages)
The Bank of Nova Scotia
scotiabk@sinfo.net
Tel.: 263-6255

Caja De Ahorros
http://www.cajadeahorros.com.pa

Citibank, N.A.
www.citibank.com/panama

Taiwan Republic of China
The International Commercial Bank of China
Tel.: 447-1888

Banco Santander Panama
Calle Ricardo Arias y 51 Este
Tel.: 264-6066

The Bank of Tokyo-Mitsubishi, Ltd.
Via España
Tel.: 263-5055

Banco Cuscatlan
Tel.: 208-8300

Global Bank
Tel.:800-0006
http://www.globalbank.com.pa

HSBC (subsidiary of NY HSBC USA)
Tel.: 263-5877
http://www.pa.hsbc.com

Credit Card Safety

At the end of this section there are a number of suggestions for making safe transactions at the ATM, opening an account and general credit card safety. In addition, keep in mind that a number of credit card scams exist in which the thief only needs your credit card number. In Panama, these credit card thieves copy your number and sell it to others who then make credit card purchases world-wide. To safeguard your cards, never let the card out of your sight. If you are making a purchase and the employee must take the card to another area of the store, service station or restaurant, follow your card. Despite this precaution, should you discover your card number is being used fraudulently, report it immediately and notify all merchants where you have recently transacted business in an effort to stop such theft.

Home Mortgages

A number of financial institutions in Panama offer home mortgage loans for those that qualify. As previously mentioned, mortgage rates for new construction on properties $62,600 or less are offered at a preferred rate over mortgages on existing properties. Check around for the best rate in the area you are planning to live. Mortgages are based on the *rule of 75*. In other words, you can get a loan based on your age and the number of years the loan will be in effect. If you are 60 years old, the maximum length of the loan will be fifteen years. The younger you are the more years you can finance your mortgage all things being equal. Mortgages generally are of two types, fixed and floating. While both actually float, the fixed or managed rates are for properties up to $65,000 and are subsidized. Current rates are between 7 3/4 and 9 percent.

A recent report out of the U.S. advised loan applicants that loan insurance is not required (in the U.S.) nor is it a benefit to anyone other than the mortgage lender. Keep this in mind when applying for a mortgage. A bank cannot require you to purchase insurance from them (in fact it is illegal for them to sell insurance) or their recommended source. If desired, you can provide your own source for mortgage insurance.

Taxes

While Panama does not have an income tax on foreign income or an inheritance tax, it does have a variety of other taxes that affect locals and *extranjeros* alike.

Property Taxes

Until very recently Panama had a twenty-year exemption on property taxes to encourage new construction. In today's market, such an incentive seems ridiculous and the law has changed. New properties do get an exemption but it is based on the cost of the property and the maximum exemption is fifteen years. The more expensive the property, the shorter time allowed for the exemption. For example: a property purchased in 2000 for $145,000, with six years remaining on its twenty year exemption, began paying property taxes in 2006 at a rate of $300 per year.

Property Capital Gains Taxes

Sale of residential property incurs a two percent transfer tax on the total sales price plus a capital gains tax of ten percent on the calculated: sales price less expenses of sale (and perhaps less cost of improvements.)

Tax Return Preparation

There are numerous accounting and tax preparation firms available for assisting with preparation of Panama Tax requirements. Some law firms also provide this kind of assistance especially for business clients. Additionally, H&R Block in El Dorado provides assistance with both Panama and U.S. tax preparation. Check their website for details at http://www.hrblock.com.

Sales Taxes

Cigarette and Liquor tax

Ten percent collected at the point of purchase.

ITBM

Sales tax on most items except food. Five percent collected at the time of purchase.

GRV

Sales tax on other goods and services. Five percent collected at the time of purchase.

Employment

Unemployment in Panama has dropped from a high in 2003 of 18.5% to 9.6% (13.2% for women and 7.5% for men) in 2006. For every position advertised there are hundreds of applicants. Additionally, many professions and jobs are reserved for Panamanian nationals only, including: doctors, dentists, nurses, lawyers, accountants, pharmacists, translators, engineers, architects, public relations executives, and journalists, just to name a few. In order to qualify as a realtor, you must be a Panama citizen or a legal resident having resided in Panama five years and have subsequently passed the real estate exam (in Spanish). Practicing real estate without the required license carries stiff fines and jail time.

If you are retiring in Panama and seeking a retirement visa, you must have a minimum monthly income to qualify for that visa which will insure you do not become a burden to the country. This minimum, $500-$700 per month, is not sufficient to maintain any more than the most basic life style. (66.3% of Panamanians earn less than $400 per month.) A good rule of thumb for a reasonable housing and living allowance would be $30,000-$35,000 per year. Foreigners in Panama on a *jubilado/pensinado* (retiree) visa are not permitted to work by law. If you cannot maintain your lifestyle on your personal retirement income and need to work, you cannot do so legally in Panama on a retirement visa.

If you wish to move to Panama to work, you need to consider one of the other visa options. This would require being hired by someone currently doing business in Panama who can legally hire you (a bank, an embassy, international corporation, for example) who would then move you in and provide your legal status. Once you are in Panama, finding a job is difficult as the employment laws are tough with such restrictions as requiring that the job a foreigner holds must be something no Panamanian is qualified to do, there must be at least ten Panamanian employees to each foreign employee, and you must have a work permit. Keep in mind you will be competing with all those Panamanian college graduates who are currently unemployed.

Employment Taxes

Social Security Tax (Planilla)—paid by both the employee and employer.

Credit Card Safety

Credit cards are easy to use in Panama but remember to take proper safeguards to protect yours.

Sign your new credit card as soon as you receive it.

Keep your credit card in a separate zipper compartment in your purse or wallet.

Keep a record of all credit cards including card number, date of expiration, and telephone numbers to report loss or theft.

Report lost or stolen credit cards as soon as you discover their loss.

Completely destroy any incorrect charge slips and make a note to check your bill to be sure you are not incorrectly charged when the statement arrives.

Destroy all credit card slip carbons.

Keep your credit card receipts to compare with your statement.

Verify your credit card statement monthly.

Report credit card discrepancies by telephone and in writing.

Notify your credit card issuer of any change of address immediately.

Do not:

Give your credit card to anyone to use.

Leave your destroyed cards or torn up receipts where someone could pick them up.

Sign a blank credit card slip.

Give your credit card number to anyone calling on the telephone to verify your account.

ATM Safety

Automatic Teller Machines are extremely convenient and are to be found all over the city and the country. Because they are so numerous, select one that affords the best security.

1. Use ATMs located in well-lit areas with good visibility.

2. Use an ATM that allows you entry and a door to lock rather than one on an open sidewalk.

3. Stand well behind the person currently using the machine when there is a line.

4. Cancel the transaction at the first sign of suspicious activity.

5. Take all paperwork with you and do not throw away anything that has your account number imprinted.

6. Do not carry your ATM card with you unless you are going to use it.

Check Writing

1. Checks may be written in either Spanish or English.

2. Write out the year in full, i.e. 2007, not '07.

3. A cedula, carnet or passport is required as identification.

4. Sign your checks exactly like the bank signature card on file. Any variation will result in a returned check.

5. Write your cedula or passport number and telephone number on the back of the check. (If the person accepting the check does not know you, they will also ask to see the cedula or passport).

6. Verify all the information on new checks at the time you pick them up at the bank.

PANAMA ON LINE

Lost Credit Card
http://www.consumers.com

Ministerio de Gobierno y Justicia
Immigration and Visas
http://www.gobiernoyjusticia.com.pa

Allied International Moving Services
http://www.amertrans.com

Focus Publications
http://www.focuspulicationsint.com

Financiero
http://www.prensa.com/mf

Happy Copy
http://www.happycopy.com

Metro Por Metro
Real Estate Guide
http://www.metropormetro.com

Superintendancy of Banks
http://www.superbancos.gob.pa

Prescriptions

All narcotics and antibiotics require a doctor's prescription. While doctors write prescriptions for all medications they may prescribe, including medications considered *over-the-counter* in the U.S., many of these items (other than narcotics and antibiotics) can be purchased without a prescription as long as you know what to ask for at the Pharmacy. Other than vitamins, all medicines are behind the counter and will require your asking by name or presenting a prescription.

A great variety of brands from around the world exist for numerous drug products. However, the specific brand available at any time may change based on import availability. In other words, generics are common, shortages not unusual and substitutions are expected.

In general generic drugs are very reasonable. However, the latest wonder drug may not be available or if it is, it will be at a premium price.

X

MEDICAL ISSUES

The standards of private medical facilities in Panama are excellent and the patient can expect to get medical treatment for 98 percent of his medical needs including coronary by-pass surgery. The exceptions are transplants for which Panama is not equipped. Panama has a three-tiered medical system with good private hospitals, the government Social Security Hospital (CSS) and the public hospitals. The private facilities have modern equipment and excellent doctors and dentists, many of whom have studied in the U.S., Mexico or Europe.

Similar to other places in the world, the term clinic is used for private institutions that generally include doctors' offices, laboratories, radiology, pharmacy and outpatient services. Hospital generally refers to inpatient medical/surgical facilities that also provide laboratory, radiology, pharmacy and related services. These facilities provide outpatient procedures as well.

Unlike many other places, doctors in Panama take time with patients to answer questions and listen. While the clinic setting may be large, the individual doctor's office and examination room may be very small. Expect your doctor to give you his office, home, and cell phone numbers as well as mobile or paging number. It is usual practice for the doctor to call the patient at home to follow-up on care and medications and they will even make house calls. You are expected to pay prior to seeing the doctor for your appointment.

Hospitals

There are four Class A private hospitals in Panama City, which are well equipped. They are **Paitilla Hospital, Hospital Nacional, San Fernando Hospital** and **Hospital Punta Pacifica**. The public hospitals in Panama City are Santo Tomás and Hospital del Niño, which are for Panamanian citizens. Santo Tomás provides services for the indigent and also houses the morgue. Additionally, the Ministry of Health has small Health Centers all over the country.

All Panamanian citizens who are employed belong to a government-health plan that entitles them to care at the *Caja de Seguro Social* **(CSS)**. This system draws on the same excellent doctors; however, it experiences a continuing problem of insufficient resources and too many patients.

In the interior the **Mae Lewis Clinic** serves the city of David and the neighboring communities of Boquete, Volcan and Cerro Punta. **Hospital Nacional** in Panama City provides support to this facility and is the usual referral facility when it is necessary to transfer a patient to a more complete private hospital. Additionally, there is a general surgeon and a pediatric clinic in the Boquete area.

There are numerous pharmacies located conveniently throughout the City many of which are open 24-hours. The two largest chains are Arrocha and MetroX, offering not only prescription and non-prescription medications, but cosmetics, house wares, stationery and school supplies. Throughout the country there are many small private pharmacies as well as those affiliated with the hospitals and medical clinics.

Laboratories providing a variety of medical tests are available in the City and Interior as well.

A typical physician office visit is $35 but some specialists charge $45. A typical X-ray is about $27 and a variety of laboratory tests range from $6-9 each. For example: a series of four shoulder X-rays cost $19.55 with a *jubilado* discount. A series of five back and spine X-rays cost $139.20. An ultra sound cost from $50 to $145. Mammograms are offered at $35. A typical five-or-six-hour emergency room experience for a kidney stone episode including iodine x-rays, painkillers, and monitoring will cost $265 in Panama vs. $2,350 in the U.S. Emergency treatment for a cut foot, not requiring stitches, cost $26.00. A typical maternity plan for a normal, natural childbirth will cost between $1,590 and $1,700. A C-Section will range between $2,890 and $2,995. Coronary bypass surgery for four or five bypasses will cost between $16,000-50,000.

Panama boasts all the usual medical and dental specialties and is a center for advanced eye surgery. People from the United States and Europe come to Panama for laser eye surgery. Cataract surgery costs $1,100.

A dental cleaning is about $35. It seems like everyone in Panama has braces, whether adults or children. The cost is reasonable and the outcome excellent. Dental implants are also available.

Hospital Nacional has long been the primary hospital offering assistance with U.S. Military Critical Care for retirees in Panama as well as being the facility of choice for Naval personnel posted in the Caribbean. Hospital Nacional offers a **TRI Care** assistance center, bilingual doctors, and both foreign and domestic medical insurance assistance with an International office equipped with translators of Japanese, French and English. They also have two doctors on staff with FDA licenses for writing prescriptions to be filled in the U.S. They regularly send out informational emails to those patients registered with their system. Contact Elsa Bermudez to be added to the mailing list. Email: EBERMUDEZ@hospitalnacional.com

Hospital Punta Pacifica opened in 2006 as a modern, totally digital, regional hospital and primary care facility, affiliated with Johns Hopkins Hospital in the U.S. The hospital offers general care in all specialties including neonatology, at this hospital with 52 rooms, eight ICU beds and large OB/GYN facility. The special baby care facility (neonatology ICU) can accommodate 20 healthy patients or eight ICU patients.

Complete with an international department currently offering English and Spanish assistance, accepting local and international insurance plans, the hospital has the capability for on-line second opinions from Johns Hopkins, as well as being state-of-the-art from the entry foyer to the last detail.

All accredited physicians are eligible to refer patients and practice in any of the various hospitals. If you have a hospital preference, make it known to your doctor.

Mae Lewis Hospital offers a full range of services including pharmacy, laboratory, two operating rooms, delivery room and intensive care unit.

Each of the hospitals recommends visiting their facilities and pre-registering before a specific need arises, particularly for patients living in the interior.

Being in the hospital, like everything else in Panama, is a social occasion. The patient may be in critical care but family and friends will gather in the waiting room to support one another. For less serious hospital stays, whether you are having gallbladder surgery or welcoming a new baby, you and your family are expected to welcome and entertain visitors. Champagne, finger food and cigars are not unusual for welcoming a new baby, for example. Some and often many family members remain with the patient all day and often all night. Private and semi-private rooms are usual in private hospitals and often have a sofa appropriate for a relative to stay the night. Receiving company also requires appropriate nightclothes, and bed coverings including matching top sheet and pillow covers. Many shops in Panama specialize in these linens or you can have them handmade, especially for a new baby. It is usual practice for all flowers to be removed from the patient's room for the night so do not be surprised to find the hospital halls lined with flower arrangements.

Emergency Situations

In case of emergency you can call ahead for your physician to meet you at the emergency room or the hospital staff will do so for you when you arrive at the emergency room (E.R.). During non-office hours, weekends and holidays, the hospital maintains a list of physicians on call to handle emergencies.

There are several ambulance services including Alerta and SEMM that provide complete service and equipment for transport to the Emergency Room or hospital. Additionally, Alerta offers service in the Coronado/Gorgona area during the busiest holiday seasons. Alerta offers a variety of membership plans for individuals and families, as well as being included in many medical insurance plans. For example, Alerta Flash offers plans for as little as $12.50 per month. Refer to Chapter I, Cat Up The Tree and Other Emergencies for lists of Emergency assistance providers throughout Panama.

Boquete has ambulance service available.

Helicopter emergency transport is available from the interior to Hospital Santo Tomas or Hotel Intercontinental Miramar where a local ambulance will meet the patient and provide transport to a City hospital.

Additional Medical Choices

The diversity of the population has resulted in the availability of a variety of health care options. You will readily find practitioners of acupuncture, acupressure, chiropractic, holistic and ancient traditional medicine.

In Case of Death

A patient in the hospital or under a physician's care will be pronounced dead by a doctor. When someone dies at home, call his or her physician **first** to make the pronouncement and provide a death certificate. Subsequently family members may contact the funeral home of choice to make necessary arrangements. In cases of questionable death or death by accident, it may be necessary to transport the body to the Santo Tomas Hospital Morgue for autopsy before it can be released to the family for burial.

Foreign citizens living in Panama should at a later time contact their respective Embassy to report the death and obtain advice on necessary procedures for obtaining a death certificate other than Panama or transporting the body to the country of origin. This service varies from embassy to embassy and from contact person within the facility. At a minimum they will need the deceased person's passport and death certificate issued from Panama in order to be of assistance. (See Appendix 16 for further details in dealing with a death.)

Unlike practices in cooler climates, burial or cremation is almost immediate in the tropics. In fact, cremation is most common, occurring the next day. The practice of viewing the body at a funeral home is not common here although it may be done at the church. In such cases the casket while open, is sealed with glass. Specific practices vary by religious tradition and since Panama has a broad spectrum of religions and ethnic groups, there are many variations.

You Can Drink The Water

Legend has it that, if you drink the water of the Chagres River, you will always return to Panama. Since the Panama City water supply comes from the rainfall collected in the Chagres River, return is a certainty. Panama is fortunate to have not only an excellent supply of water but safe drinking water. Panama has one of the better tap water supplies in the world and the purchase of filters for the tap water is not necessary—in the City. Except in the occasional El Nino year, there is never a shortage of water. While this has long been true in the City, in most of the downtown neighborhoods, it is not true in many of the outlying communities where there are continual water problems. Additionally, in the interior the water quality and availability will vary by area and will need to be investigated before you purchase land for building or before you purchase a preexisting house in an interior community. Wells are common in some communities like Boquete. In other areas, a rainwater collection system is more common. Water in Bocas town is not considered safe to drink.

Never Boring but You May be Bored

Panama offers an incredible variety of flora and fauna all over the country providing opportunities to explore and observe so your will never be bored. However, some of that same fauna may be boring you! From the mountains to the coast, from the Darien to the City, you can be exposed to these risks.

Mosquito Safety

One of the biggest problems faced by the French in attempting to build the canal was mosquitoes and all the accompanying illnesses. When the United States undertook this monumental construction task, they were fortunate to have Dr. Gorgas who is known throughout the world as the conqueror of the mosquitoes and the diseases they transmit. His medical advances resulted in not only a canal but also the habitability of this tiny nation. Today in the metropolitan areas of Panama, malaria and yellow fever are generally not a problem. However, dengue is a problem in the city as well as more remote jungle areas. As a result, precautions need to be taken.

Remember that mosquitoes are most active just before sunrise and sunset. Therefore avoiding exposure to mosquitoes at these hours will provide you some protection. Use of any of the many mosquito repellants will give you additional protection in questionable areas. Take steps to remove anything from your home and yard that could collect water as mosquitoes breed in standing, fresh water. Avoid areas known to have had outbreaks of dengue fever. Coming to Panama requires no inoculations or special medical treatments. http://www.malariaprotection.com

Leishmaniasis

One of the many boring insects found principally in Bocas del Toro causes a painful, disfiguring condition caused by Leishmania, tiny protozoa. Their parasitic life cycle includes the sand fly and the right host. Humans are one such host. Leishmania infection can cause skin disease (called cutaneous leishmaniasis), which can also affect the mucous membrane. The infection can also cause systemic (throughout the body) disease. The lesions are most common, however, on the face.

Affected mucous membranes can have a wide range of appearances, most frequently ulcers. Leishmaniasis may cause skin lesions that resemble those of other diseases including cutaneous tuberculosis, syphilis, leprosy, skin cancer, and fungal infections.

Leishmania systemic disease, called visceral leishmaniasis, can have fatal complications. When introduced into the body by the bite of a sand fly, the parasite migrates to the bone marrow, spleen, and lymph nodes. The parasites damage the immune system by decreasing the numbers of disease-fighting cells.

Systemic infection in children usually begins suddenly with vomiting, diarrhea, fever, and cough. In adults, fever for two weeks to two months is accompanied by nonspecific symptoms, such as fatigue, weakness, and loss of appetite. Weakness increases as the disease progresses.

The skin may become grayish, dark, dry, and flaky. Death usually results from complications (such as other infections) rather than from the disease itself. Death often occurs within two years.

Treatment includes the following antimony-containing compounds:

· Meglumine antimonate
· Sodium stibogluconate

Other drugs that may be used include:

· Pentamidine
· Amphotericin B

Side effects noted have been unpleasant. Recently a new pill has been developed and is available in Panama that, while costly, reduces a great percentage of the side effects and allows the patient to be treated at home. Contact the *Ministerio de Salud* for treatment.

Plastic surgery may be required to correct disfigurement by destructive facial lesions (mucocutaneous leishmaniasis). Removal of the spleen (splenectomy) may be required in drug-resistant cases (visceral leishmaniasis).

Preventing sand fly bites is the most immediate form of protection. Insect repellent, appropriate clothing, screening of windows, and fine mesh netting around the bed (in endemic areas) will reduce exposure. Numerous cases have been reported in the Bocas area.

Screworms

Screworm (Cochliomyia hominivoras) was officially eliminated in Panama in 2006 but not before boring into people all over the country. While this usually is considered a problem with livestock and farmers understand the economic and health considerations for their animals, it also can affect people. You were at risk on the lawn of your local school, in your back yard, in the jungle and especially the Darien. This little critter laid eggs that hatched and gnawed at you from the inside. Screworms can be painful and creepy, difficult to diagnose (by your doctor but not a local farmer) but now monitored and controlled in Panama.

No-see-ums

No-see-ums have a clever name and they are clever little biting flies that often live near water. You do not see them but they see you and bite. In fact looking at them under a microscope they look like flying teeth. By the time you feel them you are covered with little bites that itch and burn and can become infected with continued scratching. Avoid those high-risk times of day, sunrise and sunset. If you are out in affected areas, wear protective clothing or use insect repellants.

Screens are recommended for all windows as a further measure to keep out all but the smallest flying insects, especially flies, mosquitoes and bats. In Panama screening is available that is so *fine* that it provides excellent protection.

Bats

A variety of bats are flying around after dark looking for unsuspecting victims that are usually insects. However, a toe sticking out from the covers is not an unusual target and the next morning only a small telltale blood spot marks the nibbled toe. However, regardless of the size of the bite, the same regimen of treatment is required.

Fortunately treatment is readily available in several locations throughout the country, controlled by the Ministry of Heath. Each treatment costs less than one dollar.

Dengue fever

This condition sounds harmless enough when first encountered, as it is only a bad case of mosquito bites that get infected. However, it is very serious, especially in children. Anyone bitten will have a series of symptoms that are unpleasant and long lasting. Dengue [DEN-ghee] is a flu-like viral disease spread by the bite of infected mosquitoes. Dengue hemorrhagic fever is a severe, often fatal, complication of dengue.

Dengue fever usually starts suddenly with a high fever, rash, severe headache, pain behind the eyes, and muscle and joint pain. The severity of the joint pain has given dengue the name "break bone fever." Nausea, vomiting, and loss of appetite are common. A rash usually appears three to four days after the start of the fever. The illness can last up to ten days, but complete recovery can take as long as a month. Older children and adults are usually sicker than young children.

Most dengue infections result in relatively mild illness, but some can progress to dengue hemorrhagic fever. With dengue hemorrhagic fever, the blood vessels start to leak and cause bleeding from the nose, mouth, and gums. Bruising can be a sign of bleeding inside the body. Without prompt treatment, the blood vessels can collapse, causing shock (dengue shock syndrome). Dengue hemorrhagic fever is fatal in about five percent of cases, mostly among children and young adults.

There is **no specific treatment** for dengue. Persons with dengue fever should rest and drink plenty of fluids. They should be kept away from mosquitoes for the protection of others. Dengue hemorrhagic fever is treated by replacing lost fluids. Some patients need transfusions to control bleeding.

Prevention centers on avoiding mosquito bites in areas where dengue occurs or might occur, and eliminating breeding sites.

Hantavirus

Hantavirus pulmonary syndrome (HPS) is a deadly disease from rodents. Humans can contract the disease when they come into contact with infected rodents or their urine and droppings. The chance of being exposed to hantavirus is greatest when people work, play, or live in closed spaces where rodents are actively living. It can be contracted by breathing dust laden with droppings.

In mid-January 1999, an outbreak of HPS occurred in Panama. The Special Pathogens Branch of the CDC and the Pan-American Health Organization (PAHO) collaborated with health authorities in Panama to investigate the outbreak.

For more information on the outbreak investigation, please read the article "Hantavirus Pulmonary Syndrome -- Panama, 1999-2000", published in the *Morbidity and Mortality Weekly Report,* March 17, 2000.

Additionally, for specific information about this outbreak, please contact the Panama Ministry of Health at: hantapanama@hotmail.com

Spiders

Spiders seem to live in every nook and cranny of the average house. They range in size from the tiniest to average size and they can bite. A red, itchy patch is the usual first sign. In some cases they can cause swelling and pain which needs to be treated by a doctor. Minor bites can be treated topically.

Life in the Tropics

The good news is that all that humidity that creates problems for your house, your car and your leather goods, is of benefit to your skin. The constant moisture helps keep skin soft, pliable and less wrinkled than any applied creams. Remember Panama is eight degrees from the Equator and even on overcast days you are being exposed to the sun. Be careful in the sun, use sunscreen and benefit from the humidity.

Insurance

Medical insurance is available from a variety of sources for locals and foreigners alike. For those Panamanians eligible to participate in the *Caja de Seguro Social* (CSS) but who do not wish to take advantage of the facilities that the CSS provides, they can pay personally at a private facility or use private insurance. Many hospitals and doctors now accept foreign medical insurance as they have contracts with the major carriers including Foreign Service Carriers, Blue Cross/Blue Shield and Mutual of Omaha. However, you need to check with your individual carrier before coming to Panama to confirm their policy regarding foreign care payment.

Medical care in Panama is relatively inexpensive. Upon presentation at an Emergency Room, for example, you will be required to pay a $35 deposit and provide a credit card with sufficient limit to cover cost of service if you do not have an insurance plan. Actual charges will be presented for payment upon discharge. Similarly, many physicians will accept payment from local insurance providers. All medical providers will provide appropriate receipts for you to submit to your insurer for reimbursement.

An additional alternative to self-insurance or international coverage is to purchase national (Panama) insurance. This local insurance is significantly less expensive than its counterpart in the U.S. and either worldwide coverage or Panama-only coverage is available. The same kinds of restrictions you find in your home country for insurance coverage will apply in Panama. Additionally, you cannot purchase a new insurance plan after age 62 for either men or women. For those with preexisting plans prior to age 63, they will continue in effect with premiums to increase annually.

On average one of the four or five national companies will offer local coverage that includes doctor's office visits and hospitalization. A $1,000 deductible is usual or a co-payment equal to 20-25% of the cost of care. There is a lifetime limit on most policies of $1 million. For this coverage a person 60 years of age will pay $70 per month. For the same type of coverage on a worldwide basis the cost will increase significantly to about $180 per month.

At the time of this writing, some major foreign insurance carriers were coming to Panama to investigate what level of care is available, what it costs and subsequently to set the rates for what they will pay for their clients in this market.

Hospitals in the City

Hospital Nacional
Ave. Cuba at Calle 38 and 39
Tel.: 207-8100
Emergency 207-8110
Ambulance 207-8111
Email: mercadeo@hospitalnacional.com

Centro Médico Paitilla
Ave. Balboa y Calle 53, Paitilla
Tel.: 265-8900
Emergencies 265-8888

Clínica Hospital San Fernando
Via España between Calle 66 y Calle 69 Oeste
Tel.: 278-6300
http://www.hospitalsanfernando.com
Emergency 278-6305
Residential Geriatric 278-6340

Hospital Punta Pacífica
Affiliated with Johns Hopkins Medicine International
Boulevard Punta Pacífica
Tel.: 204-8000
Emergency 204-8110
Email: info@hpp.com.pa

Hospital Santa Fé
Via Simón Bolívar and Avenue Frangipani
Tel.: 227-4733

Hospitals in the Interior

Hospital Chiriquí
Avenida 3A y Calle Central
David
Tel.: 774-0128, 777-1020

Centro Médico Mae Lewis
Interamerican Highway and Calle B Sur
David
Tel.: 775-4616, 777-1459
Email: maelewis@cwpanama.net

Clinics in the City

Royal Center
Calle 53, Marbella
Tel.: 263-3464

San Fernando Centro Especializado
Via España, Las Sabanas
Tel.: 229-2299, 229-2477, 229-3800229-3800
Emergencies 229-2004,229-1606
Email: medicost@sinfo.net

Instituto de Rehabilitación San Fernando
Via España, 261-0891,
Tel.: 278-6608, Ext. 2813
Physical and Occupational Therapy
Tel.: 227-5444

Complejo Médico Marbella (Oshner)
Calle 53, Urb.
Condominio Royal Center
Marbella
Tel.: 263-1954

Consultorios Punta Pacífica
Boulevard Punta Pacifica, Corregimiento de San Francisco
Tel.: 204-8400

Consultorios Médicos Paitilla
Consultorios Medicos (Doctors)
Avenida Balboa and Calle 53
Tel.: 269-5222, 263-7977

Panama Plastic Surgery Center
Aesthetic and Reconstructive Plastic Surgery, Microsurgery and
Surgery of the Hand
http://www.panamaplasticsurgery.com
Email: picardami@psi.net.pa, 215-2718
Email: idcrespo@psi.net.pa, 269-9808

Clinic in the Interior

Centro Medico San Juan Bautista
Emergency Care & Outpatient Home Care
6616-2177, 720-1881
Main Street, Boquete

Special Laboratory in the City

Laboratorio Clinico Fernández
Specialized laboratory testing
Marbella 269-4413, Av. Perú 225-4497
http://www.laboratoriofernandez.com;
Email: rodfer@cwpanama.net

Laboratories Countrywide

Raly Laboratories
6 locations in Panama including:
Justo Arosemena 225-0885; La Galeria 260-9761; Los Pueblos
217-7472; San Fernando 261-2103; El Cangrejo 264-4342; Paitilla
264-0969; 2 in the interior: Chorrera 254-3764; and David 777-3401.
http://www.laboratorioraly.com

Dental Clinics

Groupo Dental de Galerias Balboa
(Dr. Charles Garcia)
Balboa Avenue and Aquilino de la Guardia Calle
Galerias Balboa, First Floor, Office No. 27
Tel.: 264-4380
Email: grupodental@gmail.com

Complete Dental Studio
Calle 53, Obarrio
Tel.: 263-8861
Email: calvo@cableonda.net

Boquete Dental Clinic
General dentistry, Periodontics & Dental Implants
Main Sreet
Tel.: 720-2867, 6673-9908

In Summary
Take responsibility for your health care management. It can be to
your advantage and your insurance carrier's for you to pay in cash and
submit your receipts for reimbursement. Many hospitals and doctors
will offer up to 30% discount for cash. Keep in mind that the Doctor
sets the price and he can be flexible on his fees for major services.
Ask for a discount. *Jubilado*s are entitled to discounts for medical

care in accordance with Law No. 6 (see Appendix 3). There are **age restrictions** for medical related discounts and discounts **do not** apply when an insurance carrier picks up the bill.

Do your homework. Health care is not free in Panama but it is affordable. You can get 98% of required care locally. Talk to your insurance company about what they cover before you come. Think of medical care and your health when considering buying a house especially in a remote area. Remember the first fifteen minutes of a medical emergency is when you need Emergency care. Is it available? Long term, excellent care is available in the city but otherwise it must be reached by car or air ambulance and time may not be in your favor in an emergency. Canadian national insurance is not applicable in Panama nor is U.S. Medicare coverage.

All of the major hospitals welcome your visit to view their facilities. They all encourage you to come in to set up a file, meet the staff and get established before you need their services. This is an especially good idea if you live in the interior and if you have preexisting medical concerns.

Comparable Thermometer Readings

Clinical thermometers are calibrated to the Fahrenheit (F) scale or the Centigrade (C) scale. The Fahrenheit thermometer usually ranges from 92 degrees F to 108 degrees F, while the Centigrade ranges from 35.5 degrees C to 41 degrees C. Digital thermometers have the capability to give temperature readings in either scale.

Temperature by Mouth		
Fahrenheit (F)	**Note**	**Centigrade (C)**
108	Usually Fatal	42.2
107	Usually Fatal	41.7
106	Critical Condition	40.1
105	Critical Condition	40.6
104	Critical Condition	40.0
103	High Fever	39.4
102	High Fever	38.9
101	High Fever	38.3
100	Moderate Fever	37.8
99	Moderate Fever	37.2
98.6	Healthy-Normal	37.0
98		36.7
97	Subnormal	36.1
96	Subnormal	35.6
95	Subnormal	35.0

PANAMA ON LINE

Weddings, Events and Etiquette
http://www.bodas-eventos.com/etiquet.htm

Customs and Manners
http://www.classymanners.com/
mexico.udg.mx/cocina/etiqueta/Uso-Cubiertos.html

US Embassy Consular Information
http://usembassy.state.gov

Canadian Embassy Consular Information
http://www.canuckabroad.com/canadian-embassy/index.shtml

Centro Istmeño de Seguros,S.A.
Email: Cidssa@cwpanama.net

Albrook Flight School
Curundu
232-7349

Boquete Service Center
Email: Boquete@sisapanama.com

El Niño

When winds don't blow, warm water wreaks havoc

Along the equator, the western Pacific has some of the world's warmest ocean water, while in the eastern Pacific, cool water wells up, carrying nutrients that support large fish populations.

But, every two to seven years, strong westward-blowing trade winds subside, and warm water slowly moves back eastward across the Pacific, like water shifting in a giant bathtub. The warm water and shifting winds interrupt the upwelling of cool, nutrient-rich water. Fish die; climatic changes affect many parts of the world.

Peruvians named this phenomenon El Niño, for the Christ child, because it first appears around Christmas. Panama is always concerned about having an El Niño year affecting rain fall.

XI

RETIREES, SNOWBIRDS AND OTHERS

Panama has been discovered as a vacation and retirement destination that creates another whole set of needs for this group **Living in Panama**. Snowbirds, the tourists from the cold north who seasonally migrate south for the winter months, generally December through March, are finding Panama a delightful change from Florida, Mexico and Costa Rica. Panama offers many of the creature comforts and conveniences they left behind, and the availability of long-term (2-3 months) furnished rental accommodations is now an emerging industry. One option is the aparthotel – a combination apartment and hotel offering maid service and limited household equipment to make living easy in your home away from home. Panama offers a great variety of these units conveniently located throughout the City.

Snowbirds generally fall within the 90-day tourist visa situation that eliminates the need for a special visa. However, many former snowbirds are now extending their stay in Panama and, as a result, are considering other types of residential status.

Temporary Relocation

Aparthotels

Torres de Alba
Ave. Eusebio A. Morales y Calle L El Cangrejo
Tel: 269-7770

Crystal Suites Hotel
Via Brasil and Calle Samuel Lewis
Tel: 263-511, Cel 6682-8848

Granada Hotel
Calle Eusebio A. Morales
El Cangrejo
Tel: 263-7477

Aparthotel Sevilla Suites
Calle Eusebio A. Morales
El Cangrejo
Tel: 213-001

Las Vegas Suites
Diagonal opposite Hotel El Panama
El Cangrejo
Tel: 269-0722

Aparthotel Suites Ambassador
Calle D
El Cangrejo
Tel: 263-7274

Coral Suites
Calle D, El Cangrejo
Tel: 269-2727

Best Western Las Huacas Hotel & Suites
Calle A El Cangrejo
Tel: 213-2222

Hotel California
Calle 43, Bella Vista
Tel: 263-7736

Furnished Apartment

Renaissance
El Cangrego
Tel: 264-1564

Retirees

For much of its 101-year history, Panama has attracted immigrants, workers, and visitors from all over the world, so it is no surprise that it is becoming a retirement destination. Just ask any of the many retired military personnel, Canal employees, embassy and business people who made Panama home over the years but left only to later return to make it their permanent or semi-permanent retirement home. In 2005, Panama's Immigration office granted 449 special retiree visas bringing the total pensioner visas issued to 2,500.

While Panama is a delightful place to live the year-round, many people spend only a part of the year here, perhaps the dry season, and the rest of the year in another location. The availability of apartments in secure high-rises in all sizes and types makes Panama ideal for this kind of retirement situation.

Additionally, many areas in the interior including Bocas del Toro, Volcán and Boquete are being considered as retirement destinations. Boquete leads the way in development for this purpose but other areas are emerging as well including Altos de María and Coronado.

Panama offers a special Visa status to those wishing to apply for retiree (*pensionado/jubilado*) status that requires many of the same basic documents as the other visas. Unlike the others, however, it requires demonstration of financial solvency in the form of an established pension, social security or other income approved by Panama immigration. This status once established brings with it many additional benefits in the form of discounts at restaurants, hotels, hospitals, doctors, and airlines. A complete list of these benefits and their restrictions is included in Appendix 3.

Support Systems

Regardless of what brings you to Panama, retirement, vacation, or work, the incredible social network will make it an easy place in which to make friends, find hobbies and just fit in. If you are a snowbird from Canada you can join the Canadian Association, volunteer with the British Aide Society or be welcomed at many other Clubs and groups active in the community.

Newcomers from the United States will want to make contact with The American Society, the United States Navy League Panama Council and the United States Army Association. For those politically oriented, there are chapters of the Republicans Abroad and the Democrats Abroad.

Those from France will find many new friends and activities through affiliation with the Alianza Francesa. Likewise, there is an Italian Club, Spanish Club, German Club, Swiss Club, Peruvian Club, Hebrew Club and many others.

Women new to Panama for whatever reason will want to join the international welcome club, Who's New. This group has been welcoming women new to Panama since 1973 and hosts a monthly welcome coffee and many other interesting activities designed to help newcomers make friends and learn more about Panama.

Service Clubs common around the world are no less plentiful in Panama and include the Interamerican Women's Club, Soroptimist, Rotary, Lions, Kiwanis, Elks, Masons and many others.

If you are here professionally, there are an equal number of professional organizations and groups for the wives as well including: Banker's Wives Club, Attorney's Wives Club, and the Rotarianns. Service clubs in particular are as prevalent in the interior as in the City with a new Rotary Club in Boquete for example.

There are also opportunities to do volunteer work at the Hospital del Nino's; numerous orphanages including Los Rios and Sister Teresa;

or the home for the elderly, *Las Brisas; Casa Esperanza; Casita de Mausi* Cancer Patient House; and British Aid Society just to name a very few.

If you are interested in knowing more about the history of Panama, the Panama Historical Society has interesting monthly meetings and is a resource for stamp and coin collectors, pre-Colombian relic (*huacas*) enthusiasts, and explorers. If birds are your interest, the Audubon Society is very active.

There are also numerous groups for bridge and mah jong or for those with a green thumb, numerous garden clubs. In fact, garden clubs exist in the city and throughout the interior with one of the newest Clubs in Bocas del Toro. The *Ikebana Internacional, Capítulo de Panamá* offers flower arranging and other Japanese art demonstrations.

Becoming involved in any of these groups or the numerous others that exist in Panama will open doors and create numerous opportunities for a full, active life whether you are here to work, accompany a spouse, enjoy retirement or an extended vacation. See Appendix 14 for a list of Associations.

Help for the Elderly or Infirm

Household help of all kinds is available in Panama and it is possible to have skilled or unskilled help with family members with medical limitations. Because of this, most people care for elderly family members at home. However, there are professional facilities available including *San Fernando Residencial Geriátrico*.

Notary

Notary offices are conveniently located all around town and can notarize documents for a nominal fee of $5 per signature. You will need a copy of your *cedula, jubilado* card or passport with the document. In almost all cases a Panamanian notarization will be perfectly satisfactory rather than a Consular notarization costing more than ten times as much. Note: the U.S. Consulate as of 2006 provides notary services only for documents going to the states.

Getting Married

Weddings, like birthdays, are special and fun to attend in Panama. In general these are formal, evening events requiring long gown and dark suit for both attendance at the ceremony and the reception following. Do not be surprised if more than half the invitees attend only the reception and not the ceremony.

Weddings are a two-step process in Panama, requiring a civil ceremony which is often several weeks before the religious ceremony. The religious ceremony is optional but usual for Catholics, Protestants, and Jews.

Requirements for legal marriage follow:

Birth Certificate & Evidence of Unmarried Status—must be authenticated by the Panamanian Consulate in the country you are leaving. Thereafter, it must be authenticated by the *Ministerio de Relaciones Exteriores* in Panama (*Departamento de Legalizaciones y Autenticacione*s).

Medical Certificate—issued by a Panamanian doctor not more than 15 days prior to the wedding. It must include a general medical examination and urinalysis, AIDS test, blood test, and V.D.R.L.

You will also need:

A valid passport or *carnet de migración* if you have been in the country for more than 30 days.

Two witnesses of legal age with passports, unrelated to those being married.

All materials must be presented to the local court handling marriages (*Juzgado de Turno en Matrimonios*), two or three days prior to the expected wedding date.

Following the legal ceremony arrangements can be made for the religious ceremony in accordance with the traditions and availability of your particular church or synagogue.

At a formal wedding, it is customary for the bride's party to pass out little programs and sometimes a little bell or bubbles to guests attending. The bell is rung or the bubbles blown after the ceremony as the couple walks back down the isle. An additional little remembrance gift will be given out at the reception. However, the traditional wedding cake has evolved into an unusual tradition. While the cake may be huge, multi-layered and incredibly decorated, regardless of how expensive, it is primarily, if not all, fake! The layers are Styrofoam and frosted to look like a real cake. Some brides at least have a small section of one layer from which to cut the traditional piece for sharing with the groom. The guests will not be so fortunate. When asked why this is done, the response from one of the major wedding planners was "tradition." There will, however, be a variety of desserts including the *sopa borracha* (drunken cake) and *sopa de gloria* (almond cake) but not the traditional piece of wedding cake for the guest to dream on.

The other different tradition at Panamanian wedding receptions is the carnival atmosphere near the end of the evening, which may be at three or four o'clock in the morning. At this time hats, horns, plastic beads and noisemakers are given to those remaining guests to celebrate with the bride and groom. Some weddings have further carnival-type entertainment at this time. A little incongruous at a formal wedding and a little shocking if you are not expecting it.

Life in the Tropics

A little advice to those *viejo verdes: Some* elderly *extranjero* men find themselves so dependent on the hired help as they do not speak the language, understand the customs or know the system, that they marry the maid, housekeeper or other employee on whom they have come to rely. The social, cultural and educational gap is generally too wide, regardless of your social standing in your home country. Additionally, the Panama government questions marriages that appear to be for the sole purpose of attaining legal status.

Exercise

The idea of exercise for the sake of exercise has caught on in Panama. Where there were just a couple of spas or gyms in the major hotels a few years ago, now there is a gym or exercise facility in every area of the City. Whether you live or work in Albrook, El Dorado, San

Francisco, El Cangrejo or Punta Pacifica, there is a gym in your neigh-borhood. While the hotels still lead the way with tennis courts, and swimming pools in addition to the traditional machines, the new gyms offer aerobics, personal trainers and a variety of programs to fit your needs. Parque Omar in San Francisco has a lighted pathway for running which is excellent for early morning and after dark exercise. It also has a Par Course with exercise stations located along a measured track. In the interior you may have to search to find anything comparable, but in Coronado the hotel has a nice facility.

A Little Help with the Paper Work

El Rey Supermarkets

Especially in the interior you will find El Rey Supermarkets of particular help with a variety of paperwork needs. You can obtain forms to request copies of Panamanian documents including a *Certificate of Nacimiento (*Birth), or Marriage Certificate, or file Public Registry doc-uments.

Additionally, they offer film development, payment of local util-ity bills, and watch repair services.

U.S. Embassy

Applicants for *jubilado* visa status based on U.S. Social Security must submit an official letter proving receipt of regular U.S. Social Se-curity payments. The affidavit form includes the dollar amount of the checks and bank where funds are being deposited. Complete the form at the U.S. Consulate, pay $30.00 in cash or by credit card and you will be one step closer to obtaining your *jubilado* visa.

A Final Word on Crime

While Panama has long had a reputation for being one of the safest places to live in the region, a word of caution is in order. As mentioned previously, petty crime, house break-ins and some crimes previously unheard of, including assassinations and kidnappings have recently become concerns. Reported crime hovers around 50 robberies per day. As a result, home security and alarm systems are becoming more popular. Many of these crimes are being attributed to the also increasing incidence of gangs or *pandillas*. While the problem is not on the scale of other Latin countries or the U.S., there are currently 80 known gangs operating in Panama City, San Miguelito and Colon.

An added complication to dealing with the crimes of these gangs comes about as a result of their using children to perpetrate the actual crimes. According to Panama law children cannot be held or prosecuted for crimes.

Recently upscale neighborhoods including Altos de Golf, Costa del Este, El Cangrejo and areas of Dos Mares have been targets of house break-ins, some involving personal injury to the occupants.

Do not make yourself a target. Use discretion in dealing with workers, shopkeepers, and the general public. Safeguard your personal possessions and do not *brag* about them or money in general. Do not tell strangers your travel plans or daily routine. (For further information see Chapter I, Safety Issues and Appendix 2, Crime Statistics.)

Multiple Exit Visa

Once you have your permanent, indefinite *pensionado/jubilado* visa you are eligible for a multiple entry visa in your passport that allows you to freely travel to and from Panama. The stamp is good for two years and cost $100. Apply for this at the Immigration office in Panama City. You will need your passport and a copy of your Panamanian *pensionado/jubilado* card. You will be asked to complete an application, make a copy of the application (in the same building) and return for your passport, with the multiple entry visa stamped therein, after two days. Upon your return, you will receive a *factura* (invoice) for $100, which you pay at the cashier. Upon presentation of your receipt, you will receive your passport with the new multiple entry visa stamped therein.

Note: Should your passport expire during the term of your multiple entry visa, you will need to carry both the old and new passport. The page on which your multiple entry visa is stamped will be preserved when the expired passport is cancelled by the issuing Embassy.

PANAMA ON LINE

Select Small Hotels
http://www.selectsmsmallhotels.com

World Headquarters
Cuba, Costa Rica, Panama
Online, store, maps, hotels, national parks, books
http://www.worldheadquarters.com/panama/

AARP International Activities
http://www.aarp.org/intl

Expresiones
Guia de Arte y Cultura
Expresiones@gmail.com

Residencial Geriátrico San Fernando
http://www.hospitalsanfernando.com
278-6340

Centro Cultural Alemán
http://www.centroculturalaleman.com
Email: centroaleman@udi.edu/centroaleman_23@hotmail.com

Out with the Old and In With the New

Spoofing the outstanding characters of the past year is a tradition in the interior of Panama at New Year's. Life-size and incredibly realistic effigies are displayed at bus stops, in yards, and along the Panamerican Highway especially between the towns of San Carlos and Chame.

These *muñecos* (dolls) can be made to resemble sports figures, beauty queens including Miss Panama, political figures including George Bush and Mireya Moscoso or Fidel Castro, even local personalities like the current President or Mayor. They may be people particularly revered by the creator or equally detested. Regardless, they live a short life as they are burned at midnight, December 31, bringing an end to what they represent and the old year.

This is just one more reason to head for the interior for a weekend, especially at the end of the year, to view these interesting displays.

PANAMA SOCIAL LIFE

"The Most Social Community"

Cultural Offerings

A friend of mine from the diplomatic corps once said to me that of all the places around the world where he had lived, Panama was the most social. There is a *club* for every ethnic, social, cultural, and sporting group you can imagine. Whether it is The American Society, Italian Ladies, or Rotary, social clubs hold regular events; and at a minimum, Tuesday and Thursday nights are busy with dinners, dances, theatre, diplomatic receptions, art gallery showings and other events. (See Chapter XI.) The big season is from September to February with many black-tie events but there is something going on all the time in Panama. Discos, more recently known as *Clubs* or *lounge bars,* exist for those looking for a more public forum for dancing the night away.

(Note: *Nightclubs*, sometimes referred to as Gentlemen's Clubs, do not mean the same thing here as in U.S. and Britain. Women, wives or dates accompanying the gentlemen are not welcome. Further, though some *extranjeros* use the Mexican term *cantina* because they think it is a cute name for a bar, never tell anyone you have been to a *cantina*, which is the name in Panama for the very lowest type of pick-up saloon.)

There are several community theaters offering stage productions in English including the Theatre Guild at Ancon, or in Spanish at *Teatro en Círculo* and the National Theatre to name only a few. Boquete boasts a new theater (Boquete Community Players) and their productions have been a great success for their English speaking audiences. The National Theatre and the Atlapa Convention Center feature visiting shows from around the world as well as local shows. These touring operas, ballets, and music of all kinds come to Panama often through the auspices of various embassies or community groups.

The Panama Canal Museum regularly is the site of special cultural exhibits including such things as a Goya Art Exhibit, Scottish Expedition to the Darien, Canadian Indian Exhibit and many others.

Movie theaters all over the City offer the latest films from Hollywood and Europe, if a few weeks behind the openings in New York. Many shows are in English. Check the local newspaper for listings and watch for whether the show is dubbed or has subtitles in Spanish. Movies especially for children are dubbed but an English version with subtitles will also be available. Movie rentals, both video and DVD, are available from Blockbuster and similar outlets all over the country. Additionally, there are museums, art galleries, parks, and native handicraft centers worth a visit. Atlapa also hosts a variety of shows monthly including the Home Show, Boat Show, Arts and Crafts, Construction, Automobiles and many more. Watch the local paper for announcements.

Tickets for the community theaters are $10-$15 and tickets for big productions range from $10 to $100. Movies are generally $3.90 but there are special rates for retirees and children. Extreme Planet boasts a unique VIP theater with reclining seats and food service at your seat (tickets $6).

Activities specifically for children are no less available. There are numerous ballet/dance schools, self-defense schools, community sports and the above theatres offer events appropriate for children from time to time. The Quadra Theater recently opened in El Cangrejo offering a children's theater in Spanish. Usually the schools provide some entertainment for children as well. Both the Brader School and the International School of Panama do at least one theatrical performance during the school year. The American Society also holds annual Christmas, Halloween and Easter events for children. Some embassies also have special events for the children of employees.

Theaters

People often ask "why choose Panama as a place to live?" The answer always involves the theatre. Panama has a reputation for community theatres doing musicals, comedies and more serious works. The following is a list of some of the possibilities:

Theater Guild of Ancon—productions in English
Located next to the Balboa PTJ
Tel.: 212-0060

Teatro en Círculo
Ave. 6-C, Norte, Urb Herbruger
El Carmen
Tel.: 261-5375

Teatro Nacional
Avenida B, between Calles 3 & 4
Tel.: 262-3525/212-2922
Concert Series

Teatro Aba
Urb Los Angeles Bethania
Tel.: 236-3258/260-6316

Teatro Balboa
Balboa, Edificio Ancón 727-C
Tel.: 228-0327

Teatro La Quadra—includes Children's Theater
Calle Albert Navarro, El Cangrejo
Tel.: 214-3695
Email: aragonch@sinfo.net

Boquete Community Players
Boquete
http://www.boquetecommunityplayers.com
Email: schmuckerbob@yahoo.com

Teatro en Colón
Calle 11 & Ave. Balboa, Colón
Tel.: 430-0101/6673-7937

Museums

Museo de Arte Religioso Colonial
Tuesday – Saturday 9 a.m. to 4:15 p.m. admission 75 cents adults, 25 cents children

Panama Canal Museum
(*El Museo del Canal Interoceánico*)
Tuesday – Sunday, 9:30 a.m. to 5:00 p.m.
Admission $2.00 adults, 75 cents children

Teatro Nacional
Avenida B, between Calles 3 & 4
Tel.: 262-3525

Afro-Antillean Museum
Calle 24 and Ave. Justo Arosemena.
Tel.: 262-5348
Tuesday to Saturday, 8:30 a.m. to 3:30 p.m.

Museo Biblioteca Archivo Ricardo J. Alfaro
Edificio Hispania, Calle 44 and Calle Colombia
Bella Vista
Tel.: 225-9332, Email: fundarja@cableonda.net

Miraflores Visitors Center
Miraflores Locks at the Panama Canal
http://www.pancanal.com
Tel.: 276-8325

Art Galleries

Panama has some excellent art galleries displaying the works of national and international artists. They regularly hold openings of one-artist shows and everyone is invited to attend. Visit your favorite gallery and sign up on their mailing or email list to be advised of upcoming shows. Notices regularly appear in the local newspapers.

It's Art
World Trade Center
Tel.: 6601-2177
Email: isabelgarciaarts@hotmail.com

Imágen
Calle 50, Edif. Imagen
Tel.: 226-2649

Legacy Fine Art
Avenida Balboa, Calle 50 Este
Tel.: 265-8141
Email: legacy@sinfo.net

Marcorama
Avenida Balboa
Tel.: 259-0643

Museo de Arte Contemporáneo
Ave. De los Martires, Ancon
Tel.: 262-8012

Sheraton Hotel and Resort
San Francisco
Tel.: 270-0477

Weil Art
Calle 48, Bella Vista
Tel.: 264-9697
Email: weilart@cableonda.net

Galeria ArteConsult
Calle 50 entre Calles 72 y 73
San Francisco
Tel.: 270-3436
Email: Artecons@cableonda.net

Mateo Sariel
Via Porras
Tel.: 270-2404

Artes José de la Cruz Gonzáles
Volcan, Chiriqui
Tel.: 6622-1502
Email: arte_cruz@yahoo.com

Arlene Lachman Galería.
Edificio Bahía Balboa, Local 4, Avenida Balboa,
Punta Paitilla.
Telefax: 215-2935.

Lachman and Charette Galeria
Edif. Don Andres, #5, Boquete, Chiriqui Tel.: 720-2886

Private Clubs

Club Unión
Calle Tomás G. Duque
Punta Paitilla
Tel.: 263-5233
Email: cunion@sinfo.net

The *Club Unión* is the oldest Club in Panama to which the "first" (*rabi blanco*) families belong. Memberships are passed from generation to generation – but still at a significant cost. Currently initiation and share purchase, if you receive a recommendation from the required members, is $50,000. The Club offers fine dining, swimming, tennis, party-rooms for private functions, catering, children's activities for the summer and all the other amenities you would expect of a private club.

City Club Panama

Credicorp Tower
29th and 30th floors
Calle 50
Tel.: 210-1366
Email: cityclub@plazapan.com

This prestigious business club is affiliated with a number of clubs and businesses around the world, including resorts, golf clubs and business clubs. These include local affiliations with the Club de Golf de Panama and Miramar Spa Health Club in the city. City Club is known for its fine dining, private meeting and dining facilities, party and reception rooms, as well as cooking classes, elegant parties, gourmet supper group, Sunday brunch and annual Civic Award Gala. Initiation fees are based on class of membership, for those fortunate enough to be recommended by a member, ranging from $8,000 for Corporate, $7,000 for Individual and $5,000 Junior (payments made in installments up to age 35 for Junior members). Diplomats pay no initiation fee. In addition, there is a monthly fee, part of which goes towards consumption.

Club Cultural Hebreo

Coco del Mar
Tel.: 226-0206 or 226-0455

Private social club with swimming pools, card and social rooms, two dining rooms which hold fashion shows, weddings and religious and social events.

Club de Golf de Panamá, S. A.

Cerro Viento
San Miguelito
Tel.: 220-9568
Email: Clubgolf@ihpanama.com

Social golf club in the country surrounded by a private, gated community. Club de Golf offers an 18-hole golf course for members and guests as well as banquet and event facilities. Members have reciprocal use of City Club. To join requires an invitation by a member. Membership cost is in the range of $12,000-$15,000 for an individual to purchase a share. Corporate membership is less but is non-voting and has an expiration date.

> ## Traje de Calle
> Litterally means *street clothes* but on an invitation it means dark suit and tie for the men and cocktail dress for the ladies.

Places of Worship

Panama offers churches, synagogues, temples, cathedrals and bible study groups to suit every need. Below are listed just a few but every neighborhood boasts at least one house of worship to serve the community needs.

Crossroads Bible Church
Calle Gaillard, Corozal
Tel.: 317-9480
Ministry in English
http://www.cbcpanama.org

La Boca Baptist Church
Ave. Julio Linares at Calle Ernesto J. Castillero (near FSU)
Tel.: 314-0375
Email: labocabaptist@excite.com
Ministry in English

Baha'I House of Worship
Via Transistmica
Milla 8, Las Cumbres
Tel.: 231-1137

First Baptist Church
Ancon Blvd., Balboa
Tel.: 272-5727

First Isthmian Baptist Church
Cristobal, 99 Colon,
Tel.: 445-1237
 Email: isthmian@cwpanama.net

Iglesia Ortodoxa Griega
Via Porras opposite Super 99
Tel.: 223-4572

Sacred Heart Chapel
Catholic
Ancon Blvd, Balboa
Tel.: 262-3076

St. Mary's Parish Church
Calle Enrique Linares
Tel.: 228-0036

Balboa Union Church
Balboa, Ministry in English
Tel.: 314-1004

Synagogue Kol Shearith
Costa del Este
Tel.: 225-4100

Iglesia del Carmen
Via España and Frederico Boyd

National Cathedral
Casco Viejo

Santuario Nacional
Calle Samuel Lewis
Tel.: 263-9833

Iglesia Episcopal San Marcos
Calle Angel Rubio
El Carmen
Tel.: 223-4820

St. Luke's Episcopal
Ancon
Tel.: 262-1280

Iglesia Nuestra Senora de Guadalupe
Calle 50
San Francisco
Tel.: 226-2434

La Iglesia de Jesucristo de los Ultimos Dias (Mormon Church)
Plaza Edison Piso 15, Service Center
Tel.: 302-1414

Iglesia Pentecostal United Pentecostal Church
Galerias Obarrio
Via España and Via Brazil
Tel.: 263-8424

Seventh Day Adventist Church
Ave. Gavilan, Balboa
Tel.: 228-4237, Email: Advenpma@cwpanama.net

Hindu Temple
Via Ricardo J. Alfaro in front of Edif. Villa Gloriela
Tel.: 236-2366/224-3304

Episcopal Services in El Valle de Antón
Casa de Lourdes Restaurant, 5:00 p.m.
3rd or last Saturday of the month

Catholic Mass
Coronado in the Park

Assembly of God
Calle 75
Tel.: 261-7660, Email: concilio@cwpanama.com

Hosanna
Via España & Martín Sosa, Bella Vista

Recreation in Panama

Panama is known as the land of a thousand activities and many of them fall under the category of recreational. Whether you are interested in fishing, scuba, surfing, boating or other water activities there is something for everyone. Portobelo on the Atlantic side offers some of the best scuba diving and the Pacific coast has the world's second best surfing. The new marina at Fort Sherman, Shelter Bay, offers everything for the day sailor and the mega yacht. There is fresh-water bass fishing on Lake Gatun with some of the best peacock bass fishing in the world. Hemingway was just one of the deep-sea fishermen to discover Panama's bounty and make it famous. The numerous islands near and far on both sides of Panama provide delightful destinations for the boating enthusiast. Whether you are off for a month in the San Blas on a private yacht, a weekend in Taboga via ferry or just an afternoon sail on Panama Bay, water activities abound in Panama. Further, destinations in the interior offer the excitement of white water rafting.

If land-based activities are more your style, Panama has some great areas for walking, roller blading, hiking, running or biking. One of the most beautiful areas is the recently improved Causeway. This manmade link to the three small islands off the Pacific side is a favorite on weekends. Here you can walk, run, ride a bike or skate along the two mile, tree-lined avenue at the entrance to the Panama Canal. Whether you run with one of several running teams or just do your own thing, the Causeway is a great option. This is also the perfect place for a family outing. There are small restaurants on both ends of the walkway where you can stop for a soda, beer or a meal. You can also just take a break and sit on one of the many benches along the way and enjoy the spectacular views of the Canal on one side or the Panama Bay and the City skyline on the other.

Also on the Causeway for the yachting enthusiast there is a beautiful marina offering full service including haul-out facilities for visiting and local boats as well as the moorings at the Balboa Yacht Club.

If flying is your thing, check out the parachute club, the model airplane club or the ultra-light club.

When you are ready to venture out of the City, there are numerous parks and nature areas to explore including *Parque Natural Summit* with its excellent Harpy Eagle exhibit and gardens; or *El Valle* where you can hike to a waterfall, swing through the jungle on a canopy tour or visit the zoo. There are numerous areas to view some of Panama's approximately 1,200 species of orchids or 1,000 varieties of humming birds. In fact, the birding opportunities are some of the best in the world. If you want to get up there for a "bird's eye view" you can hike the trails around the Canopy Tower or take the aerial tramway at Gamboa Resort. For something less strenuous, you can sit at Miraflores Locks and watch the ships transit the Panama Canal. This is a spectacular sight.

Panama has a number of golf courses and resorts offering challenging play. Whether it is Summit Golf and Resort or *Club de Golf*, you will have a great round. The courses at Coronado and Contadora offer additional enjoyment because of their equally special locations. Additionally, several planned communities with private golf courses are in development for other interior areas.

And, if sitting and less strenuous activities are your style in general, the horse races at the hippodrome may be just the thing. Panama boasts some great racehorses and they run daily (also televised). There are also the soccer teams all over town and an occasional cricket match in Paraiso to just watch and enjoy. Enjoy is the key word in Panama recreation.

Golf in Panama

Coronado Hotel & Resort
Office in Panama 264-2863
Fax in Panama 223-8513
Coronado Hotel
Tel.: 240-4444; Fax 240-4380

Open to guests of hotel and day players.
Green fees $50, cart $21 (for two people)

Club de Golf de Panama, S.A.
Cerro Viento, San Miguelito (near International School of Panama)
Tel.: 266-7777
Fax: 220-3994
Private membership Club. Requires invitation to membership by a current member. Reciprocal agreement with City Club. Green fees for Stock member: $25 weekdays, $50 weekends, $21 cart, caddy $15-20
Green fees for Corporate members double above
Two-week pass from a member $50 unlimited golf

Summit Golf & Resort
This lovely new facility opened in 2001 on the Summit Road (past Pedro Miguel Locks). Rates are comparable with other clubs in the area. Summit has a huge dining room offering buffet luncheon.

Gyms
Several gyms offer memberships especially those in the larger hotels including Miramar and Caesar Park.
Platinum Fitness Center, Albrook, 315-0645, 315-0188
Power Club, El Cangrejo, Dos Mares, 236-3897

Tennis Groups and Public Courts
Local football fields and tennis courts are available for children and adults as well as a tennis school that trains players from all over the world.

Ballbangers
Tennis group that meets weekend mornings and some weekdays.
Maintains private courts at Amador. Limited number of members.
Contact John McTaggert, Tel.: 272-5177.

Curundu Tennis Court
Tennis Pros available
Tournaments, classes for kids, clay courts

Centro de Alto Rendimiento de la Federacion Panameña de Tennis
Llanos de Curundu
Administered by the Tennis Federation of Panama
Reservations Tel: 232-7875 / 232-5196
Monday - Friday- 6:00 a.m. - 9:00 p.m.
Sat. & Sun. - 6:00 a.m. - 4:00 p.m.
7 clay courts with lights & 2 hard courts without lights
$5.00 per person per hour
Nighttime play: $5.00 per court additional for the lights
Annual memberships available:
Family (4 persons) - $350.00 (free court fees, however have to pay extra light fee at night)
Individual - $240.00

Parque Omar Tennis Courts
Administered by the Panama Tennis Club, annual memberships available
$3.00 per playing session
2 hard courts with lights

Albrook
Administered by the Associacíon de Propietarios de Albrook
$5.00 per person per hour
4 hard courts with lights

Diablo
Administered by the Club de Tenis de Diablo
$5.00 per person per hour
3 hard courts with lights

Clayton
Administered by Ciudad del Saber
Darlene Kahn´s Tennis Academy
3 hard courts with lights

Amador
2 hard courts

Private Clubs with Courts

Club Union
hard courts with lights

Club de Golf de Panama
4 hard courts with lights

Sheraton Hotel Panamá - Club Nogui
For guests and members
3 hard courts with lights

Hotel Miramar Intercontinental
Guests and members only
1 hard court with lights

Sailing

La Cresta Sailing Team
Sailing enthusiasts, with a dream of seeing Panama Bay dotted with sailboats, meet every Saturday afternoon. Currently there are 6 local yachts that sail. Contact David Wilson, http://www.tantoes.com, Email: tantoes@pobox.com. (See Appendix 6 for Yachting Facilities and Services.)

Horseback Riding

Horseback Riding Club
Offering boarding and some horses available for riding. Instruction is available. Across from Parque Nacional in Curundu. Offers classes, training and riding.

Club de Equitación Clayton
Offering lessons twice a week and membership after six months. Membership is $1,200 per year.
Via Juan Pablo II, Tel.: 232-6071

Coronado Stables
Facilities in Coronado for boarding and competition shows

El Valle

Informal arrangements may be made for riding. Look for the horses along side streets.

Horse Racing

The Hipódromo

Offers horseracing and all the amenities of a first-class racetrack including the Jockey Club. Panama boasts some excellent stables and champion horses.

Running Club

Hash House Harriers

http://www.geocities.com/hasherctt/PCHHH.html
Email: RobertML@cwpanama.net; hash@alairelibre.com

Hiking Clubs

Panama Rovers (Chiriqui)

Alex Marin Montilla, Tel.: 6524-2802

Club de Orientación de Panamá

Irving Bennet, Email: bennett@aldetall.com

Club Excursionistas del Istmo

Gilbert Ceballos, Tel.: 6637-0467

Club Eco Aventuras

Abdiel Barranco, Email: info@clubecoaventura.com

Panama Rappel Club

Mitchell Gonzalez; Tel.: 6600-5530/225-2260

Surfing/Diving

For more than 70 years the call has gone out, "Surf's Up." Playa Santa Catalina, Rio Grande, and the Soná district in the province of Veraguas are the places for surfing in Panama. Waves here are reported in the range of 2 to 25 feet. March, April to September are the best waves. They are smaller in September and October. On Isla Colon,

Bocas del Toro, Bluff Beach and Paunch Beach are also easy to reach for great surfing.
Tel.: 507-240-9128 or 675-2526.

Organización Panameña de Surf
Calle 63 B
Los Angeles
Tel.: 260-6012

Kitesurf and Windsurf Club and School
http://www.puntachamewindsurf.com

Scuba Diving
Portobelo, San Blas and Coiba Island National Marine Park offer diving opportunities.
Email: Info@panamawatersportadventure.com; http://www.scubapanama.com; http://www.panamadivers.com
Tel.: 261-3841/4064

Riomar Surf Camp
http://www.riomarsurf.com
email: riomarsurf@hotmail.com

Fishing and Exploring

Panama Bay Charters
Email: MolokaiPanama@aol.com
http://www.Panama-Bay-Charters.com
US Tel.: 305-852-6353; Panama Tel: 011-507-228-4348

Jungle Land Explorations in Lake Gatun
Email: gatunexplorer@gmail.com; http://www.gatunexplorer.com;
Cel: 6615-4773; Boat: 6612-5823
Carl Davis—a unique opportunity to visit and explore Lake Gatun.

Panama Jet Boat Explorer
Yariela Sánchez de Anciauxd
http://www.panamajetboatexplorer.com
Travel the route Columbus discovered in Bocas del Toro.

Cayuco Regatta

Once a year since 1954 this famous *cayuco* regatta, the world's only ocean-to-ocean boat competition, has taken place and many of the boats are as old as the race itself. The unique *cayuco* (long, narrow wooden boat) has a crew that varies in number and age depending on size of the boat. The race begins at the Cristobal Yacht Club on the Atlantic Side with as many as 78 boats in various categories and ends the third day on the Pacific side. But the training for this multi-day event every April actually begins months before. It takes many hours of training to build the strength necessary for this competition and as a result you will see crews out training on the Canal early in the morning. If you are not up to this vigorous paddling, this is a fun event for the whole family to watch from many spots along the banks of the Canal. This is a real family activity providing an opportunity for athletic competition, teamwork and continuing tradition. Sponsored by *Club de Remo de Balboa*/Balboa Paddle Club. http://www.cayucorace.org or http://www.cayucorace.com

Yacht Clubs—See Appendix 6

Bird Watching

Audubon Society

The Panama Audubon Society (SAP) is an independent non-governmental organization that supports education about, and protection of, the environment. The Society was founded in the 1970's and has continued to address the conservation needs of the Panamanian fauna and flora along with its habitat. This is accomplished by providing a forum dedicated to education of adults and children on the importance of the environment.

SAP maintains an affiliation with several International Conservation groups and Birding organizations.

The activities sponsored by the Society are:
Field trips (birding and educational)

Monthly meetings (business and social)
Scientific Forums
Bi-monthly Newsletters
Website
Scholarships
Library (reference and sales)
Annual Christmas Bird Count

Office Tel./Fax: 224-4740, 224-9371. Email: audupan@pananet.com, Website: http://www.pananet.com. Birding International. Tel: 270-3110. Email: ecoconsult@pty.com or Tel.: 226-8032, Email: wmsnyder@cwpanama.net

Panama Forever Growing and Changing

Living in Panama is always interesting and full of changes. During the time this book was being written the telephone rates and the train schedule changed, one newspaper went out of business, the planned continuation of the *Corredor Norte* was begun, the new *Centenario* Bridge over the Canal opened as well as the interchange at Albrook. New people are continually coming to Panama and discovering that Panama has something for every one. However, if you do not find what you are looking for, the opportunities are endless for starting your own activity, group or club.

This is particularly true in the interior where many newcomers are settling. At the time of this edition the following groups were forming:

Altos del Maria/Coronado Dinner Social Club, meets 4th Wednesday of the month
Boquete Rotary Club
Who's New Sister Club Boquete
Who's New Sister Club Bocas del Toro

Great Running/Walking Locations

Location	Distance	Time Required
Parque Omar	3.5 kms	25—40 min.
Ave. Balboa Extreme Planet to Miramar	1.0 kms	7—8 or 10-12 min.
Alrededor ATLAPA	0.7 kms	5—8 min.
Amador Causeway Museum to Flamenco	8.0 kms	55—90 min.

National Festivals of Some Countries with Embassies in Panama*

Canada—July 1

United States of America—July 4

Venezuela– July 5

France-July 14

Colombia-July 20

Egypt-July 23

Peru-July 28

Brazil-September 7

Costa Rica-September 15

Nicaragua-September 15

El Salvador– September 15

Honduras-September 15

Guatemala-September 15

*check further listings by month in *Mundo Social*

Fairs (*Ferias*) in Panama

January— Panama, Festival de Jazz
Panama, Fiesta Don Bosco (religious)
Penonomé, Orange Fair
La Chorrera, Feria Internacional
Chepo, Feria Agricultural
Veraguas, Feria de Santa Fé
Bugaba, Feria de la Candelaria
Boquete, Feria de las Flores y del Café

February- San Blas/Kuna Yala, Anniversary of the
Tule Revolution
Panama and Interior, Carnavales

March - Veraguas, Feria de Chitre
David, Feria Internacional
Darién, Feria de Santa Fé
Feria Nacional de Colón
Atalaya, fiesta religiosa de Jesus el Nazareno
Colón, Feria Nacional

April - Boquete, Expo Orchids

April-May- Azuero, Feria Internacional

May - Capira, Feria de Villa Rosario

July - Santiago, Patronales de Santiago Apostol
Las Tablas, The Pollera National Festival
Coronado, Champion's Parade, Equestrian Club
Panama, National Handicraft Fair

August-   Herrera, Festival del Manito, Ocú
                 Darién, Fundación de la Provincia

September- Bocas del Toro, Feria del Mar
                 Guararé, Festival Nacional de la Mejorana

October-   San Blas/Kuna Yala, Feria de Isla Tigre
                 Herrera, Feria de la Flor del Espíritu Santo,
                 Las Minas
                 Portobelo, fiesta religiosa del Cristo Negro
                 (Black Christ)
                 Antón, Festival del Toro Guapo (Beautiful Bull)

November- Bocas del Toro, Anniversary of the founding of
                 the Province
                 Volcán, Feria de Tierras Altas

Specific dates vary from year to year. For additional information check the local paper or call:

Bocas del Toro, 757-9642   Coclé, 993-3241
Azuero, 966-8013   Panamá, 226-2861
Colón, 441-9644   Chiriquí, 775-2839
Veraguas, 998-3929

PANAMA ON LINE

The American Society
http://www.amsoc.org

The Navy League of the U. S.
Panama Council
http://www.navyleague-panama.org

Who's New
International Women's Welcome Club
http://www.wnpan.org

World Trade Center, Panama
http://www.wtcpn.com

National Association for the Conservation
of Nature ANCON
http://www.ancon.org

La Biblioteca Nacional
Ernesto J. Castillero R.
infobinal@binal.ac.pa

Parque Natural Summit Panama
http://www.summitpanama.org

Almacenajes Mini-warehouses
261-6111/224-0517/232-5203/290-4480

Association of the U.S. Army (AUSA)
Email: fmpc@pancanal.com

3.3 million Panamanians

Approximately July 1, 2007, Panama's population will reach 3,339,781 according to la Dirección de Estadística y Censo de la Controlaría. The current indication is that there will be 105 males born to every 100 females.

Summing It All Up

So you think you want to come to live in Panama

Everyone who knows me knows that I always start out by saying Panama is a perfectly delightful place in which to live. It is also the most social place where you will ever live. In fact, Panama has so much to offer, whether you are looking for a location with wonderful beaches, beautiful mountains, challenging rivers, an incredible collection of flora and fauna to enjoy, or social activities, Panama has it all and no hurricanes. Finding out how that *works* for you is the challenge.

So if Panama sounds like just the place you want to live, I offer the following advice before you pack up and move.

Come and visit. Come often and travel around the country. Some people think they want to live in the mountains only to find they are too isolated, too underdeveloped, or just not what they imagined. However, they may find that the City suits them perfectly or the coastal areas are inviting. Every area of Panama is different whether the city or the interior - the climate, the services available, and the local culture. You cannot *know* if you will be comfortable in any one area until you spend some time in that area. Once you think you have found the place for you and your family, **rent**. Find an apartment or house and rent for a month, a season, or a year before you make a commitment to buy. I have friends that have lived here a lifetime and are still renting. There are advantages.

Rent before you commit to buy. Think of buying real estate in Panama the same way you would when purchasing jewelry or art. Years ago a jeweler gave me a very good piece of advice. While many jewelers will tell you that you are *making an investment* when you buy gemstones or expensive jewelry, the fact is, that if you decide to sell that *investment* at some future date, there may not be a market. He said buy jewelry because you love it, because it is worth the price *to you* that you have agreed to pay and because you are going to enjoy the purchase. Do not buy it with the idea of making a killing on the sale at some future date.

I give you the same advice on Panama real estate. Traditionally, Panama real estate has not been easy to resell. Ask any local. They own the first piece of property they ever purchased and not always because they want to, but because they cannot sell it. The same laws that look so friendly going into a purchase, work to your disadvantage when you go to sell. The major one of these disadvantages is the tax exemption and another is the preferential mortgage rate for new construction. Both these laws make selling older properties difficult. I will not say impossible but definitely difficult. Further, look around you, especially in the City, new buildings are going up daily and every one of them is competing for the same purchaser.

Bank at home. One of the suggestions I make to newcomers is to open a local bank account. After all, Panama is a major banking center. It is well worth the effort expended to get through the paperwork required in order to have the convenience of a local checking account. You can then pay your rent, telephone bill, buy groceries, pay your children's school tuition, and pay your club dues or any one of a dozen other things that will come up during the month. Transfer on a regular basis a convenient amount of money in order to meet these expenses but keep your money in your home country or wherever you have had it during your adult life. While the major Panama banks are perfectly safe, they do not pay much in interest on deposits (2-4%). In fact, contrary to most savings account plans that encourage saving, the Panama system requires activity on a regular basis or the bank will access charges that will deplete your savings account balance. In other words, if you deposit $1,000 in a savings account and expect it to stay in the bank and grow with interest and do not either make more deposits or withdrawals, the bank will charge a monthly fee and over time your $1,000 will disappear. Further, a variety of other investment options back home such as certificates of deposit or treasury bills will pay significantly more interest with less hassle.

Adequate financial resources. While the residency requirement for monthly income is $500 or $750 per month depending on the type of Visa you obtain as a *jubilado*, this is not adequate for any more than a very basic lifestyle. Panama is a bargain when it comes to many things – health care, food, and entertainment. However, electricity is expensive and housing prices vary based on what you are willing to spend. Most locals do not live in totally air-conditioned homes. Keep in mind that a middle-class Panamanian earns between $16,000 and $35,000 per year. For this he lives a nice lifestyle and so can you.

Health Care. Panama has excellent doctors, dentists and hospitals in the City. You as an *extranjero* or foreigner are expected to pay for your care. The Panama health care system, the *Caja Seguro Social* (CSS) is designed for employees who pay into the system through their jobs. Panamanians who can afford to do so also use the private health care system and either have local insurance to cover expenses or pay out of pocket. Either way, health care here is incredibly inexpensive compared with other developed countries, especially the United States. Therefore, plan to pay through your own resources. Check with your individual insurance carrier before coming to Panama to determine what coverage if any is applicable. Do not expect to find a government system here to cover you. Additionally Medicare is not available in Panama or elsewhere outside the U.S. Similarly, Canadian medical coverage is only provided in Canada. Local health insurance is available and at a reasonable cost; but, it has limitations concerning medical conditions as well as age restrictions. However, the health care system here is so good and so inexpensive we do not want the insurance problems that exist in other parts of the world. Additionally, some prescription drugs are significantly more expensive than you may be accustomed to and other newer drugs may not be available at all.

Lastly, in the words of one hospital administrator, "it is the first fifteen minutes of a medical emergency that are critical." In the City, help is available within that first fifteen minutes. Outside the City, is a different story. While there are clinics and doctors, even the occasional hospital in the interior, they are not equipped to handle the kind of emergencies that your hometown hospital sees on a daily basis. They may also be located at a distance that will determine whether you have a positive or negative outcome in time of emergency.

Retirement. If you are thinking of coming to Panama to retire, that is wonderful. Panama is a place that makes retirement fun. There are so many clubs, groups, activities, and things to do that life need not be dull no matter what your interests. If you are thinking of doing a little work on the side, do not. Retirement, *jubilado, pensionado* status means just that. You must have adequate resources to quality for this status. Therefore, you are not working to support yourself and you should not be taking a job from a local. If you want to come to Panama to open a business, work for a company or earn income from your labors, you need to apply for a different kind of Visa and meet those specific requirements.

Fitting in. While it is possible to live in Panama and not speak Spanish, it will not be easy and it will be really difficult in the interior. If you do not speak it before you come, make it your number one goal to learn to speak the language.

Dress. I read recently about a couple who moved here and planned to "wear shorts and sandals for the rest of their lives"—and live in the City! While you will be perfectly dressed at the beach, in your own home, or even in the mountains on a warm day, shorts and Birkenstocks are not appropriate attire in the city except on weekends. As I have mentioned before, you will be judged by how you are dressed and treated accordingly. In order to enjoy Panama, to be a part of the community and not just another awkward tourist, DRESS appropriately.

Lastly, I suggest to you when coming to Panama leave at home your preconceived ideas and home cultural expectations. Come here with your eyes and ears open and experience what Panama has to offer and seek to fit in. Do not expect everything to work like it did in your home country. Do not expect to change Panama to be like your home country. After all you came here looking for something different and Panama certainly is that. Do your homework before you come and spend some time here to understand how it works. Panama is a wonderful place to live as long as you understand what to expect.

Appendices

Appendix 1

Panama City Climate

Temperature

Month	Average Daily Degrees Fahrenheit	
	Maximum	Minimum
January	88	71
February	89	71
March	90	72
April	90	74
May	87	74
June	86	74
July	87	74
August	87	74
September	86	74
October	85	73
November	85	73
December	87	73

The Traveling Woman, New York Times Company, ISBN 0-385-15681-2

Precipitation

Month	Relative Humidity Percent	Ave. Monthly Rainfall Inches	More than 0.4 in. rain Days
January	84	1.0	4
February	81	0.4	2
March	78	0.7	1
April	81	2.0	6
May	88	8.0	15
June	90	8.4	16
July	91	7.1	15
August	91	7.9	15
September	91	8.2	16
October	92	10.0	18
November	92	10.2	18
December	89	4.8	12

Highlands Altitudes

Altos de María	**1540-3750 feet**
El Valle Antón	**2500 feet**
Boquete	**3713 feet**
Volcán	**4524 feet**
Cerro Punta	**5400 - 7506 feet**

Adiabatic Rate : temperature decreases 3.5 F per 1000 feet

Appendix 2

Crime Statistics					
Incidences of Major Reported Crime (2006)					
Category	Santa Ana	Calidonia	Bella Vista	El Chorillo	Pueblo Nuevo
Total	1,016	727	842	497	424
Property Robbery	587	442	694	215	307
Personal	229	112	52	161	43
Homicides	11	9	1	19	0
Drugs	50	67	7	38	11
Sexual	4	3	5	3	2
Other	146	103	84	80	61

La Prensa, July 4, 2006

The *Policia Tecnica Judicial* (PTJ) reports that from January to April 2006, they registered 989 cases of armed robbery, 6 kidnappings (*secuestros*), 228 rapes and 106 homicides. Additionally, 80 known gangs (*pandillas*) are in Panama, Colón and San Miguelito. About 50 robberies per day are reported.

Panama is not unique in the number of scams in operation. Below are just a few current ones in operation, as well as a number of web sites offering information and assistance to help you avoid being the next victim.

Web Sites for Assistance and General Information:

http://www.alianzaprojusticia.org.pa
http://www.Scam Busters.org
http://www.cia.gov/cia/contact.htm
http://www.interpol.int/Public/Wanted/fugitiveInvestServ.asp
http://www.usdoj.gov

Web sites for specific Scams in operation:
http://www.crimes-of-persuasion.com
http://www.avatar.nl/engels/organ.html
http://www.avatarScam.com
http://www.petitiononline.com/avatar06/petition.html
http://www.prophet.co.nz/avatar

In Panama report suspicious activities:
Tel.: 207-7161 or 6616-4576 or 104
Denuncialo/Report Domestic Violence: Tel.: 800-0014 or 147
Policia Tecnica Judicial (PTJ): Tel.: 212-2222

Appendix 3

Benefits for Retirees, Annuitants of the Third Age (Senior Citizens' Benefits)

Law No. 6 of June 16, 1987, Official Gazette #20.827 of 22 June 1987. modified by Law #18 of August 7, 1989; O. G. 21,368 of 4 Sept. 1989, Law 15 of 1992, Law 37 of 2001 and Law 14 of 2003.

1. Panamanians and foreign **residents** of this country who are 55 years of age or more if they are women.

2. Panamanians and foreign **residents** of this country who are 60 years old if they are men.

3. Retirees (*Jubilados*)/*Pensionados,* regardless of age

4. Disabled people on pensions or handicapped people regardless of age. It is necessary to present your *cédula* and retiree card or carnet of pension for disabled.

50% off the price of recreation activities, movies, theaters, sports and special public events. This **discount does not apply to charitable events that benefit children, old people, homeless and other authorized charitable events.**

30% off public transport: intercity buses

30% off trains

30% off launches and ships

25% off for passengers on airlines, both public and private, national or international

50% off at hotels, motels and pensions Monday through Thursday

30% off at hotels, motels and pensions on Friday, Saturday and Sunday

25% off the individual's meal in a restaurant

15% off the individual's meal at national and international franchised fast food restaurants*

10% off the total bill for hospitals and private clinics

10% off the cost of prescription drugs (17% at some pharmacies)

20% for general medical consultation

15% off dentist services

15% off optometrist services

Medical Insurance companies shall adjust their fees to include the benefit of these discounts for insured members: females 55 and males 60, as well as Pensionados and Jubilados.

20% off fees of technical and professional specialists (for example lawyers, architects, physical therapists, nurses etc.)

20% off the price of prosthesis

50% off commissions involving personal and commercial loans in your name at banks, financial and savings and loans institutions. Lenders do not have to give the discounts.

50% off the cost of (Panama) passports

25% off monthly electrical consumption of private or public entity up to 600 kw's and normal tariffs applied to anything above.

25% off basic phone service when the phone is in the name of the individual, is for a residential phone, and for one and only one phone.

25% discount off water bill as long as consumption does not exceed $30.00, the bill is in the individual's name and is the prime residential property.

15% is the maximum interest that can be charged for personal and commercial borrowing

*Age requirements apply in hospitals (women 58 and men 60), *jubilado* lines at the bank (55 for women and 60 for men).

Discounts apply solely to the expenditures of the retiree and not the entire group in a restaurant or the entire bill of a family or group.

You must be a legal resident of Panama.

APPENDIX 4

The Local Cuisine

It is easy to get to know the local foods as they show up at dinner tables and restaurants at all levels. No party is complete without at least one kind of Ceviche on the hors d'oeuvres selection. You will never recover from a cold or the flu without adequate Sancocho and no meal is complete without plantains prepared in one of many different options.

Panamanian Food - Comidas de Panamá

Arroz con Pollo	Rice and chicken
Carimañola	Cooked and ground yuca with ground meat filling
Ceviche	Fish, squid or shrimp marinated for 24 hours in lime juice with salt, hot red peppers and onions. Served in little pastry cups or on crackers
Empanadas	Half moon shaped pastry tarts filled with meat, chicken, cheese, mushrooms or potato
Patacones de Plátano Verde	Slices of fried green plantains, pounded and refried
Sancocho	Chicken soup with yuca, name and corn on the cob. The national dish
Tamales	Ground corn pie with meat or chicken fillings

(continued on next page)

Panamanian Food - Comidas de Panamá

Churros rellenos	Long, crinkled sugar-coated pastry (tastes like a donut) . Enjoy them plain or with cinnamon, or filled with cream
Michas de pan	Long, rolls about the size of a hot dog roll
Plantain	Baked with sugar and cinnamon
Yuca Frita	Fried yuca (like potatoes)
Arroz con Guandu y Coco R	ice and pigeon peas with coconut
Flan	Custard
Hojaldres	Fried dough served with honey
Tres Leches	Three milk cake

Appendix 5

<u>Cost of Living</u>

Living in Panama offers many advantages and pleasant surprises. The cost of goods and services is just one of those surprises. I recently took my husband's dress shoes to the repair shop (*zapateria*) for new leather soles. When I returned home, I mentioned to him that the cost for the repairs would be $17.00, to which he replied, "That is exactly what I paid in the U.S. twenty years ago!" A shoeshine from this expert is $1 but a shine at the airport is fifty cents.

Fruits and vegetables are plentiful and varied and at prices below the cost in the United States. Many basic toiletries, household products and canned goods are cheaper than their equivalents in the U.S. Panama is a crossroads of the world and as a result the selection of products available is truly international. You will find canned peaches from Greece, products from China and Japan, toiletries made in Colombia, Guatemala, and Mexico. The wine selection starts with Chile, Argentina, Spain, and U.S. and extends through France.

Water is plentiful and inexpensive and the same should be said of electricity with the large installed capacity for hydroelectric. However, electricity prices are high by U.S. standards. Telephone service is good and prices for basic residential service are reasonable. Cell phone service plans are much more expensive than U.S. prices. (But include all the amenities).

The following is a sampling of prices on typical goods and services. This sampling was made *August* 2006.

Rice, long grain, 5 lb bag 1.85
Sugar, granulated, 5 lb bag......................................1.54
Cornflakes, 500G box 2.85
Shredded Wheat, Post...3.71
Coffee, ground 425.2 gr 2.55
Coffee, Nestle Instant, 100 gr 3.59
Tomatoes, whole canned, 14.5 oz 1.35
Tomatoes, fresh, lb 90
Apricot halves, 15 1/4 oz 1.10
Tea bags, 150 gr 2.17
Tomato Ketchup, 14 oz, Hunts 1.25
Tuna fish, canned, 6 oz, Bumble Bee...................... 1.92
Olive Oil, 34 oz, Extra Virgin, Bertolli.................. 5.65
Milk, whole, ½ gal. 1.79
Soft drink, 335 ml, can, Coca-Cola, Pepsi.................45
Eggs, 12 large...1.22
Cheese, cheddar, natural 12 oz............................... 3.95
Danish Blue Cheese, 100 grams.......................2.22
Bananas, lb...14
Onions, lb...55
Olives, Lindsay Large pitted, 6 oz....................1.95
Tomato Soup, Campbell's, 10 1/4 oz.................1.04
Whole kernel sweet corn, 8.75 oz........................65
Yogurt, Bonlac natural, 200g............................50
Potatoes, red, lb...78
Fresh mushrooms, quart. 3.15
Ham, lb...1.95
Fish, corvina, whole, lb...2.05
Pork chops, lb...1.85
Chicken, whole, lb 89
Beer, canned, Panama 38
Beer, bottled, Balboa...55
Wine, Cabernet Sauvignon, Concha Y Toro 4.75

Wine, Sauvignon Blanc, Casillero del Diablo 7.60
Toilet paper, 6 pkg. Scott 3.92
Aspirin, Bayer, 20 tablets...1.08
Provera, 5 mg, 20 tablets............................... .6.36
Estrogen, .625 mg, 28 tablets...........................8.15
ABC Plus Multi-Vitamin & Mineral, 100 tablets....7.88
Toothpaste, 100 ml Colgate 1.85
Lipstick, MaxFactor...12.95
Camera film, 35 mm, 400 ....4.46
Dry Cleaning men's trousers.....................................1.75
Dry cleaning ladies dress...............................4.25
Dry Cleaning Ladies skirt...............................2.05
Men's hair cut 6.00
Cinema ticket 3.50
Theatre ticket 10.00
Newspaper, daily, local 35
Manicure..3.00—10.00
Leather resoles, Men's shoes.........................17.00
Whiskas Dry Cat Food 1.5 kg..........................4.75
Scoop Away Clumping Cat Litter 14 lb..............7.67

Prices vary by area within the city and in the interior as well as from market to market.

Appendix 6

Yachting Facilities and Services

Yachting Facilities

Pedro Miguel Boat Club
Port Meigs on the Panama Canal
Pedro Miguel
Tel.: 232-4509
http://www.pmbc.ws
small boat storage

Panama Canal Yacht Club
Cristóbal
Tel.: 441-5882

Balboa Yacht Club
Ft. Amador
The Causeway
Tel.: 228-5794
Fax: 228-5446

Club de Yates y Pesca
Balboa Avenue
Tel.: 227-3505

Fuerte Amador Resort & Marina (Flamenco)
The Causeway
Tel.: 225-3515 or 225-3512
http://www.fuerteamador.com

Diablo Spinning Club
Calle Walker
Ancon
Tel.: 232-6882, 232-6926

Shelter Bay Marina
Fort Sherman, near the Caribbean
Entrance to the Panama Canal
Tel.: 433-3581
Fax 322-0439
http://www.shelterbaymarina.com

Boat Launch Ramp
Gamboa, Nelson or Mayo
Tel.: 231-8656, 6634-8088,
6656-694

Bocas Yacht Club and Marina
Bocas del Toro
Email: Bocasyachtclub@yahoo.com
http://www.bocasmarina.com
Tel.: 507-757-9800

Careening Cay Marina
Bocas del Toro
Lat 9°20' N, Long 82°15'W
http://www.careeningcaymarina.com
Tel.: 507-757-9242
Email: Stay@careeningcaymarina.com

Yacht Services

Panama Yacht Services
Tel.: 229-7110 – 613-6337
Email: ariasjul@pananet.com

Taxi Driver Yacht Guide
Colon
Stanley Scott
Tel.: 507-447-0065
Cell: 6680-7971
VHF Chanel 74
Email: sscott@cwpanama.net

Tina McBride Yacht Services, S.A.
Let your agent handle your
Panama Canal Transit
Tel.: 507-6637-2999 or
507-232-8843
Email: Tinamc@sinfo.net
http://www.panamacanaltransit.com

Enrique Plumber
Taxi Driver Guide
Balboa Yacht Club
Cell: 6674-2086

Yachting Goods

Abernathy S.A.
Via Transístmica 260-1222
Amador, Tel.: 314-1432
Yates y Pesca, Tel.: 227-8621

Centro Marino
Ave. Nacional
Email: Chikos@cwpanama.net
wttp://www.centromarino.panama.net

Cromados Panamá, S.A.
(Chrome replating)
At the entrance to Costa del Este
Cl Z Parque Lefevre
Tel.: 224-1056

Fiberglass Corp
Cl 1 Juan Díaz
Llano Bonito
Tel.: 217-6546

Fire Extinguisher Recharging
Tel.: 800-Fire

Friolín Segundo, S.A.
(Refrigeration products and Services)
Cl Abel Bravo Urb Obarrio, 1
Email: ventas2@cableonda.net
Tel.: 269-3804

Islamorada Internacional, S.A.
Nautical and Air Charts & Guides
Edif. 808, Balboa, Ancon
Tel.: 228-6069
Email: Info@islamorada.com
http://www.islamorada.com

La Casa de las Baterias
The greatest assortment of (marine)
batteries in Panama
Via España 264-0904
David, Tel.: 774-4826
Colon, Tel.: 445-3476

Metálica Pérez, S.A.
Ave 7 Central
Tel.: 227-1352

Pesqueros, S.A.
Ave. Balboa & Cl 27
Tel.: 227-3097
Email: Ventas@pesqueros.com
http://www.pesqueros.com

Appendix 7

Chambers of Commerce

American Chamber of Commerce and Industry of Panama
AMCHAM
Tel.: 301-3881 or fax 301-3882, Email: amcham@panamcham.com
http://www.panamcham.com

Canadian Chamber of Commerce
Email: Info@pancanada.org, Tel.: 223-7222

Panama Chamber of Commerce of Industry
and Agriculture, Tel.: 227-1233

Tourism Chamber of Commerce
Tel.: 211-3268
Puerto Rico Commercial Office
Tel.: 269-2415
Mining Chamber of Commerce
Tel.: 228-9385
Spanish Chamber of Commerce
Tel.: 225-1487
Maritime Chamber of Commerce
Tel.: 264-7996
International Services Chamber
Tel.: 223-2061
Chamber of Transportation
Tel.: 215-2483
Chamber of Construction
Tel.: 265-2500

Appendix 8

Community Services

Mother-to-Be Classes
Clínica Hospital San Fernando
Tel.: 229-3800, Ext. 4129 or 4229

Parroquia Cristo Redentor de San Miguelito
Gran Via Crucis Juvenil (Juvenile Crisis)
Tel.: 267-1370

Fundación Socorro
The Colombia Confict
Tel.: 261-0675 or 698-5320

Dirección de Correos y Telégrafos
(Post Office)
Department of Filatelistas/Stamp Collecting
Tel.: 225-2803
Email: filatelia@cwpanama.net

Panama Municipal Government
Panama offers the following 800 phone numbers to report the following:
Trash pick-up large items (refrigerators, stoves, junk cars)
Tel.: 800-ASEO (800-2736)
Suggestion Line, 800-IDEA (800-4332)
Corruption Hot Line 800-ALTO (800-2586)
Complaints concerning tree trimming and cutting
Tel.: 800-TALA (800-8252)
Discrimination Hot Line 800-IDEM (800-4336)

Cruz Roja Panameña (Red Cross Panama)
http://www.panama.cruzroja.org

Appendix 9

Handy Food Terms

ENGLISH	SPANISH

Staples — Básicos

Baking powder	polvo para hornear
Baking soda	bicarbonato
Buttermilk	leche agria descremada
Cheese	queso
Coffee	café
Cornstarch	maicena natural
Cream, sour	crema cultivada
Cream, whipping	crema de batir
Dough	masa
Eggs	huevos
Flour	harina
Flour, self-rising	harina leudante
Flour, sifted	harina cernida
Flour, wheat	harina de trigo
Gelatin, unflavored	gelatina sin sabor
Juice	jugo
Milk, whole	leche pura
Milk, skimmed	leche semidescremada
Pepper	pimienta
Salt	sal
Shortening, vegetable	manteca vegetal
Sugar, powdered	azúcar micropulverizada
Sugar, refined	azúcar refinada
Tea	té
Yeast	levadura seca
Yogurt	yogurt

Fruits & Vegatables — Frutas y Vegetales

Apple	manzana
Apricot	albaricoque

Artichoke	alcachofa
Avocado	aguacate
Banana	banana
Bean	frijol
Beet	remolacha
Bell pepper	pimentón
Blackberry	mora
Broccoli	brocoli
Brussels sprouts	repollo de bruselas
Cabbage	repollo
Cantaloupe	melón
Carrot	zanahoria
Cashew	pepita de marañón
Cauliflower	coliflor
Celery	apio
Chayote	chayote
Cherries	cerezas
Coconut	coco
Corn	maíz
Cucumber	pepino
Eggplant	berenjena
Garlic	ajo
Grape	uva
Grapefruit	toronja
Guava	guayaba
Kiwi	kiwi
Leek	ajoporro
Lemon	limón
Lettuce	lechuga
Lima bean	haba
Lime	limón
Mango	mango
Onion	cebolla
Orange	naranja
Papaya	papaya
Passion fruit	maracuyá
Pea	petitpois

Peach	durazno
Pear	pera
Peanut	maní
Pineapple	piña
Plantain	plátano
Plum	ciruela
Potato	papa
Prunes	ciruelas pasas
Pumpkin	zapallo
Radish	rábano
Raisins	pasitas
Raspberry	frambuesa
Spinach	espinacas
Strawberry	fresa
String bean/green bean	habichuelas
Sweet potato	camote
Tangerine, mandarin	mandarina
Tomato	tomate
Watercress	berro
Watermelon	sandía

Seasonings & Spices / Condimentos y Especias

Allspice	pimienta guayabita or pimienta gorda
Anise	anis
Basil	albahaca
Bay Leaf	hoja de laurel
Brown Sugar	Azúcar morena
Chamomile	manzanilla
Caper	alcaparra
Caraway	comino holandés o alcaravea
Cinnamon	canela
Clove	clavo de olor
Coriander	cilantro
Cream of tartar	crema tártara
Cumin	comino

Dill	eneldo
Fennel	hinojo
Garlic	ajo
Ginger	jengibre
Horseradish	rábano picante
Mace	macis
Marjoram	mejorana
Mint	yerba buena
Mustard	mostaza
Nutmeg	nuez moscada
Onion	cebolla
Oregano	orégano
Paprika	pimentón húngaro
Parsley	perejil
Rosemary	romero
Saffron	azafrán
Sage	salvia
Salt	sal
Tarragon	estragón
Thyme	tomillo
Tumeric	curcuma
Vanilla	Vainilla

Meats   Carnes

Fowl   Aves

Chicken	pollo
Duck	pato
Goose	ganso
Turkey	pavo

Beef   Carne de Res

Escalopes	milanesas
Ground beef	carne molida
Filet Mignon	filete
Roast Beef	rosbif
Standing Rib Roast	Pierna de res

| Steak | bistec |
| T-bone | T-bone |

Pork	**Cerdo**
Bacon	tocino, bacon
Chops	chuletas
Crackling	chicharrón
Ham	jamón
Spareribs	costillas

Lamb	**Cordero**
Chops	chuletas de cordero
Leg of Lamb	pierna de cordero

Seafood	**Mariscos**
Blue fish	corvina
Clams	almejas
Crab	Cangrejo
Flounder	lenguado
Lobster	langosta
Mussels	mejillones
Octopus	pulpo
Oysters	ostras
Red Snapper	pargo
Sardine	sardina
Sea Bass or grouper	mero

Shellfish	**Mariscos**
Shrimp (prawns)	langostinos
Squid	calamares
Trout	trucha
Tuna	atún

Veal	**Ternera**
Chops or Cutlets	Chuletas de ternera
Roast	Asada de ternera

Appendix 10

<u>Tried and True Restaurants</u>

One of the delights of Panama is the opportunity to experience a variety of restaurants. Whether it is a fast burger and fries, or filet mignon and a fine wine that you are looking for, Panama restaurants provide the answer. The following are just a few favorites but the possibilities for you to discover are extensive and you will want to get started soon!

Italian

Café El Pomodoro
Spaghetteria
Aparthotel Las Vegas
Calle 55, El Cangrejo
Tel.: 263-9400

Restaurante Las Americas
Italian and International
Avenue Ira. Sur & Calle 58
Obarrio
Tel.: 223-7734

Napoli
Avenue 13, No 24262-2446
Calle 57, Obarrio
Tel.: 263-8800

Tre Scalini
El Dorado Boulevard
El Dorado
Tel.: 260-0052

Tre Scalini
Bella Vista, Calle 51
(behind Maduros)
Tel.: 236-5303

Romanaccio
Ristorante and Pizzeria
Calle 57 y Via Brasil,
Obarrio
Tel.: 303-2633/302-2644

Japanese

Matsuei
Calle Eusebio A. Morales
El Cangrejo
Tel.: 264-9562

Mexican

La Mexicanita
Calle 50, El Dorado
Tel.:223-2157

Sol Azteca
Calle 51, Bella Vista
Tel.: 214-3910
Email:Restsolazteca@hotmail.
com

Continental

Las Bóvedas
Casco Viejo
French Plaza
Tel.: 228-8068

La Posta
Calle 49 con Calle Uruguay
Tel.: 269-1076/269-4225
http://www.lapostapanama.com

Peruvian

Machu Picchu
El Cangrego, Tel.: 264-9308
Boquete, Tel.: 6676-0757

El Velero de Salinas
Esquina Samuel Lewis Y Via
Brasil, Tel.: 214-3739

Panamanian

Las Tinajas
Calle 51, Bella Vista
Tel.: 263-7890

Al Tambor de la Alegría
Brisas de Amador (Causeway)
Tel.:314-3380

Breakfast and all round

Manolo's Churreria
Via Argentina & Obarrio
Tel.: 264-3965 or 214-3986 http://
www.churreriamanolo.com

Boulevard Café
Albrook Mall
Look for a new location 2007

Executive Hotel
Calle A De La Guardia and 52nd
Obarrio
Tel.: 264-8011

Greek

Jimmy's
Via Cincuentenario
Tel.: 226-1096

Ice Cream

Granclement Gourmet Ice Creams & Sorbets
Ave. Central Y Calle Tercera,
Casco Viejo
Tel.: 228-0737

Seafood

Siete Mares
Calle Guatemala, El Cangrejo
Tel.: 264-0144

Le Bistro
Marbella, Tel.: 269-4025

Chinese

Restaurante Sunly
Calle Miguel Brostella
El Dorado, Tel.: 260-1411

Great Salads, Wraps and More

Greenhouse
Cl Uruguay, Tel.: 264-6484 Via
Argentina, Tel.: 214-7475

Ozone Café
Calle Uruguay
Tel.: 214-9616

Steak Houses

Gaucho's Steak House
Calle 48 & Ave. Uruguay
Tel.: 263-4469

Viejo Pipo
Bella Vista
Tel.: 225-7924 Email:
Viejopipo@cableonda.net

**Shamrock's Grill &
Restaurant**
Edif. 791, La Boca
Tel.: 314-1436

Los Años Locos
Calle 74 (& 50 at KFC)
San Francisco
Tel.: 226-6966, 226-3996

Interior

Casa de Lourdes
El Valle de Anton
Tel.: 507-983-6450
Email: Golosinas@cableonda.net

Restaurante Pappassitos
Tex-Mex
Interamerican Highway, one
kilometer out of Capira at
mile 48

Interior

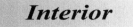

Bistro Boquete S.A.
Central Avenue Boquete
Email:
Bistro_boquete@yahoo.com
Tel.: 720-1017

El Rancho Restaurante
Argentina Steak House
Boquete

Bambito Hotel Restaurante
Cerro Punta (Fresh trout)

Los Camisones
Beyond Coronado, and just
past Corona, over the bridge
and up the hill. On the right.
(gas station on the left if you go
too far.)

Appendix 11

<u>Handy Dandy Household Tips</u>

Living in the tropics presents numerous challenges, especially around the house. Mold is a particular problem – on walls, on leather goods, in the toilet bowl, in closets. Ants and insects of all kinds are not daunted by tall buildings or perfectly sealed walls. Whole boxes of envelopes will stick before you can use them, wine will not keep from one day to the next once it is opened, vegetables will rot in the warm air, bread molds, and salt and sugar melt. Everyone has a suggestion for attacking these problems. The following are some suggestions collected from those that have attempted to meet the challenge.

General
Flies or bees buzzing - Spray them with hairspray and they will take a quick dive.

Sealed envelope - Put in the freezer for a few hours, then slide a knife under the flap. The envelope can then be resealed.

Cords - Use Empty toilet paper roll to store appliance cords. It keeps them neat and you can write on the roll the name of the to which it belongs.

Ink on clothing—spray with hairspray and wash. For more difficult ink stains soak in milk and then wash.

Crayon marks on walls - A damp rag, dipped in baking soda.

Permanent marker on appliances/counter tops rubbing alcohol on paper towel.

S.O.S Pads – Use scissors to cut each pad into halves. No more rusted and unused halves. The scissors get sharpened at the same time.

Opening brand new jars can be a feat in itself. Use the nutcracker, as it will adjust to the size of the jar and simply give it a good twist and off pops the lid!

Blood stains on clothes - Pour a little peroxide on a cloth and proceed to wipe off every drop of blood.

Windows - Use vertical strokes when washing windows outside and horizontal for washing inside windows. This way you can tell which side has the streaks.

Straight vinegar will get outside windows really clean. Don't wash windows on a sunny day. They will dry too quickly and will probably streak.

Fresh rooms and drawers - Spray a bit of perfume on the light bulb in any room to create a lovely light scent when the light is turned on. Place fabric softener sheets in dresser drawers and linen closets and your clothes will smell freshly washed for weeks.

Candles will last a lot longer if placed in the freezer for at least 3 hours prior to burning.

Artificial flowers – to clean, pour some salt into a paper bag and add the flowers. Shake vigorously as the salt will absorb all the dust and dirt and leave your artificial flowers looking like new.

Burnt food - To easily remove burnt on food from your skillet, simply add a drop or two of dish soap and enough water to cover bottom of pan, and bring to a boil on stove top.

Tupperware – Spray with nonstick cooking spray before pouring in tomato-based sauces and there won't be any stains.

Flour the pan - When a cake recipe calls for flouring the baking pan, use a bit of the dry cake mix instead and there won't be any white mess on the outside of the cake.

Celery -Wrap celery in aluminum foil when putting in the refrigerator and it will keep for weeks.

Fresh Corn -When boiling corn on the cob, add a pinch of sugar to help bring out the corn's natural sweetness.

Headache Cure: Take a lime, cut it in half and rub it on your forehead. The throbbing will go away.

Leftover wine- Freeze into ice cubes for future use in casseroles and sauces.

Itch from mosquito bites- try applying soap on the area and you will experience instant relief.

Ants, ants, ants everywhere - Well, they are said to never cross a chalk line. So get your chalk out and draw a line on the floor or wherever ants tend to march. Or, try the same trick by rubbing the area with fabric softener cloths.

Mirrors- Use air freshener to clean. It does a good job and better still, leaves a lovely smell with the shine.

Splinters - Simply put the scotch tape over the splinter, then pull it off. Scotch tape removes most splinters painlessly and easily.

Bounce Fabric Softener Sheet Uses

*Repel mosquitoes. Tie a sheet of Bounce through a belt loop when outdoors during mosquito season.
*Eliminate static electricity from your television screen - wipe your television screen with a used sheet of Bounce to keep dust from resettling.
*Dissolve soap scum from shower doors. Clean with a used sheet of Bounce.
*Freshen the air in your home. Place an individual sheet of Bounce in a drawer or hang one in the closet.
**Prevent thread from tangling. Run a threaded needle through a sheet of Bounce to eliminate the static cling on the thread before sewing
*Eliminate static cling from pantyhose. Rub a damp, used sheet of Bounce over the hose.

*Prevent musty suitcases. Place an individual sheet of Bounce inside empty luggage before storing.
*Freshen the air in your car. Place a sheet of Bounce under the front seat.
*Clean baked-on food from a cooking pan. Put a sheet in the pan, fill with water, let sit overnight, and sponge clean. Not recommended for plastic pans and dishes since the odor of the fabric softener might stay in the plastic.
*Eliminate odors in wastebaskets. Place a sheet of Bounce at the bottom of the wastebasket.
*Collect cat hair. Rubbing the area with a sheet of Bounce will magnetically attract all the loose hairs.
*Eliminate static electricity from venetian blinds. Wipe the blinds with a sheet of Bounce to prevent dust from resetting.
*Wipe up sawdust from drilling or sandpapering. A used sheet of Bounce will collect sawdust like a tack cloth.
*Eliminate odors in dirty laundry. Place an individual sheet of Bounce at the bottom of a laundry bag or hamper.
*Deodorize shoes or sneakers. Place a sheet of Bounce in your shoes or sneakers overnight so they'll smell great in the morning.

Alka Seltzer Uses

* Clean a toilet- Drop in two Alka Seltzer tablets, wait twenty minutes, brush and flush. The citric acid and effervescent action clean vitreous China also.
*Clean a vase- to remove a stain from the bottom of a glass vase or cruet, fill with water and drop in two Alka Seltzer tablets.
* Polish jewelry- Drop two Alka Seltzer tablets into a glass of water and immerse the jewelry for two minutes.
* Clean a thermos bottle- Fill the bottle with water, drop in four Alka Seltzer tablets, and let soak for an hour (or longer, if necessary).
* Unclog a drain- Clear the sink drain by dropping three Alka Seltzer tablets down the drain followed by a cup of Heinz White Vinegar. Wait a few minutes, and then run the hot water.

Mold and Mildew

On Wicker/rattan rub the spots with a cloth dipped in diluted ammonia (don't saturate the wood.)
On walls wash in a solution of water, soap and Clorox or water and vinegar.

In closets keep a low watt light bulb burning.

Sugar and Salt

For bulk storage, keep in an airtight container. Try rice in the saltshaker or buy a shaker with a screw cap. Keep your sugar bowl or saltshaker in the refrigerator between uses.

Appendix 12

United States Embassy Assistance

The U.S. Embassy offers a variety of services to its citizens. Following are details for securing new or renewed passports, reporting lost or stolen passports, obtaining a marriage license, registering to vote, registering with the Embassy, and complying with Selective Service registration requirements.

Passports

American citizens residing or traveling abroad who require issuance of a U.S. passport are issued the latest, state-of-the-art passport incorporating a photo-digitized image and other enhanced security features. U.S. Embassies and Consulates will send the applications to the domestic U.S. passport facility. This will increase processing times at some U.S. Embassies and Consulates, but the Department is committed to ensuring that American citizens receive secure documents in a timely manner. American citizens are encouraged to apply early for renewal of expiring passports.

U.S. Embassies and Consulates will continue to issue passports in emergency cases. Such passports will be limited in validity, and cannot be extended. Bearers will be required to exchange their limited validity passports for a full-validity photo-digitized passport upon completion of their emergency travel, either through passport facilities in the U.S. or U.S. Embassies and Consulates abroad. http://travel.state.gov/passport/get/renew/renew833.html.

First-Time Passport Applicants

To apply for a U.S. passport, a native-born, U.S. citizen must present a certified copy of his or her birth certificate, two passport photos measuring 2 inches by 2 inches, (color or black and white with a light background,) photo ID and the applicable fee ($67 application fee plus $30 execution fee for a total of $97 for adults at the time of this writing). To apply for a U.S. passport, if a naturalized citizen, present the certificate of naturalization along with the photos, photo ID, and fees.

Passport Renewal

You will need your current passport as evidence of citizenship, two passport photos measuring 2 inches by 2 inches, (color or black and white with a light background). To be eligible you must have been issued a U.S. passport in your name within the past 15 years. Fees for those under the age of 16 are $82 total.

Lost or stolen passport

You will need to report the loss of your passport to the police and obtain a copy of the police report. In addition to the two passport photos, you will need to present proof of identity and proof of U.S. citizenship. The proof of identity could be any photo ID such as a U.S. driver's license. Proof of citizenship could be a certified, sealed copy of your U.S. birth certificate and/or old canceled U.S. passport. The fee for a replacement passport is the same as above.

Marriage in Panama

Take the following documents and fill out the application for a license to enter into marriage before the court in the jurisdiction where at least one of the parties lives (Marriage Courts (*Juzgado de Turno en Matrimonios*) two-three days before the expected wedding date.

1. Health Certificate, including: General Medical Exam, Lab Tests: Hemoglobin Electrophoresis, Hematic Biometry, VDRL, Urinalysis, and AIDS

A registered physician must issue the above documents within the last 15 days prior to the ceremony

2. Birth Certificate

3. If the parties have not been married previously, a certificate (*Certificado de Solteria*) to that effect must be presented.

For Panamanian citizens: The aforementioned certificates can be obtained free of charge at the Civil Registry Office.

For foreign citizens: The Birth Certificate must be issued in your country of origin. The certificate stating your civil status (*Certificado de Soltería*) must be issued in the country where you have been residing the last 2 years. Both certificates must be authenticated by the Panamanian Consulate in the country you lived in. Thereafter, they must be authenticated by the *Ministerio de Relaciones Exteriores* in Panama.

4. Two witnesses of legal age not related to any of the parties (i.e. within the fourth grade of consanguinity or second degree of kinship or by adoption). Therefore, the following cannot be a witness: brother/sister, cousin, uncle/aunt, nephew/niece, son/daughter-in-law, father/mother- in-law or brother sister-in-law-of the couple to be married.

5. *Cédula* or passport with corresponding visa.

Voter Registration

Information on absentee voting and regulations for each state can be obtained by contacting the American Citizens Services Section.

In Presidential Election years, the Republicans Abroad in Panama (http://republicansabroadpanama.org) hold voter registration activities in order to assist in the process. The Federal Voting Assistance Program has trained members of this organization and they maintain copies of all pertinent forms and guidance materials for registering. Additional information may be found by email: Email: vote@fvap.ner.gov or http://www.fvap.gov.

You may request an absentee ballot by completing a voter registration form on line or in person at least 60 days before the election.

Selective Service Registration

In order to register, males who have attained the age of 18 years may bring their U.S. passport and Social Security number and fill out the application for Selective Service registration.

US Embassy Warden's List

Throughout Panama nineteen Wardens have been designated by the U.S. Embassy in order to disseminate information of interest to American Citizens in a timely manner. Information for voters by state, visa and passport changes, social security issues and much more is regularly sent to the Wardens for dissemination to the American community. Contact the American Citizen's office (207-7000) for the Warden in your area. In Panama City Email: canaltransit@pobox.com.

Real Estate Purchases in Panama

The U.S. Embassy Panama has excellent guidelines for foreigners considering purchasing property in Panama. Please review and utilize these guidelines before making any purchase. http://panama.usembassy.gov/panama/property.html

Appendix 13

<u>Assistance from the Canadian Embassy</u>

The Canadian Embassy and Consulate in Panama offer a variety of services to both Canadian citizens living in Panama and Panamanian nationals. Canadians planning to travel to Panama whether for vacation, retirement or business are encouraged to utilize the website at http://canadaonline.about.com/od/travel/a/embpanama.htm for helpful information.

Warden's List

Once you have arrived in Panama, be sure to register with the Embassy. This free service will assure that you receive current information of interest to Canadians including voter registration, local security, and notice of community activities. In case of emergency, the registration assures that family members in Canada will be able to locate you in Panama.

Canadian Citizen Services

Through the Consul, Canadians residing in Panama can obtain or renew their passport, request a Certificate of Citizenship for children born abroad, receive assistance in case of robbery, obtain emergency passports, receive assistance in case of death of a family member, as well as assistance with medical evacuation.

The Consulate administers the federal elections voting process and handles return of ballots. Ballots can be downloaded and printed from the web site.

Prisoners

The embassy assists in assuring the equal treatment of Canadians arrested and imprisoned, including overseeing of processing and eventual compliance with transfer of prisoners agreement.

Commercial Sector/Trade Commissioner

Canadians coming to Panama for business and those in business in Panama can utilize the services of the Commercial Sector. The Commissioner can provide information on exports, joint ventures, investments and other business activities in Panama.

Canadian Chamber of Commerce

Contact the Consulate office for information on the Chamber or see Appendix 7.

Canadian Association

Canadian citizens are encouraged to join the Association and participate in the community activities. Each year a Thanksgiving dinner is held as well as other social events.

Real Estate Purchases in Panama

Refer to the U.S. Embassy Panama recommendations for foreigners considering purchasing property in Panama. Please review and utilize these guidelines before making any purchase. http://panama.usembassy.gov/panama/property.html

Medical Care

Canadians residing abroad or considering moving abroad need to consider the impact on their medical coverage. Medical care in Canada is administered by each Province although applicable throughout the country. However, once you are no longer residing in Canada, you lose your coverage. Those that qualify for a government health plan or private plan may retain some coverage from those plans. Additionally, once having given up residency, even if you return to Canada you will not be able to use the National health care without prepaying and then filing for reimbursement.

Safety issues

A number of web sites include helpful information about security in Panama. Panama is currently the safest country in the region. However, big city considerations apply. See Appendix 2 for crime statistics. Avoid areas where crime is more common including San Miguelito, Rio Abajo, El Chorrillo, Ancon, Curundu, Playa Veracruz, Panama Viejo and Madden Dam. Further information is available at the following web sites: http://travel.state.gov/travel/cis_pa_tv/cis/cis_994.html and http://www.voyage.gc.ca.

Appendix 14

Associations

Aero Club of Panama (AOPA)
http://www.iaopa.org/info/enews/0311.html

Alcoholics Anonymous
Tel.: 264-8962

Alianaza Francesa
Tel.: 223-7376 or 223-5972, Email: alliance@cableonda.net

American Society
http://www.amsoc.org

Asociación Panameña de Aeromodelismo (ASPADA)
Model Airplane Club of Panama
http://www.geocities.com/aspada_02
Email: aspada_02@yahoo.com

Asociación Amigos de Los Animales
Friends of animals
Tel.: 233-6401

Asociación Bancaria de Panamá/Bankers Association
Tel.: 223-7630, also **Bankers Wives Association**

Asociación Médica Nacional
Medical Association
Tel.: 263-7622-263-7758
Email: amenalpa@sinfo.net

Asociación Nacional de Scouts De Panama
Tel.: 261-4026

Asociación Panameña de Diabéticos
Diabetics Association
Tel.: 225-6239

Association of the United States Army (AUSA)
Email: fmpc@pancanal.com

British Aid Society
Email: Borer@c-com.net.pa
Tel.: 264-1751

Business Women International
Email: Aepdorado@hotmail.com

Camara de Turismo de Panama
Chamber of Commerce of Tourism
Tel.: 211-3268 or 211-3269

Canadian Association of Panama
Email: Pmaloney@fondoperegrino.org
Tel.: 225-0751/6517-3431

Casa Esperanza Pro Rescate Del Nino En La Calle
House of Hope for Street Children
232-7367/64 or Email: cesperanza@cwp.net.pa
http://www.casaesperanza@org.pClub Activo 20-30 De Panama
Tel.: Tel.: 270-2030

Club De Leones de Panama
Lions Club
Tel.: 225-0721

Club Kiwanis de Panama
Tel.: 232-6286

Club Panama Freefall (Parachute Club)
http://www.panamafreefall.com/contacto.htm
Email: info@panamafreefall.com, Tel 6615-9720

Club Rotario Panama
Tel.: 226-2684 or 270-0147

Democrats Abroad
http://www.democratsabroad.org

Harley Davidson Club
Biker's Cafe
Via Brasil & Av. Ricardo Arango
Tel.: 264-0081

Historical Society of Panama
Email: Jcarlson@cwpanama.net
Tel.: 211-0186, 674-2622

Ikebana International
Email: ArtTable@Artiemail.ne.jp
http://www.ikebanaHQ.org

Interamerican Women's Club
Tel.: 223-1749

Ivy League Mixer
Brown, Columbia, Cornell, Dartmouth, Harvard, Penn, Princeton, Yale
Email: info@pennalumnipanama.com

Navy League of the U.S. Panama Council
http://www.navyleague-panama.org

Panama Amateur Radio Association
HP2CTM or HP1XRO

Petalos Garden Club
Tel.: 270-7088

Puruvian Women's Club (Asociación de Damas Peruano-Panameñas)
Tel.: 264-8348

Republicans Abroad
http://republicansabroadpanama.org/
Email: panama@republicansabroadpanama.org

Soroptimist International Panama Pacific
Sheraton Hotel and Resort
2nd and 4th Wednesdays, 7:00-9:00 p.m.

Tuesday Morning Group
10:00 a.m., Panamonte Hotel
Boquete

Union de Triatlon (Colón)
http://www.triathlon.org
Tel.: 507-615-3919 Fax: +507-224-8049
Email: camiloamado@gmail.com

University of Pennsylvania Alumni
Tel.: 263-5489

Veterans of Foreign Wars
http://www.geocities.com

Vino Club Panama
http://www.vinoclubpanama.com

Who's New Panama
Tel.: 264-0567
Email: whosnew@wnpan.org
http://www.wnpan.org

Appendix 15

Embassies in Panama

Embajada de Alemania
World Trade Center
Edificio World Trade Center
Piso 20
Cl. 53 Urb. Marbella
Tel.: 263-7733
Fax: 223-6664

Embajada de Argentina
Calle 50 y 53, Obarrio
Tel.: 264-6989

Embajada de Austria
World Trade Center
Piso 14
265-3855

Embajada de Bélgica
Edif. Cocige, el Crisol
Vía Domingo Díaz
Tel.: 301-5200

Embajada de Bolivia
Cl, Eric Arturo del Valle
Bella Vista
214-6438

Embajada Británica
P H Swiss Tower, Piso 4
Cl. 53 Urb. Marbella
Tel.: 269-0866
Fax: 223-0730

Embajada de Brasil
Calle Elvira Méndez, 24
Tel.: 263-5322

Embajada de Canadá
World Trade Center
Panamá, Panamá
Galeria Comercial, Piso #1
Cl 53-E Marbella
Tel.: 264-9731
Fax: 263-8083

Embajada de Colombia
World Trade Center
Edificio World Trade Center
Oficina 1802
Tel.: 264-9266
Fax: 223-1134

Embajada de Corea
Cl Ricardo Arias
Tel.: 213-9857

Embajada de Costa Rica
Av. Samuel Lewis
Tel.: 264-2980

Embajada de Cuba
Calle 33 Ave. Cuba y Ecuador
Frente al Parque Porras
Tel.: 227-0359
Telefax: 225-6681

Embajada de Chile
Cl Elvira Méndez
Edificio Banco Boston,
Piso 11
Tel.: 223-9748
Fax: 263-5530

Embajada de China
Av Samuel Lewis
Tel.: 263-3092
Consulado de Dinamarca
Via Cincuentenario, Calle 50
Tel.: 270-0944

Embajada del Ecuador
Cl Manuel M Icaza
Tel.: 269-0477

Embajada de El Salvador
Apartado 8016
Panamá 7, Panamá
Cl Manuel Espinosa Batista
Tel.: 223-3020

Embajada de España
 Apartado 1857
Panamá 1, Panamá
Cl 33 y Av Perú
Frente al Parque Porras
Tel.: 227-5122

Embajada de Estados Unidos
Ave. Balboa and Clayton
Tel.: 207-7000

Consulado de Finlandia
Calle 64 y Via Simón Bolívar
Tel.: 279-9802

Embajada de Francia
Plaza de Francia
Tel.: 228-7824
Fax: 228-7852

Embajada de Grecia
Ave. Manuel Espinosa Batista
Tel.: 263-0932

Embajada de Guatemala
Edificio Altamira, 9 Nivel, 925
Via Argentina
Tel.: 269-3406
Fax: 223-1922

Embajada de Haití
Apartado F
Panamá 9A, Panamá
Cl Manuel M. Icaza
Tel.: 223-1767

Embajada de Holanda
Edif. Tower Plaza, Piso 3
Calle 50
Tel.: 264-7257

Embajada de Honduras
Av Justo Arosemena
y Cl 31
Edificio Tapia, Piso 2,3-80
de Banco General
Tel.: 225-0878
Fax: 225-8200

Embajada de Hungría
Calle 64 y Via Porras
Tel.: 229-7575

Embajada de Israel
Ave. Manuel Maria Icaza
223-6268

Embajada de Italia
Av Balboa, 25
Tel.: 225-8948
Fax: 227-4906

Embajada de la India
Av Federico Boyd
Tel.: 264-2416

Embajada del Japón
Encargado de Negocio, a.i.
Cls 50 y 60-E Obarrio
Tel.: 263-6155
Fax: 263-6019

Embajada de la Republica
Arabe de Egipto
Cl 55 El Cangrejo
Tel.: 263-5020
Fax: 264-8406

Embajada de la Republica
Arabe de Libia
Av Balboa y Cl 32
Tel.: 227-3365

Embajada de la Republica
Arabe Saharaui
Cl Manuel M. Icaza y Av Samuel
Lewis
Tel.: 263-1199

Embajada de la República de Polonia
Urbanización Marbella, T- B
Tel.: 263-5097

Embajada de México
Apartado 8373
Panamá 7, Panamá
Cl 50 Edif. Credicorp Bank P. 17
Tel.: 210-1526

Embajada de Nicaragua
Apartado
Panamá, Panamá
Quarry Hights Amador 16
Tel.: 211-1700

Consulado General de Noruega
Edif. Comosa, Piso 5
Ave. Samuel Lewis
Tel.: 263-1955

Embajada de Paraguay
Via Italia, Paitilla
Tel.: 215-0238

Embajada de Perú
Edif. World Trade Center, Piso 12
Tel.: 223-1112

Embajada de República Dominicana
Cl 75 Este San Francisco
Tel.: 270-3884

Embajada de Rusia
Av Samuel Lewis
Edificio Omega, Piso 7
Tel.: 264-1408
Fax: 264-1558

Embajada de Suecia
Calle Aquilino de la Guardia
Tel.: 264-3748

Embajada de Vaticano
Paitilla
Tel.: 269-1530

Embajada de Venezuela
Encargada de Negocio
Av Samuel Lewis
Torre Hong Kong Bank, Piso 5
Tel.: 269-1244
Fax: 269-1916

Embajada del Uruguay
Av Justo Arosemena y Cl 32
Tel.: 225-0049

Appendix 16

When all Else Fails

Keep in mind living in another country presents many opportunities and challenges. Herein I have tried to address a variety of issues in order to make your transition as smooth and pleasant as possible. However, there is still lots of room for unforeseen happenings. The allure of Panama is the appearance of freedom and simplicity. Where you may feel the laws in your home country are oppressive, rules in Panama are flexible. Often they appear no more than a suggestion, a mild inconvenience, rather than an absolute. Everyone thinks this translates to a better life for less money. However, it can also bring stress.

When Life Ends

We do not like to think about it too often but eventually we all face the death of a loved one, a friend, or a neighbor and discover the process required to deal with the situation personally and legally. A brief guideline was included in Chapter XI and this section will provide more detailed information should you need it.

The death certificate is the most important document you need to obtain in order to keep the process moving in a timely way. It will facilitate every other step. At the time of death, if the person is not in the hospital, immediately, call their physician to come to issue the death certificate.

The Death Certificate consists of the following sections and information:

A. General Information

Complete name, Sex, Cedula No. or Pensionado/Jubilado Visa No., Panama Social Security Number, Occupation, Age, Date of Birth, Date of Death, Marital Status, Place of Death (City, town, hospital, etc.), Usual residency.

B. Other Information (completed when there is no physician certifying the death)

Symptoms of the illness when the deceased died, probable cause of death, if medical assistance was received provide the name of the institution and the physician, name of the informant and relation to the deceased.

C. Information for Children less than one year old

List of questions pertaining to the identification of the child and cause of death.

D. Medical Certification. This section is completed by the attending physician. Any certified doctor under Panama Law can complete this form and certify the death. If you do not have a physician to call and the death occurs in your place of domicile (residence) of natural causes, not violent in nature, or accident you may call a reliable funeral home and they can provide you with a physician to go to your home. If there is any doubt or question of the cause of death, the police authorities need to be called and an autopsy will possibly be ordered.

Disposal of the Remains—Stay in Panama

A. Private Burial: If the deceased is to be buried in a private cemetery, arrangements should be made with the funeral home and the administration of the cemetery. A cemetery plot and service in a garden such as Jardin de Paz can cost $1,800 depending on the location of the plot and services required. Burial in a municipal cemetery is more economical.

Municipal burial—the person acting on behalf of the deceased must go personally to the municipality with a *Paz & Salvo* from the municipal showing the person making the request has no municipal debts owed. A copy of the Death Certificate will also be required. A reliable funeral home can assist you with this process.

B. Cremation: The remains, a copy of the Death Certificate, and a relative or someone capable of personally identifying the body as the person identified on the Death Certificate, must all be presented at the Crematorium. The cost of cremation ranges between $500-$1,000 depending on special services or containers desired.

In Panama there are reliable funeral homes that will take care of all the necessary paperwork as well as preparation of the body, transportation, church services, cost of the morgue and all related costs. There are morgues at Santo Tomas Hospital, the Social Security Hospital, and David. Should the body be held at any of these facilities, it is to your benefit to have it removed to the morgue of the cremation institution, as it will be less expensive.

Disposal of the Remains– Shipped to Another Country

A. Remains in Bodily Form

Same basic requirements apply plus:

The body must be embalmed and certified that it has been adequately prepared for shipment; obtain Permission of the *Ministerio de Salud*; contact *Ministerio de Relaciones Exteriores;* Contact Consulate of the country to which the body is to be shipped; arrange transportation and for receipt of the body by a funeral home at the other end. The protocol for each country varies. Most reliable funeral homes should have the current rules for compliance. The home Consulate of the deceased may be of further assistance as well. Cost depends on a variety of factors.

B. Remains in the Form of Ashes (Cremated)

The same basic steps apply but are much simplified. The *Ministerio de Salud* will provide a certificate stating that you have cremated human remains. You will also need permission from the airline that you are shipping with. If you are hand carrying the ashes you will require a copy of the death certificate, certificate of cremation and the certificate of *Ministerio de Salud*.

Remains Returning to Panama from Another Country

Human remains to be returned to Panama require processing through the procedures outlined in a special handbook for shipping human remains. The local funeral home can be of assistance in complying with all the local laws and making the necessary paperwork as well as moving it through the nearest Panama Consulate. Arrangements need to be made for a Panama funeral home to receive the remains when they arrive.

Ashes fall under a simpler procedure as all that is required is a death certificate and certificate of cremation. If the ashes are to be shipped and not hand carried, you must check with the carrier to determine what other requirements may be necessary.

Funeral Homes

Funeraria Alvarado
Ave. Mexico y Calle 34
Tel.: 225-4484, 227-1286

Funeraria Leblanc, S.A.
Ave. 7a, Central 33-20
Frente a la Basilica Don Bosco
Tel.: 225-6244, 225-3887, 6612-0395

Cremations
Incresa, Servicios Internacionales de Cremaciones, S.A.
Ave. Santa Elena y Jarden de Paz
Tel.: 221-4184, 221-4932

Cemeteries

Jardin de Paz
Ave. Santa Elena 224-1266
Complejo de Nichos Jardin de Paz
Tel.: 221-0333

Parque del Recuerdo
Milla 8, Panama 231-7526
El Dorado 236-8748

After Shopping Till You Drop
Shopping in Panama is fun, most of the time. However, when you get home with your new purchase only to find it does not fit, is not the item advertised on the package, or failed the first time you tried to use it, there is always the return. A little known fact in Panama, the store **does** have to give you your money back. Assuming you have a legitimate

claim for the return and they have already agreed to at least give you a store credit, you can insist on a return of the money or a credit card credit. Law 29 is the answer.

Http://www.clicac.gob.pa, Click on *Normas Legales, Disposiciónes en Materia de Protección al Consumidor, Leyes, Ley 29 de Defensa de la Competencia, Article 49.*

Living Wills

Living Wills, Medical Directives or Advance Directives are commonly in use in many parts of the world providing a means of expressing ones desires at the end stages of life. Panama law currently does not address Living Wills. However, in practice, doctors and hospitals do recognize properly executed Living Wills and comply with them. To be effective the will must be in Spanish and notarized. The Internet has many sites with sample Living Wills, in a variety of languages, or you can write your own, in Spanish, and have it notarized. If you have a current Living Will in some language other than Spanish, have it written as an original document in Spanish. You will also want a copy in English for your own records.

Things to Consider Before Purchasing Real Estate (Bienes Raices)

The U.S. Consulate web site in Panama offers some excellent tips to consider before making any property purchase in Panama. It is well worth the effort to check out:

http://panama.usembassy.gov/panama/property.html

Click on American Citizen Services, then Panama Info, then Purchasing Property and finally go to:

Useful Tips on Buying Property in Panama.

Prison Is No Fun!

Prison in Panama is no fun. Photos showing incredibly over crowded facilities always accompany any article about prison life. Add to that the long waiting time to be charged and tried, the lack of facilities and it should be sufficient deterrent. Panama has a zero tolerance policy for drugs. No drugs are acceptable. Do not bring, use or sell drugs. Do not be confused into thinking you can do otherwise because drugs are widely available and appear to be in use.

Should you end up in prison, representatives of your respective Embassy **may** be able to expedite your trial assuming they have such an agreement. They may further be able to arrange for you to serve your sentence in your home country, if they have such an agreement. Otherwise, you will need to rely on friends and family to provide you with pocket money, basic toiletries including toothpaste, toilet paper, deodorant and anything else you need for the duration of your sentence.

Be sure you understand what *over crowded* means in this situation: a room with four-high bunk beds, side-by-side and end-to end. There is no privacy, hardly any room to stand, no air conditioning and minimal toilet facilities.

Some churches and social organizations work with prisoners, especially women prisoners, to attempt to provide some assistance, especially to foreigners.

Index

currency 29, 191
customs agent 51, 52

D
Dance schools 143-144
David 25, 121
death 209, 317
Death Certificate 318
December 8 31
Democrats Abroad 228, 310
Dengue fever 214
Dental 220
departure 44
departure tax 45
diablo rojos 185
departure tax 45
dictionaries 98
diplomat clause 107
Direct TV 66
discontinued goods 160
discounts, 81, 160, 185
districts 29
Do-It-Center 121, 162
dog kennels 157
dogs 108
domestic airport 40
Do's and Dont's 89
Dos Mares 114
downtown 105, 110
dress, 77, 90, 266
dressmakers 159
drivers 173-174
driver's license 104, 178
dry cleaning 92

dry season 28
dual citizenship/nationals 134

E
Easter 31, 95, 239
Easy Mail 62
economy 33
EDEMET 152
El Cangrejo 105, 110
El Carmen 105
El Dorado 105, 114, 158
El Dorado Mall 158
El Hombre de la Mancha 62,
102
El Niño 224
El Panama Hotel 44
El Pomodoro 94, 292
El Valle de Anton 116, 120, 121,
128
El Visitante/TheVisitor *64*
Elderly help 229
electricity 152,
email 61
Emancipation Day 31
Embassies 65, 68, 232, 257, 302,
306, 313
Embassy Services 64
Embera 27
emergency generators 106
Emergency numbers 38, 175
emergency treatment 208
employment 154
Employment taxes 154, 198-199
enrollment 137Entertaining 79
Espacio Magazine 62

ADVERTISERS

ABC
Aerocasillas/Air Box Express
Air Panama
Balboa Academy
Boutique Helene Breebaart
Café Pomodoro Spaghetteria
Centro Medico San Juan Bautista/Dr. Leonidas Pretelt
Complete Dental Studio/Dr. Ernesto Calvo
Copa Airlines

DEFG
Dr. Louis Picard Ami
Farmacias Revilla, S.A.
Arlene Lachman Galería
Gamboa Rainforest Resort
Grupo ArteConsult, S.A.
Grupo Dental de Galerías Balboa/Dr. Charles Garcia

HIJKL
H&R Block
Hospital Nacional
Hospital Punta Pacifica
Joyeria Barakat
La Posta Restaurant
Lic. Nixia Guerra
Lic. Vanessa Cornejo de Marsh
Los Capitanes—El Valle

MNOP
Mauad & Mauad Attorneys at Law

Oxford International School
Panama Canal Railway
Panama International Packers
Panama Plastic Surgery Center/Dr. Luis A. Crespo

QRS
Rancho Los Sueños
Restaurante 1985
Rincón Alemán
Rincón Suizo
Romero Supermarkets
San Maló
Scotiabank
Seasons
Solomon's International
Supermercados Rey

TUV
The Insurance Center
The International School of Panama
The Wine Bar
Tropical Services Corporation

Grupo Dental
de Galerías Balboa

Seen here are Dr. Mario Chalhoub (Periodontist), Dr. Pascuale Calvosa (Prosthodontist), Dr. Jean Marie Guardia Zeimetz (General Dentist), Dr. Francisco Sousa-Lennox (Orthodontist), seated Dr. Charles A. Garcia (General Dentist). Not shown , Dr. Jesus Ruiz Najera (Endodontist).

Excellence, Economic Sense, Quality Care, U.S. Licensed Providers, OSHA Standards of Sterilization & Infection Control.

Family Practice Environment, with emphasis in: Orthodontics, Periodontics, Endodontics, Pedodontics, Oral Surgery,Cosmetic Dentistry & Oral Rehabilitation, Implants, Veneers, Porcelain Crowns & Routine General Dentistry.

30-50% less expensive than in USA for same quality care.

Balboa Avenue and Aquilino
de la Guardia Street
"Galerias Balboa"
First floor, Office No.27

Tel: (507)-264-4380/3348
Fax: (507)-223-5834
e-mail: grupodental@gmail.com
www.grupodentaldegaleriasbalboa.com

Discover the Secrets of the Rainforest...

- Resort • Spa • Aerial Tram
- Corporate Meetings
- Fishing • Ecological Tours
- Bird Watching • Honeymoons
- Family Reunions
- Much More...

GAMBOA
RAINFOREST RESORT
AT THE PANAMA CANAL

www.gamboaresort.com
Resort: (507) 314-9000 • Fax: (507) 314-9020 • Reservations: (507) 206-8880
Toll Free US: 1-877-800-1690 • reservations@gamboaresort.com

THE BEST
EUROPEAN CUISINE
IN PANAMA

Caffè Pomodoro SPAGHETTERIA

120 different ways to eat pasta

Pizza, Pasta & Wine Outdoor Dining

Via Veneto
Tel: 269-5836
Las Brisas de Amador, Causeway
Tel: 314-3340

Rincón Suizo

Traditional Swiss Cuisine

Cozy atmosphere!

Calle Eusebio Morales
Tel: 263-8310

Restaurante 19 85

French Cuisine and Seafood

Elegant & Stylish!

Calle Eusebio Morales
Tel: 263-8541

The Wine Bar PANAMA

Wine & Cheese Bar Live Music

Via Veneto near
Hotel & Casino Veneto
Tel: 265-4701

The Wine Bar Amador

Wine & Cheese Bar Live Music

Las Brisas de Amador, Causeway
Tel: 314-3340

Rincón Alemán
DEUTSCHE KNEIPE • GERMAN FOOD

Deutsche Kneipe German Food

Calle 51, Bella Vista
Tel: 264-0590

GANADOR DEL FIVE STAR
DIAMOND AWARD

Taste Chef Willy's delicious creations!
www.1985.com

Believe in your dreams,
and *make them come true.*

Get advice from the experts! We have the right solution for your financing and savings needs.

Scotia Plaza Branch
Federico Boyd Avenue & 51st Street
Tel: (507) 208-7700 / Fax: (507) 208-7702

El Dorado Branch
Camino de Cruces Mall, #26
Tel: (507) 360-2190 / Fax: (507) 360-2199

Condado del Rey Branch
Multimax Mall, Ricardo J. Alfaro Avenue
Tel: (507) 236-6445 / Fax: (507) 236-7447

Albrook Branch
Centro Comercial Pancanal Plaza
Ave. Omar Torrijos H., Albrook
Tel: (507) 315-6700 / Fax: (507) 315-6711

Contact us at:
scotiabank@cwpanama.net

Scotiabank
Life, Money. Balance Both.

for those Who love LIFE

At Hospital Nacional
we are ready to provide
excellent service,
a highly professional staff
and the ultimate
medical technology,
unpararell in Central America.

We also offer
International Insurance.

There are a lot of benefits
available for our
international patients.

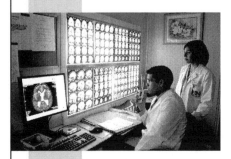

HN 1973
HOSPITAL NACIONAL
centro médico integral

For those who love life.

Feel free to call us for more information

(507) 207-8345 / (507) 207-8354
(507) 207-8100 / (507) 207-8102

Cuba Avenue between 38th & 39 Street,
Panama City, Panama.
www.hospitalnacional.com
e-mail: sinternacional@hospitalnacional.com
mercadeo@hospitalnacional.com

Panama Plastic Surgery Center

Aesthetic and Reconstructive Plastic Surgery, Microsurgey and Surgey of the Hand

Recognized for its high level of medical and ethical care the Panama plastic surgery center has helped hundreds of patients obtain the best possible results.

Patients appreciate the individualized attention, the well appointed accommodations and the absolute privacy.

We will be happy to answer any questions you may have regarding the latest techniques in:

- Facial Rejuvenation
- Breast Surgery
- Body Contouring
- Hair Transplantation
- Lasers and non surgical ancilary procedures
- Reconstructive Facial and Hand Surgery

Luis A. Picard-Ami, Jr, MD., FRCSC, FACS

Luis D. Crespo, M.D., FACS

Fellowships in:
Cosmetic Plastic Surgery, University of Miami.
Cranio & Maxillofacial Cleft Lip/Palate Surgery, University of Miami.
Plastic Surgery Residency McGill University, Montreal, Canada.
General Surgery Residency McGill University, Montreal, Canada.
Certified:
Fellow, American Board of Plastic Surgery, FACS.
Fellow, Royal College of Physicians and Surgeons of Canada -FRCSC.
Member:
American Society of Plastic Surgeons.
American Society of Aesthetic Plstic Surgeons.
American College of Surgeons.
Panamanian Society of Plastic Surgeons.
Medical Licenses:
Florida (Active), USA Federal DEA (Active).
Panama Rep. of Panama (Active).
Work Experience:
Private practice Miami, FL 1992 to 2000.
Private practice Panama City, Panama 2000 to present.
Operation Smile/ Healing The Children.
Anatomy instructor, McGill University School Of Medicine, 1987

Phone: (507) 215-2718 Office • (507) 215-2719 Fax
E-mail: picardami@psi.net.pa

Fellowships in:
Cosmetic Plastic Surgery, University Miami.
Plastic Surgery Residency, Harvard University.
General Surgery Residency, Tuft University.
Certified:
American Board of General Surgery.
Fellow, American College of Surgeons, FACS.
Member:
American Society of Plastic Surgeons.
American Society of Aesthetic Plastic Surgeons
Panamanian Society of Plastic Surgeons.
Medical Licenses:
Panama, Rep. Panama (Active).
Massachusetts, USA.
Work Experience:
Private practice, Panama City, Panamá from 1991
Academic practice, Univ. Panama 1991 to 1996.
Medical Director - Operation Smile, Panama.
Clinical Instructor, School of Medicine, University Panama 1993-1996.

Phone- (507) 269-9808 Office • (507) 269-9809 Fax
E-mail: ldcrespo@psi.net.pa

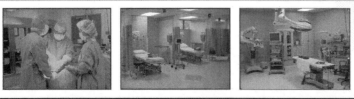

Visit us: www.panamaplasticsurgery.com

www.panamaintlpackers.com

PANAMA
iNTERNATiONAL
PACKERS

Door to Door
We specialize in Local and
International Relocations

Our services:

- Packing of Free Hand Articles
- Local Moves
- Packing and Transportation of Art Work
- Moving of Household Goods
- Receiving of Household Goods
- Custom Broker Services

Call us at:

PANAMA:
Albrook Commercial Park
Tel.: (507) 232-7153 / 232-7154
Fax: (507) 232-7151
caridad@ptypackers.com

Now in
BOQUETE
Edificio Don Andrés, Of.5
Tel.: (507) 720-2886
ptyboquete@cwpanama.net
CORONADO
Tel. 507-6708-7497
robscott82@yahoo.com

TROPICAL SERVICES

PANAMA   COSTA RICA   EL SALVADOR

Don´t risk the cleanliness of your home.
Leave that in our hands!

Now Tropical Services Corporation, with 35 years of experience in cleaning services, will solve your housework problems. We have trained personnel, to make your home a good, safe and healthy place to live.

- General residential cleaning.
- Antiseptic disinfection of bathrooms and toilets.
- Thorough kitchen cleaning.
- Sanitation of mattresses, furniture and rugs.
- Temporary replacement of domestic personnel.

| Panama 227-0311 | Boquete / David 774-6685 | Colon 441-7961 |
| tscpma@tropicalservices.net | chiser@cwpanama.net | tsccolon@tropicalservices.net |

For your *health and beauty needs* at your **SERVICE IN CHIRIQUI.**

FARMACIAS *Revilla* *Orgullosamente Tuya!*

Parque: 777-8513 / Obaldía: 777-8555 / Cinco Esquinas: 777-8551 / Mercado: 777-8550 / Concepción: 777-8558 / Boquete: 720-2995

THE INTERNATIONAL SCHOOL OF PANAMA

Preparing Students for Tomorrow's Challenging World

International Learning Environment:
Students representing 5 continents and 38 countries
Multicultural curriculum
Instruction in English
Fully Bilingual Staff
International Baccalaureate Program
Graduating accepted to prestigious Colleges and Universities
Outstanding facilities :
8-hectare school property
Spacious air-conditioned classrooms
Library of 14,000 volumes
Computer & Science Laboratories
Outdoor covered courts area
Gymnasium / Track & Field

Scholastic Excellence:
Small Class Size
Highly committed, well trained teachers
Ongoing staff development program
Regularly updated curriculum
College Preparatory program
Meets Panamanian and International Requirements
Accredited by Southern Association of Colleges and Schools

Parental Involvement:
Board of Directors elected by parents
Parent-Teacher Association
Close home-school connection

FOR ADDITIONAL INFORMATION WRITE OR CALL:
P.O. Box 0819-20588
Panama, Rep. Panama
Tel. (507) 266-7882/9532/7037
Fax: (507) 266-7808
Website: www.isp.edu.pa

Centro Medico
San Juan Bautista

Dr. Leonidas Pretelt

Serving Boquete since 1992

General Medicine & Surgery
Internal Medicine & Family Medicine

24 / 7

Emergency Care & Outpatient Home Care

We treat adults,
teens, children and newborn

We are always willing
to serve you

6616-2177   720-1881
We speak English

Located on Main Street in Boquete

Romero brings you the best of Panama

For 85 years, Romero has offered the best quality in products and services to the Chiriqui province, and now Bocas del Toro. Our Supermarkets in David, Boquete, Concepcion, Volcan, Puerto Armuelles and Changuinola are your one-stop solution for groceries, pharmacy, bakery, meat, produce and more. Discover the very best our land has to offer: quality of products, and a smile!

ROMERO
SUPERMARKETS
775-2131 • WWW.ROMERO.COM.PA

RANCHO LOS SUEÑOS

COUNTRY LIVING AND HOUSING DEVELOPMENT

Eco-Community:
Lots available with absolutely breathtaking mountain and ocean views.

- 1/4, 1/2 & 1 Acre Lots available
- 3 models of houses to choose from
- 45 minutes from Panama City and 5 minutes before Bejuco
- 12 minutes from the beaches, major golf course and restaurants

Next to Campana National Park

www.realestateinpanama.com
e-mail: ranchofdreams@yahoo.com
Call us at: **(507)236-7724 Cel: 6672-7736**

arlene lachman
G A L E R I A

Artistas Contemporáneos de Panamá
Contemporary Artists of Panama

Edificio Bahía Balboa en Avenida Balboa y
Vía Italia en Punta Paitilla, local 4, Panamá

Telefax (507) 215-2935 Celular (507) 6618-0307

alachman@cwpanama.net y arlenelachman@hotmail.com

ʙᴀʟʙᴏᴀ ᴀᴄᴀᴅᴇᴍʏ

Balboa Academy is a private, co-educational day school, which offers an American college preparatory educational program from Pre-Kindergarten (3/4 year old programs) through 12th grade for students of all nationalities.

The school year consists of 185 days of classroom instruction divided into two semesters extending from August to June. School vacations are four weeks at midyear, December to January; one week at Carnival; and one week at Easter.

Our installations are located in Clayton, City of Knowledge
Phone: 211-0035   Fax: 211-3319

For more information, please visit our website at www.balboaacademyweb.org

Come ride the famous
Panama Canal Railway
The World's first transcontinental railroad.

Schedule: Monday – Friday
Panama City – Colon: 7:15 am
Colon – Panama City: 5:15 pm
Phone: 317-6070 • Fax: 317-6061
e-mail: Info@panarail.com

Cornejo March Quijano & Asociados

Vanessa Cornejo Quijano
Attorney at Law

- Immigration Assistance: All types of Visas & Naturalization
- Establishment of Anonymous Societies and Foundations
- Civil Documents: Assistance with obtaining a Cedula, Marriages and Death Issues
- Work Permits
- Free Zone Operations: Brand and Trademark Registration
- Family Assistance

Edificio Bahía Marbella # 1 Oficina 3B • Marbella • Republic of Panama
Tel: (507) 213-2641 • Cel: (507) 6680-0093
E-mail: vaneq7@hotmail.com
P.O. Box 0819-05867 • El Dorado Panama • Republic of Panama

San Maló

Exclusive representation in Panama of...

The House of

WEDGWOOD · VERA WANG · Villeroy & Boch · TRAPP PRIVATE GARDENS · Hagerty

The best bridal registry for brides in Panama!

Fabulous gifts and great discounts for all brides

Fine China - Crystal - Sterling Silver - Flatware - Tableware
Bakeware - Candles - Aromas - Decorations - Details - Gifts

Open 9:00 a.m. - 6:00p-m. Monday - Saturday Obarrio 57th Street, Diagonal from the Bingo 90
Tels: (507)223-5937 / 213-1853 Fax: (507) 263-2315 e-mail: sanmalo@cableonda.net

Prepare 1.2 million business tax returns and something happens...

...you get really good at it.

Whether you're a wedding planner or own a planning
supply company, we're here year-round to help you with:

- Bookkeeping
- Payroll
- Tax Preparation
- Advise

H&R BLOCK | business services

To learn more call:

H&R Block Panama
Colonial Gallery El Dorado
2nd Floor Office 3-A
Tel: (507)260-1052
Fax:(507)260-1037

Monday - Friday   8:00 a.m. - 5:00 p.m.
Saturday   9:00 a.m. - 1:00 p.m.

José Manuel Chu
Franchise Owner
Cel: (507)6674-1037
jchu@hrblock.com

INDIA EUROPA INDONESIA

MARRUECOS Mediterraneo

The world's finest in accessories and furnishings are here for you

Furniture • Accessories • Carpets • Linens • China • Glassware

Salomon's
INTERNACIONAL
Desde 1934

Vía España. Tel. 264-0044 / Fax 264-4471   Open Monday through Saturday from 9 a.m. to 6 p.m.   salomons@cwpanama.net

Living in paradise?
Airbox Express Aerocasillas can deliver at affordable rates.

P.O. Box in USA
Internet Purchases
Magazine & Catalog
Subscriptions
International Courier
Urgent Parts
Air & Maritime Cargo
Shipments

AIRBOX EXPRESS *AEROCASILLAS*

Panamá: 269-9774 Albrook: 315-1226 David: 775-4512 Boquete: 720-1027
Coronado: 304-1431 / www.airbox.com.pa - expat@airbox.com.pa

HOSPITAL PUNTA PACÍFICA
Afiliado a Johns Hopkins Medicine International

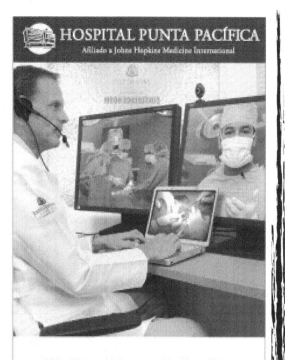

What does it mean to have the assurance of a second opinion, simultaneously, from one of the best hospitals in the world?

It's an option offered only by Punta Pacífica Hospital, to count with a team of more than 2,000 specialists from the Johns Hopkins International Hospital in every operating room through our simultaneous time virtual technology.

This is another innovation from Punta Pacífica Hospital for your benefit.

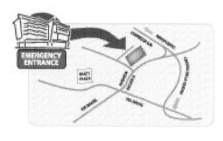

EMERGENCY
204-8181

Central: 204-8000 · www.hospitalpuntapacifica.com

Art Gallery
*specializing
in Contemporary
Latin American Art*

27 years
*serving the Panamanian
community with all
their art needs*

Frame Shop
*wide selection of frames
museum quality mounting
acid free materials*

Professional Services
*corporate and private consulting
appraisals by certified professionals
art packing and shipping
professional restorations
installations of art work
art rentals*

arteconsult

ALEMÁN Y GRIMBERG
Calle 50 between Calle 72 and 73
tel: 302-2646 / 302-2647   fax: 302-2648
e-mail: artecons@cableonda.net
www.galeriaarteconsult.com
vonage tel: 305-735-2316

HOTEL & RESTAURANTE

Los Capitanes

El Valle de Anton

Hospitality in a Natural Setting
- El Valle de Anton -

128 KM FROM THE CITY

A comfortable place where your hosts are a retired German sea captain and his friendly Panamanian and European staff who offer you first class service.

- Comfortable suites & family rooms

- Restaurant serving excellent German, local and international food

- Internet service

- Coffee & cocktail bar

- Facilities for conventions and small groups

Tel: (507) 983-6080 - Cel: (507) 6687-8819 - Fax: (507) 983-6505
capitanes@cwpanama.net - www.los-capitanes.com

NEED INSURANCE

CALL 236-3940 FOR A QUOTE
E-mail: cidssa@cwpanama.net

The Insurance Center
All forms of insurance:

Automobile, Fire, Theft,
Medical Expense, Life Insurance
and Pension Plans

Lowest rate, Payment terms

**Serving Panama's English
speaking community for
over 30 years.**

Nixia J. Guerra C.
Attorney at Law
Consulting & Legal Services

Visas for Retirees,
Investments, Technicals
and others
Set up Corporations
Establish Foundations
Comercial Licenses
Title Searches

Boquete, Chiriquí, Republic of Panama:
Located in the Anayansi Building
next to the Crafts Store
nixiaguerra30@hotmail.com
Cel: 011 (507) 6-667-7197

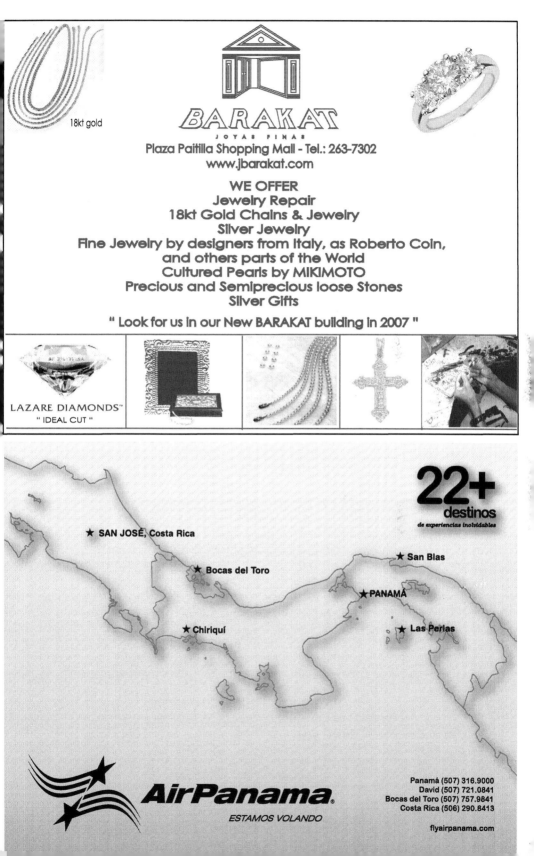

BARAKAT
JOYAS FINAS

Plaza Paitilla Shopping Mall - Tel.: 263-7302
www.jbarakat.com

WE OFFER
Jewelry Repair
18kt Gold Chains & Jewelry
Silver Jewelry
Fine Jewelry by designers from Italy, as Roberto Coin,
and others parts of the World
Cultured Pearls by MIKIMOTO
Precious and Semiprecious loose Stones
Silver Gifts

" Look for us in our New BARAKAT building in 2007 "

18kt gold

LAZARE DIAMONDS™
" IDEAL CUT "

22+
destinos
de experiencias inolvidables

★ SAN JOSÉ, Costa Rica
★ Bocas del Toro
★ Chiriquí
★ San Blas
★ PANAMÁ
★ Las Perlas

AirPanama.
ESTAMOS VOLANDO

Panamá (507) 316.9000
David (507) 721.0841
Bocas del Toro (507) 757.9841
Costa Rica (506) 290.8413

flyairpanama.com

Oxford International School

Cutting edge technology

- *Authorized by the Ministry of Education in Panama*
- *Accredited by the Northwest Association of Accredited Schools*

Instruction in English

Phone: (507) 265-6422
Fax: (507) 265-7446
P.O. Box 0831-01996
Panama, Rep. of Panama
www.ois.edu.pa
e-mail: oxford@ois.edu.pa

Cultural emphasis

MAUAD & MAUAD

Abogados - Attorneys at Law
Fundada – Established
1984

* Company Formation (Panama - Offshore)
* Trusts and Private Interest Foundations
* Commercial and Tax Law
* Energy, Telecommunications and
  Regulatory Matters
* Trademarks, Patents and Intellectual Property
* Banking - Finance - Insurance
* Labor and Immigration Law
* Litigation and Arbitration
* Administrative Law
* Public Bids
* Asset Planning
* Vessel Registry and Maritime Matters
* Project Finance and Investments

Main Office
Dresdner Tower, 50th Street, 7th and 9th Floors
P.O. Box 0853-05791, Tel: (507) 269-3555 / Fax: (507) 264-5741
e-mail: mym@mauad.com.pa / www.mauad.com.pa
******

CORRESPONDENT OFFICES
ASIA * EUROPE * LATIN AMERICA * NORTH AMERICA

SEAS☀NS

Furniture • Antiques • Home Accessories
Silver • Gifts

El Cangrejo Calle 55
Edificio 21 Planta Baja
Telefax: 011- (507) 265-8007

Boutique Breebaart

Hélène Breebaart transforms
Panamanian craftsmanship
into art.

🍍 Fashion
🍍 Accessories
🍍 Home
🍍 Gifts

Calle Abel Bravo
Casa Duplex #5
Obarrio
Telefax:
264-5937
e-mail:
lananas@sinfo.net
P.O. Box 0823-00736
Panamá,
Republic of Panama

Complete Dental Studio

Dr. Ernesto Calvo
General Dentistry (Oral Rehabilitation)

Dr. Graciela Arosemena V.
Oral Hygiene, Bleaching & Cosmetic Dentistry

Dr. Aldo Correa
Endodontics (Root Canals)

Dr. Manuel Ortíz
Oral Surgery

Dr. Gloria Marengo
Orthodontics

Dr. Ricardo Orillac & Dr. Gabriela Eisenmann
Periodontics & Implants

Dr. Gilda Chanis de Crespo
Children´s Dentistry

Calle 53, Obarrio
(Opposite to the Santuario Nacional)
Tel: 263-8861   Fax: 223-0741   Cel: 6626-7353
calvo@cableonda.net

LA POSTA

Restaurant & Bar in the oldest house in Bella Vista

Reservations suggested
269 - 1076 / 269 - 4225
6678 - 4052

* Fish and Seafood
* Homemade Pasta
* Pizza from our wood
  burning oven

David Henesy
Founder of
La Vitrola, Cartagena

Hours
Lunch
12:00 p.m. - 3:00 p.m.
Dinner
7:00 p.m. - 11:00 p.m.

LA POSTA

PRIVATE ROOM FOR 24 PEOPLE

Calle 49 con Calle Uruguay
www.lapostapanama.com
mail@lapostapanama.com

Notes

Sandra T. Snyder

is a native of Virginia, with a B.S in Management major and English minor, San Jose State University, California; graduate work at Hawyard State University, California. Her professional career spanned some twenty years in management.

Before settling in Panama, Sandra and her husband, spent many years living and traveling in Central and South America. Through her numerous affiliations with organizations in Panama over the last eleven years, Sandra has been known as *the information resource* for newcomers to Panama. She served as a board member for numerous clubs and organizations including five terms as President of the Who's New Club. She is regularly invited to speak to relocating corporate executives, diplomats and individuals newly arrived in Panama.

She has been a contributor to the *South American Handbook, Corporate Relocation News*, the American Chamber of Commerce *Business Panama* magazine, *ABC's of Investing in Panama, La Prensa, Panama Eagle* and *Bajareque Times*. Often sought out as a resource by national and international press, she is quoted as an authority on Panama in both the *Boston Globe* and *La Prensa*.

She is a recipient of the U.S. Ambassador's Distinguished American Citizen Award (Panama 2002).

LOOKING FOR MORE BOOKS
FROM
TANTOES, S.A. and SANDRA T. SNYDER

Order Direct: tantoes@pobox.com;
 http://www.livinginpanama.net

Order from Exedra Books: info@exedrabooks.com
 http://www.exedrabooks.com

Order on Line: http://www.amazon.com

COMING
PANAMA CULTURE SHOCK,
A LOOK AT A PEOPLE AND A COUNTRY
by
SANDRA T. SNYDER

Made in the USA
Lexington, KY
26 December 2009

4140806